UNGRATEFUL IMMIGRANT DAUGHTER

AF896058

UNGRATEFUL IMMIGRANT DAUGHTER

A Memoir from the Child of a Mail-Order Bride

Katya Suvorova

alcove press

Books should be disposed of and recycled according to local requirements. All paper materials used are FSC compliant.

Copyright © 2026 by JUNESPOON LLC

All rights reserved.

Without limiting the exclusive rights of any author, contributor or the publisher of this publication, any unauthorized use of this publication to train generative artificial intelligence (AI) technologies is expressly prohibited.

To protect the privacy of certain individuals, some names and identifying details have been changed.

Published in the United States by Alcove Press, an imprint of The Quick Brown Fox & Company LLC.

Alcove Press and its logo are trademarks of The Quick Brown Fox & Company LLC.

Library of Congress Catalog-in-Publication data available upon request.

ISBN (hardcover): 979-8-89242-684-8
ISBN (paperback): 979-8-89242-685-5
ISBN (ebook): 979-8-89242-686-2

Cover design by Emily Mahar

Printed in the United States.

www.alcovepress.com

Alcove Press
34 West 27th St., 10th Floor
New York, NY 10001

First Edition: September 2026

The authorized representative in the EU for product safety and compliance is eucomply OÜPärnu mnt 139b-14, 11317 Tallinn, Estonia, hello@eucompliancepartner.com, +33757690241

10 9 8 7 6 5 4 3 2 1

My wish for everyone who reads this
book is that they have someone in their
life to whom they can dedicate their art.
And if you don't feel that you have
anyone, please let my book inspire
you to find your people. I am lucky
enough to have three.

First, for my Babushka, Valentina.

You taught me to love reading in a
language you didn't know, so
that I could survive in a country
that didn't want me.

Second, for my sister, "Masha."

I am alive today only because
I couldn't imagine going somewhere
you couldn't follow.

Third, for my husband.

I am brave only because
you believe I am.

Table of Contents

Author's Note

A CONTENT WARNING—
This memoir contains discussions of rape, kidnapping, and the physical and sexual abuse of a child. It also includes references to suicide, substance abuse and homelessness. These topics may be distressing or triggering for some readers. Please take care of yourself as you read.

Also, please note that this is a work of nonfiction, but this memoir is drawn from the author's memory. Names, places, dates, and identifying details have been changed to protect the privacy of the individuals portrayed. Memory is subjective, and this account reflects the author's experience and understanding of the events as she remembers them.

The pseudonyms used in this book are, in alphabetical order:

Adam, Alana, Ayana, Catherine, Chanel, Chris, Dream, Ivan, Jerry, Joe, Kristina, Layla, Lenora, Liam, Maritzia, Masha, Megan, Mr. Clark, Mrs. Sandy, Ms. Lopez, Ms. Lynn, Ms. Nancy, Rachel, Sophia, Yuliya.

Lastly, references to the *Harry Potter* book series serve solely to mark the time period and cultural phenomenon, without endorsing the author.

Prologue

Eleventh Grade, 17 Years Old

It's Houston humid and my skin is boiling off my bones. I hate being outside right now—it feels like you're stuck in someone's mouth and they've gargled with gasoline. And the worst part is that it's not even summer yet.

My stepdad says I need to spend the day cleaning the garage. I hate being out here, but I like this chore because my nosiness is sanctioned for the sake of organization.

Halfway through rifling through his stuff I've decided my stepdad has never been interesting in his life. This whole four car garage is filled with his shit and all of it sucks. There is a box of Megan McLachlan CDs and posters, another box containing "Most Improved" awards from what looks like a summer camp he went to 100 years ago, and a binder with several emails printed out and put in plastic sleeves of other people giving him kudos at his job. I don't know what I was hoping to find, but it's not this garbage.

When I go to put everything on the curb for trash collection, I find a box belonging to Mom. It's not marked as hers, but I can tell it is because it looks like a family of rats was living inside of it. The lid is torn, there is a weird, peppery smell coming from the opening that I'm sure is probably her Russian witch medicine. Everything Mom owns is disheveled, but it surprises me that she has a box in here, because she usually keeps all her things in her closet behind lock and key. After her last husband tore and burned her clothes and the family photos, she is vigilant about her things.

I flip open the box, hungrily. There are some tiny Russian horoscope pamphlets, Houston newspapers from the 90s, and a magazine I would recognize anywhere. Mom showed it to me when I was little. I remember it as her modeling catalogue. I was so enthralled with it.

Rose Russians.

"Rose Russians," I mumble. "Rose Russians?"

I scan the pages.

This does *not* look like Russian Vogue.

This doesn't look like a fashion magazine at all.

This catalogue is clogged with women, but they don't look like they're advertising clothes. They're posing in front of beds, in front of houses, up close, on chairs, crossing their legs.

My hands are buzzing as I slide down to the concrete floor of the garage.

I flip to a dog-eared page and find Mom's face quickly. Her photo takes up a quarter of a page. It's tiny compared to some of these other women's photos. There is a smattering of text next to it. I read the words slowly, carefully. *I'm looking for a family and eternal love.*

My stomach drops.

"Son of a bitch," I whisper. "She's a mail-order bride."

PART 1

The Border

Spring, Late '90s, Three and a Half Years Old

I REFUSE TO LEAVE my grandmother. I hold on to her pants as tight as I can. I know my mother hates when I cry, so I sob loudly. Mama is trying to rip my hands away from Babushka's legs, but what she doesn't know is that I am stronger than she thinks I am.

Babushka told me so.

Dedushka, my grandfather, says something I can't hear to my mama. Hopefully he is telling her to leave me alone.

"Katya, let go of her!" Mama yells. "We're going to be late for our flight!" We're at the airport. There are lots of people here.

"I don't want to leave!" I wail.

Mama pulls on my arm, using her nails to bite into my skin. I hold on tighter.

"I am your mother. You need to listen to me! We're going somewhere nice!"

Babushka swats Mama away from me. "Stop Yuliya! Can't you see she is scared?"

Mama steps back. I can hear Dedushka telling her that she is screaming as loud as I am. I can't see if Mama is upset by what he said to her because my face is buried in Babushka's legs. Her pants are wet from my tears, but I don't care.

Babushka moves, bending down to my level. I keep my eyes squeezed shut. I have a feeling Mama is going to win this fight.

"Katyusha, look at me," Babushka says.

I squeeze my eyes even more closed.

Babushka sighs. "You will be back soon, my Katyusha. You are only going for a short time. A vacation to a warm place where it's better for your health." I feel Babushka brushing the hair from my face. She is using her softest voice.

"When will I be back home with you?" I ask, opening my eyes. My snot is salty in my mouth.

"So soon you will forget you even left us!" My grandmother brings me to her chest, squeezing me tight. "Listen to your mama, okay? Be careful. Don't talk to anyone you don't know. Stay with Mama, always."

"OK, Baba," I promise her.

Babushka stands up and tells Mama that she needs to watch me carefully.

"Come on!" Mama says, grabbing my arm. "We need to get on the plane."

Babushka lets me go. The last thing I see before we are swallowed by the crowd is Babushka waving to me and Mama.

I will never go back home again, but I don't know that yet.

Mom and I arrive in Mexico from Russia in the late '90s. Mom is in her twenties, and I'm close to four years old.

Until Mexico, Mom is just a woman who visits my grandparents' house occasionally. A stranger with a life lived mostly out of my sight. I know her as "Mama" but the name means nothing. My grandmother is who I reach for when I need comfort.

Now, in my grandmother's place, is this woman with fiery orange hair and red lips who feels hot, like the end of the cigarettes she won't stop smoking.

When I start asking when we'll go home, Mama tells me the place we are going is the most beautiful place in the world. She says I'll love it so much I won't ever want to go back home again.

"America has freedom like you can't imagine, Katya," Mama says in Russian. We have been in Mexico for a few days. We are lying on a bed with a shiny, purple quilt. Bananas and oranges from the tiny grocery store across the street are spread out like treasures in front of us. The motel room we are in is full of Mama's smoke, because she smokes more than she eats. That's what Babushka says. After leaving the airport in Mexico, we only went outside one other time, and that was to get food.

In the motel room, Mama paints me her dream of our perfect future.

"In America everyone is happy. Americans can say whatever they want and no one will put them in jail for their opinions. And the police? The police don't take bribes there. Neither does the president. Or anyone. When we get inside, we will truly be safe. We will be protected."

America, as advertised to my mother and the rest of the world, was a place steeped in justice for every human being. There was no corruption there, like there was where we were from.

"I want you never to be scared," Mama says to me. "I want you to grow up and have too many choices to pick from when you want a job. I don't want anyone to ever tell you there is something you cannot do."

I can understand now why these values were important to her, but as a toddler, I did not think about human rights and how rare they were in so much of the world. I only thought about my life with my grandparents. I did not feel scared when I was with my grandparents. I would live on the street if it meant I could be with them.

I am shocked when a knock comes on our motel room door.

I jump up from the bed, excited, because I think maybe it's my grandmother. When Mama opens the door, Babushka isn't there.

"Privet," a large man says from the frame of the door. "Ya Joe." *Hi. I'm Joe.*

Joe is wearing a black shirt tucked into blue jeans and chunky white sneakers. His face is the face of a dedushka, or grandfather, but he's not mine. Mama tells me that Joe can speak Russian, our language, unlike everyone else we've run into in Mexico, but I can't understand him at all.

"Joe is a good man, Katyusha," Mama says. The small trash can in the corner of the room smells rotten because Mama doesn't want to throw the peels from our fruit away. She's too scared to go back outside. "He will be your new father soon."

Joe is the man who helps my mother and me cross the Mexican border into the United States illegally. He never becomes my dad.

The United States' first red flag was letting Mom and me in.

Granted, it was on the third try. Mom was determined that someone at border patrol would slip up and let us through without asking for our documents because we "look American," and she was right.

Our easy entrance based on our white skin was foreshadowing what would come—a warning to us that America was not the utopia of justice and equality my mother was hoping for. A warning she ignored.

The first time we try crossing the border, I am under a heavy blanket in the trunk of Joe's white Suburban. Mama tells me not to move or breathe. Border patrol opens the trunk and finds me, and, after asking us a few questions Mama can't answer because she doesn't know English, sends us back. The second time we try crossing, the very next day, border patrol tells Mama to come with them. We are taken into an interrogation room with armed guards, and then we are sent back into Mexico, guards in tow. The third time, a few days later, the patrolman waves us through after Joe lowers his window and shows him my mother's and his smiling white faces. Mom told me later that she would have tried a hundred more times to get through.

Maybe it's because Mom is going to tell me about this moment a million times throughout our life, or maybe I will really remember it, but I will always have an image of her kneeling on the ground, kissing the dusty California dirt after we cross. I will grow up and think her mouth was planting a seed with every desperate kiss, little wishes for us in this country.

Someday, I will understand those kisses weren't wishes. They were promises. She was laying herself bare before the American altar, she was bargaining herself in exchange for freedom. Money. Comfort. Things she couldn't get in Russia.

One day, I will realize she was sacrificing me too.

I don't remember much about our time in California, but I do remember Joe opening his arms wide when we arrive at his house, like we didn't know what a house is. "Have you ever seen anything this nice before?" he asked us, in choppy Russian.

The house was small and had pink bricks. What was I supposed to be excited about?

I didn't know it then, but there will be many, many men opening their arms in front of their apartments, town houses, homes, and saying the exact same thing. *Have you ever seen anything this nice before?* Only Joe will be able to say it in Russian, but we will understand. Their eyes will shine, looking for amazement in Mom's expression. They will assume Mom has no standards because she came here desperate, that they are our saviors, and we should be grateful for basic necessities. We had a *dacha*, a summer home, on the sea in Ukraine. I wasn't impressed with Joe's house.

We stayed with Joe for a few months. Getting into America from Mexico took a week from landing at the airport to being inside the United States. Mom and Joe applied for their marriage visa during this time, but we left Joe before we found out if they were approved. When Mom and I talk about Joe a decade later she will tell me we weren't with him for as long as she had planned for, but I'll never find out why. Some disagreement or other. Maybe Mom thought she could do better.

My memory jumps from Joe's small, pink house to me and Mom alone in a motel room in California. It is now summertime. The last time we were in a motel, it was spring, and we were in Mexico. Our room is similar to the one we had in Mexico, except there are two big beds instead of one. Mom will be getting dressed to go to a bar and look for a new husband since Joe didn't work out. Later I will find out the only way she could get our green cards so we could stay in the United States permanently was by being married. Her visa had been rejected for everything else you could get a visa for.

Mom will talk a lot about how I was a great toddler because she could leave me by myself for hours at a time, and she would come back, and I'd be in the same spot.

Where my mom remembers me as a perfect child, I will remember never knowing if she was going to come back for me once she left.

The room is lined with orange wood. I'm sitting on a bed, one of two big beds with green covers the same color as the seaweed that washes up at the beach at the Black Sea. I'm frustrated because I don't understand what the cartoons are saying on the television, but I'm still enamored by them, my eyes following a man with big, blonde hair and sunglasses. He has a pink car, which I like. The cartoons here are on a larger screen than at home, so I stare, wishing I knew what was being said.

Mama is coloring her lips red in the mirror next to the television. She's making a kissing noise as she opens and closes them. I copy her, enjoying the sucking feeling my mouth makes and the little "pop" that comes after it.

Mama starts brushing her bangs with her fingertips, separating each strand of hair. I watch her watch herself.

I feel tears kiss my lids but I blink them away. I miss my Babushka. I want to go home.

I try to focus on the man with the yellow hair on the TV until Mama turns around and smiles at me.

She is wearing a white dress, and it is very tight. I don't know how she is even breathing. It looks like it is tape, holding her body together. She takes her big, black purse and puts it over her shoulder with one hand, and with the other hand she grips the room key tightly. "Katyusha, wait here for me, OK? Be good. I'll be back soon."

She stubs out her cigarette and puts a piece of minty gum in her mouth. I hold my hand out for a stick, but she shakes her head.

"You'll choke," she says.

I start to cry again. Not because of the gum. Because she's leaving. My whole body feels cold with her words.

She bends down to my level, her hands on my knees, wiping snot from my nose as it leaks out. "Katyusha, be a big girl, OK? I will only be gone for a little while."

I look away from her, trying to swallow my tears.

"Katyusha. Only babies cry. You aren't a baby anymore," she says, her voice cracking. She looks like she is going to cry too. Maybe she also misses Babushka. I thought America, the place we left Babushka for, was supposed to be the best place in the world. It does not feel that way here.

I nod, putting on a smile. I want water but I don't want to ask Mama for anything, so I try not to swallow anymore.

"Just pay attention to the television, OK? And don't open the door for anyone."

I nod.

She kisses me again, and I watch her walk out the door.

Now she is gone.

I am calm, but I start crying when the cartoon is over. Being here feels bad.

Mom will not come back for me until the next day.

I don't know how many days it has been. I am on the floor of a closet. The carpet's curly hair is burning hot against my knees. I can hear Mama crying, loudly, and I am scared, so I open the door and start toward her voice. Mama told me not to open the door to this closet when the man put me in here. She said she would come get me. Her voice was shaky so I know she was scared.

The door opens into a hallway. I move toward another door I can see is open because I think I hear Mama's voice. I crawl because I am too tired to stand. Finally, I reach the opening. Inside the room I see a white bed, and my mama naked, her hands tied to the golden posts on the headboard. There is a large man at the foot of the bed. He is smiling, wearing a white shirt with suspenders. He has a knife in his hand, the blade glinting at me.

The large man, I will realize, is the man Mama met at the bar she went to the night she left me. He told her he wanted to marry her, but first she needed to come home with him. She told him she needed to get her kid. He agreed.

I stand on shaky legs and move toward Mama, fast. I must have made a tiny noise, because the man turns around. He walks toward me, fast, and grabs my hair, pulling me away from my mother. I scream "Mama!" as he trails me away. She disappears from my view.

"Katyusha!" She yells.

"Mama!"

"Katyusha, stay in the closet!" I will remember her words but none of his, the English words not yet having taken root in my mind.

The man drags me back to the tiny closet, the triangle of yellow light folding in on itself as the door snaps shut in front of me.

I don't know how long I stay in the closet. I am itchy and wet with pee. I am cold but I can't move. I lie on top of the wet spot, curled like a snail on the floor, listening to Mama sobbing and screaming. I don't have any more tears in my eyes to cry. The room is dark, and I try twisting the doorknob but it doesn't open so I have to lie on the floor and listen. I want to put my hands over my ears so I don't have to hear Mama screaming anymore but I am afraid not to hear her. I need to hear her voice so I know she is still there.

Mom and I will escape. One day she tells me how she thought that all American men were good and kind and trustworthy. She wasn't afraid of going home with a stranger she met at a bar because the men here were supposed to be like "Superman." America, she said, was supposed to be the promised land. Americans, the saviors. Not the bad guys. The United States was supposed to be the place where justice wasn't just an idea, but a truth.

She wanted to be saved.

We escaped by hopping the man's fence. Mom found our suitcase, and we fled when he left the house. She said she knew he had no plans to let us go.

This was my mother's first lesson that America was not the place she thought it was.

I will grow up and mull over this memory. I will hold my stomach every time I think of it, as though I am still in that closet. I will ask myself what I would have done in my mom's situation, and then I will get angry. How could she let that happen? How could she be so naive, to think so highly of a place that let us in based on their biased idea of what an American is "supposed" to look like? If her bet was to slip into the country based on the color of our skin, then how could she believe that same country would have the freedom and equality she harped on about?

With time, I will realize how scared she was. I will realize that my mother knows desperation in a way I never will. I will also come to understand how red flags are ignored when you're only focus is surviving.

Jerry

Summer, Late '90s, Four Years Old, Kindergarten

MOM WILL NEVER be specific about how we get from California to Nevada, whether we took a bus or a taxi after we escaped the man who tied Mom to a bed and locked me in a closet, but she will recall how the moment we got there, she knew we had to get out as fast as we could. She was running out of money, and we had to have a plan for when she did. She chose Nevada, she said, because she heard it was cheaper than California.

This time, Mom had standards. She made the next guy she met at a bar wait for two weeks before we went home with him. She also called Babushka and let her know where we were for the first time since we said our goodbyes at the airport in Moscow.

Our first husband in the United States was named Jerry.

After Mom married Jerry in Vegas, he drove us to his apartment in Idaho, where Mom and Jerry somehow managed to forge my documents to say that I was older than four so I could attend kindergarten. I am not sure how Jerry and Mom were even able to communicate, but when I look back at my records, I have Jerry's last name. When I ask Mom, years later, why she sent me to kindergarten a year early, she will tell me it is so I could teach us both English.

We are in America for a year and a half when I realize we're not allowed to be here.

My Russian has become rusty at this point, the English words filing my teeth down with wear. Mama and I practice English every day. She has completely stopped speaking to me in Russian. We do my homework together, but she does not help me like all the other Mamas help their kids in my class. She is learning with me.

My memories of the place where I was born have started to fade, but I still know Russia is where Babushka is. I still know it is where home is. I know it is better than hiding in closets to avoid getting beaten with a belt, which is what Jerry starts to do to me. The bits and pieces of memories I have of home comfort me. The taste of Babushka's chicken soup, with potatoes so soft they melt on my tongue and carrots so sweet they taste like apples. I still remember the feel of the Black Sea on my toes. I know Russia and Ukraine are home, and I want to go back so bad it hurts.

One of my last times speaking Russian without thinking about it was when I was five. In an emergency, I ran back to my first language, the place I felt most safe.

At five years old, my favorite toy is my red-haired Barbie. I like this Barbie the best because she looks like Mama. She also has a beautiful, velvet, blue dress and dark blue sparkly shoes.

Her shoes are so pointy and clean, with all the right angles. I like them so much. When I look at them, I don't know what to do with myself. I decide to stick one of her shoes up my nose, because maybe it will feel good up there. I stick it so far up my nose I can't get it out. When I reach in with my finger, I feel a stinging, and I lose hold of the heel of the shoe. I've pushed it even further up. It starts to really hurt. I try blowing my nose into my shirt. I blow hard. Nothing comes out.

I go to Mama, who is watching *Murder She Wrote* on TV.

"Moy noss," I say crying and pointing to my nose. "Shtoneeboot tam." *My nose. Something is in there.* I realize I am speaking in Russian, which I'm not allowed to do, but I don't have the right words in English. Not right now.

Mama frowns, finally turning to me. "What? Why are you speaking Russian?"

"Ya palashella shtoneebot na moy noss," I say. *I put something up my nose!* I don't have the English words to give her.

Her eyes get wide when she finally comprehends that I've stuck something up my nose.

"Vytashchit eto!" She shouts. *Get it out!* Maybe Mama lost her words too.

I yell to her that I can't get it out, I've tried.

She runs to the bathroom and gets some toilet paper, scrunches it up, and tells me to blow. I blow as hard as I can. She yells at me in Russian to blow, and I blow so hard my chest gets tired.

Blood starts speckling out.

"Katya!" She shouts.

"I'm calling Babushka," she says, in Russian, running over to the phone.

After a few minutes and dialing several times, she says, "No one is picking up. It's too late," her voice tight. We're still speaking in Russian, but the rules don't matter right now.

Mama's eyes get so big they remind me of plates.

Mama grabs me and runs downstairs to our neighbor's door who is also our only friend in the United States. We're on the second floor of our apartment, and our friend lives right below us, on the first floor.

Mama bangs on her door, hard. Normally she lightly knocks.

Our neighbor opens her door with a red lipped smile. She must be getting ready to go somewhere since she has make- up on and her brown, shiny hair in a tangle of curls around her shoulders.

"Yuliya?" She asks. "Are you OK?" Her face drops its smile.

"My . . . daughter . . ." Mama says, fast, pointing at her nose. "She has," and she points to my face frantically.

Our friend bends down to my level, frowning.

"What's the matter?" She asks me.

"I have . . . something in my nose." I say, remembering my English.

Mama nods. "Yes! There is something in her nose!"

The woman looks up the stairs, to where our apartment is. "Is he . . . not home?"

Our friend is talking about Jerry, who sometimes comes home for dinner and sometimes doesn't. Mama says he likes to drink at the bars after work.

Mama shakes her head.

"OK," our friend says, calmly. "Let me see."

She takes my head gently and looks inside my nose. "What is it?" She asks.

"A shoe," I say. "Barbie."

She frowns, examining my face, her fingers soft against my chin.

"I think . . . We're going to have to call the ambulance. I don't know how to get this out, and she is bleeding," she looks to Mama.

Mama shakes her head. "No, no!" She begs her, tears running down her cheeks. She turns to look at me.

"Yuliya," the woman says, putting a hand on Mama's shoulder. "She's hurt."

Our friend takes Mama's arm and herds us inside her apartment, where she picks a phone off of a machine. I've been in here a lot, especially when Mama goes to her job as a masseuse. Our friend has a basket of toys for her dog that I also like, because they are stuffed animals. I walk over to the basket automatically.

"Wait," Mama says to me. I walk back over to her. Now is not the time for toys. Mama looks at the phone that is in our neighbor's hand, then back at me, then at the phone again, like she doesn't know which one to choose.

The woman takes Mama's hand and says, "It will be OK, I promise. We have to take care of her," she nods at me.

"No!" Mama says, pulling the phone away from the woman. The woman gently removes Mama's hands and starts dialing.

"No!" Mama says, but she doesn't take the phone away. She puts her hand under my nostrils and tells me to keep blowing.

"Please!" She says, looking at our friend, then at me.

I blow with all the force I can muster. I don't know who the lady wants to call for help, and I don't know why Mama doesn't want her to call them. The lady says something about needing help, then gives what I recognize as our address. She hangs up.

After a few minutes we hear wailing in the distance. Mama says "Please!" to the lady, forcefully, like she is demanding something. The woman nods her head and points upstairs to our apartment. As we go up the stairs I can feel Mama shaking. "Do not speak to the police," she says to me, in shaky Russian. This means she doesn't want our friend to know what she is saying.

"Do not say a word. We can get in big trouble," she adds. "They're not supposed to know we're here; no one is supposed to know we're here."

I am suddenly not afraid of the Barbie shoe stuck in my head. Why aren't we supposed to be here? Where are we not supposed to be?

We get inside our apartment. I sit on the floor in front of the TV. Mama sits in front of me, holding a napkin to my nose, yelling at me to blow. Our friend is on the edge of our brown, sticky, couch, watching us.

After a few minutes, there is a knock on our door. Mama doesn't get up to answer, so our friend does. Our friend opens the door to a man who looks like a police officer. She tells him that I have something in my nose, and I need help getting it out.

He nods and comes inside, walking right over to me. Another man follows after him. The first man has short, spikey, brown hair. It looks like rose thorns are coming from his head. The rose thorn man bends down gently, smiling. His eyes go up and down on my face and then he tilts my head without asking if he can.

He says something to the blonde guy behind him, and the guy gives him a long metal thing that looks like a pen. He pulls it out of a briefcase. I wonder what else he has in there. The rose thorn man sticks the metal thing up the nostril hole that has the shoe in it.

I wince, thinking it will hurt. It doesn't hurt. I feel something moving around in my face, and suddenly, the Barbie shoe is out. It is covered in snot and blood in the man's gloved hand.

Mama is crying next to me. The man says something I don't understand to Mama, and she smiles and nods.

The man gives the shoe to me.

"I bet your Barbie doesn't want that on her foot," he says.

I frown at him because it's still a good shoe even if its covered in boogers.

He gets up to go.

"Thank you," our friend says, and closes the door after him.

"See? They weren't the police, even though they looked like them," our friend says, when they're gone. "They were the paramedics."

"Thank you," Mama answers, hugging her. "Thank you, thank you."

"No more Barbie shoes for you," the neighbor says to me, taking the shoe out of my hand.

At night I cradle the jacket I wore on the airplane when we came from Russia. It's called a wind breaker, and it's pink, blue, and white. It makes a lot of noise when I squeeze it, but I don't care. I shut my eyes, feeling hot tears on my pillow.

The door to my room creaks open slowly, and I see that Mama has come in. She tiptoes over to my bed and crawls under the covers. Her feet are cold, but I don't complain because I like that Mama is cuddling me.

"Prastee meenya," she whispers. Forgive me.

She sniffles very loudly. I bring my wind breaker up to her nose so she can blow. She laughs and wipes her face. When she's done, she brings my forehead to hers.

"I can't survive this without you," she whispers, in Russian.

I don't know what she means. I think my Russian is getting bad.

"Everything will be OK, Mama," I say, in English.

I do not know why yet, but I have an inkling that we are not going home because Mama is afraid of home. As scared as she is to be in the United States, whatever is at home is worse.

Babushka

Spring, Late '90s, Five Years Old, Kindergarten

I AM SITTING IN the middle seat in the back of Jerry's small car. It's the color of sand in here and so hot that droplets of sweat fall from the tip of my nose and into my mouth. We are on the way to the airport to pick up Babushka. It's April. I turned five a few months ago, but I'm not supposed to tell anyone that since I'm not really supposed to be in kindergarten until next year.

Jerry doesn't let us turn the car cold because he says it's too much money, and he is going to have to feed an extra mouth since Babushka is coming to stay with us. I want to tell Jerry that maybe we could turn on the air conditioner if he could try and stop eating for three people.

Mama says I will not recognize Babushka when I see her. She tells me I have grown up too much to remember her well. At least I can still hear her voice in my mind. We talk on the phone every week. Only enough to say "I love and miss you" and "kisses," because Jerry says it's too expensive for Mama to call home for too long.

Mama is very happy today. Her smile is as big as a slice of watermelon, and she keeps thanking Jerry for letting Babushka stay. Mama doesn't smile very often anymore. She cries a lot, which she says she's allowed to do, but I can't because I sound like a baby. I want to tell Mama that when she cries, she sounds like when the drain in the bath is slurping up water, but I know not to do that.

"The apartment will be very clean," Mama says to Jerry, from the front seat of the car. "Mama can clean better than me." Jerry doesn't answer her. He keeps his eyes on the road.

His bald head is shiny in the rearview mirror, his skin pink and pocked like a grapefruit.

Mama sounds like she is trying to make him feel better about Babushka coming. I don't know why she is doing this, since there is nothing bad about Babushka.

"I will be able to work more and bring in more money for us," Mama says, looking at him. Mama has a job where she works rubbing people's backs. No one is supposed to know she is working, but Mama says her boss is nice and taught her what to do to make people feel better.

"Mama cooks very well. She will learn all your favorite dishes." Jerry's face doesn't move.

"She will watch Katya, so Katya will not bother us," Mama continues, her voice small. Her words sound like they are scared and hiding and she has to show them how to walk out from behind her teeth.

I am upset by what Mama said last. I don't bother anyone. Jerry bothers *me*. Jerry yells a lot, especially when he clinks his bottles of beer. Mama bothers me too, sometimes. The only time we talk is when she's asking me how to say different words in English.

Safety, I will learn, will mean a roof over our heads and food in our stomachs. It means it's OK that I am getting beaten, that Mom is being abused, that we are scared. Being beaten doesn't mean we are not safe, but having food means we are.

After a long time, Jerry parks the car. Mama practically leaps out. I follow after her. My chest feels like there is an engine rumbling inside of it, ready to go fast. Jerry grunts out of the car, struggling to lift himself from the seat.

"Don't open your doors too fast," he says, after we have already closed the doors to the car. "You'll hit the car next to us."

Babushka has been like a dream to me. Every time I think of her my heart jumps in my chest, but I don't know why. Babushka is someone I know I love, but her face is so fuzzy to me.

When we arrive at the airport doors, Jerry reads the signs out loud slowly and directs us to a large room. Bigger than where we do gym in school. It's a giant open space, and we sit in little gray chairs. I sit next to Mama, and she holds my hand. It feels nice to have her hold my hand. I see other mamas at school giving out hugs and kissing the top of my classmates' heads, but Mama does not do this for me.

Mama's hand is cool, even though it is hot outside. It feels smooth, and I want to bring it against my forehead, but I'm scared moving in any direction will make her go away from me so I sit still.

After a little while, people start coming out of a door that is blocked off by ropes. They all have lots of bags with them piled on top of each other on metal carts. Mama stands up as soon as she sees the first person walk out of the door.

Jerry says, "Sit down," but she ignores him and walks over to where people are now pouring like spilled water from the doors.

Suddenly, Mama starts shouting. "Mama!" "Mama!" "Mama!" She's waving her hands in the air, her arms like wings on a bird.

I hear a gasp from far away. "Yuliya!"

"Mama!" Mama shouts.

I look at Jerry, who is frowning. I should probably stay where I am, but I want Mama, so I get up and follow to where she is.

That is when I see her.

She is at the mouth of the door.

Babushka. Her face clicks into a place in my mind that has been empty. A space in the shape of her.

Babushka's hair, a thunderstorm like Mama's, except instead of a fiery red, it is like my favorite part of the night, when everyone is asleep, and I am alone. She has glasses in her right hand and with her left she is wiping her eyes. She wears a gray shirt and brown pants and something in my body tells me that I have seen the pants before. They are familiar.

I feel like a cloud is lifting me up into the sky.

My eyes get warm, and I start to cry. I want to go to her but I'm afraid I will get into trouble so I stay with Mama. Mama keeps waving her hands in the air.

I have never cried like this. I'm not scared or upset. I feel good.

I watch as Babushka rushes through the ropes and leaves her bags, running to Mama and pulling us into her so hard I can't breathe. Babushka takes the cold of the airport away from me. She feels like when I'm in my closet, and Jerry doesn't know where I am. She feels like when I'm home alone.

"Katyusha!" She wails. "Yuliya!"

"You told me you were leaving only for a little while!" She says, in Russian, a language I haven't heard for so long. "You were supposed to come home," she sobs, into Mama's shoulder.

"I know, Mama," Mama says. She is also crying.

I feel Jerry behind us.

"You're making a scene," he says in Mama's ear. His voice is low.

Mama stiffens and turns to him slowly. She looks at him, and I see that she put her mad face on. Mama's eyes get sharper than the tips of knives. Her lips turn long and thin like swords.

She's not mad at me, but at him. She is always mad at me and scared of him.

I am scared of this Mama.

"I haven't seen my mother in two years," she says, her voice low, matching his.

He is unphased, taking her by her elbow and leading her to the chairs where he was sitting. He waves his hand at Babushka, who is still holding me, indicating at all of us to follow. Babushka looks behind her to all her bags.

She smiles down at me and hugs me, tight, releasing her arms from my shoulders. She moves to carry her luggage to our chairs.

I hold her shirt as we move toward Jerry.

"Jerry," he says, holding his hand out to Babushka when she reaches the chairs.

Babushka makes no face at all. I can't see if she is happy or sad or mad.

"Valentina," Babushka says, and shakes his hand.

We all walk back to the car, Jerry's hand on Mama's arm. They're walking in front while me and Babushka walk behind them, holding her luggage.

"He looks older than her father," Babushka says, in Russian.

I giggle.

"Katyusha te menya ponimayesh?" *Katya, can you understand me?* she asks, looking down at me.

"Koneshno," I say. *Of course.*

I understand her. How could I not?

"Te moya Babushka." *You're my Babushka.*

"Te uznal menya?" *Did you recognize me?*

"Da," I answer. *Yes.*

"Maya Lastichka. Maya Sonsa. Ya vas ochen lyublyu." *My bird. My sun. I love you very much.*

She kisses me on the head.

I feel like everything will be better now.

Add Friend

Spring 2020, Late Twenties

I STALK HIM FIRST.

Only a little.

Just enough to verify it's him.

I hold my breath and click Facebook's blue ADD FRIEND button, then shut my laptop. My brow squishes into a frown.

"What's wrong?" My husband, Liam, asks, walking from our bedroom into our tiny apartment's living room, where I am sitting. There are boxes everywhere because we're preparing to move into our first house. It's April, and it's finally not raining. I'm on a green futon I hate because I can't comfortably lie down on it, and lying down is my preferred way of being. Especially right now.

I cock my head, considering his question. I'm worried because I just did something really impulsive and maybe dumb. I blame the pandemic.

"I added my bio father on Facebook," I say.

Liam stares at me for a moment, then he sits down next to me, studying my face.

"Oh," Liam says. "Your father has Facebook? I thought he was in Russia."

"Everyone has Facebook," I say, exasperated. I bite my thumb.

"Are you sure it was him?" he says, ignoring my reaction.

I didn't ask myself this question before I added him, but I don't want Liam to know that.

"*Yes,* I'm sure. I know my own father."

He frowns. "Do you?"

I mean, it *looked* like him. From what I remember. White blonde hair. Square glasses. Blue eyes, my eyes. Round face, my face. It was his name.

I hope it was him. I think. Maybe it was a Russian bot. Those are common since 2016, right?

"Can I see?" Liam asks, holding his hand out for my laptop.

I shake my head no, pushing my laptop further away from us.

Liam frowns, retracting his hand. He is wearing a green "Ireland" shirt my mom got him eight years ago, when we were nineteen. His black glasses are pushed back on his nose. He recently grew a beard I'm getting used to, but I've decided I like. Right now, he is running his hands through his dark hair, and when he's done it's sticking up in a way he hates, but I like because it looks rugged.

Liam is likely going through the rolodex in his mind of everything Mom ever said to him about my father. How my father killed his own sister. How he caused the scarring on her arm. How he gave her custody of me because he wanted to focus on his career.

I grew up knowing these things, but with an emphasis on how I got my bad skin from him (thank God I got her nose).

Liam sighs. He bites his lip. He gets up. He sits down. He squints.

I meet Liam's eyes, trying to decipher what we should do.

"Why aren't you talking?" I ask him. His hand is on his chin, like he's thinking.

He shrugs. "Going through all the possibilities."

We are quiet for a few moments when Liam asks, "Why? Did you add him, I mean."

I pause, thinking for a moment, and decide to blame the computer.

"Facebook shouldn't make adding people so easy," I say, defensively.

Liam raises an eyebrow.

"I don't know," I concede. "His face popped up on the 'suggestions' list at the bottom of my page." Facebook should really fix that too. I don't need a computer's opinion on how well my social life is going.

"Huh," Liam says. "Well . . ."

"That's helpful," I snap.

We're quiet for what feels like ten minutes.

"Maybe it's not the worst idea," he says, finally. "Maybe we'll definitively find out if you were vaccinated."

"You make me sound feral," I say, rolling my eyes.

"You are," he says, smiling and rubbing my back.

I playfully punch him.

"Just a little," he adds.

My eyes wander to the pile of Russian language books I have in the corner of the room. The ones I thought about throwing away. Why keep them? My first language is vestigial. I don't have anyone to practice Russian with. Russian is no longer a living thing inside of me. It is a ghost in my throat. Each day it becomes more transparent until it will cross to the other side. I probably won't even notice.

"I—" but there's a knot in my throat that surprises me. I feel my eyes start to heat up. The lids cradling my tears release them and suddenly my face is soaked. Liam brings me a tissue that wrinkles immediately.

He puts his arms around me.

"I miss my Babushka. I miss everything," I say, folding into his shoulder. He smells like the lavender soap we got from France a few years ago.

"I know you do," he says, holding me tighter.

"I'm alone here," I say.

"I know you feel that way," he says.

"You don't understand what it's like. You don't understand what *alone* means."

"You're right," he says, and I cry until I start to hiccup. "I think this is a good thing," he continues, as I wipe my snot on his shirt. "I think this is a way for you to get some answers. Fill in some blanks."

I cry some more, and when I tire myself out I decide to hide my computer from myself until I have five boxes packed for our move. My husband ends up packing those boxes because, naturally, I find my way to the few photos that I took from Mom's house the last time I saw her.

I look at a picture of me, my mom, sister, and Babushka. It was before my mom's last husband came into our life. Her face is fuller, she's smiling, and it reaches her eyes, her cheeks are pink. I think about who my mom was before she met Adam. Not a perfect mom by any means, still broken by life, but she hadn't given up.

I pick up a different photo. This one has me and my babushka. She's holding a baby-me by my stomach in the Black Sea. I'm smiling. In another, my great-aunt is pointing at something in the distance, my little mouth open in amazement. There's an older photo of me sitting on the lap of a woman I recognize as my great-grandmother and another sepia—colored photo of my grandfather embracing me as I drink from a bottle. I find one of my uncle grabbing my legs as a toddler, and I'm laughing, like he's tickling me. There are photos of my mom and bio father signing documents and another with my mom holding red roses and wearing white gloves, looking at my father adoringly while he stands, pridefully, his arm wrapped around her. I count twenty people, spread throughout these photos, that I don't know. Twenty people who are my family, who know me, but are strangers to me.

I start to sob. When I went no contact with my mom, I gave up my family too. And my culture.

I pull my computer out from its hiding place in the side table next to the futon I hate, open the screen, type in my password. The loading screen automatically morphs into my Facebook profile page, where I have a notification for a new message.

My heart accelerates.

I click on the notification.

My father's (I think) photo pops up next to a small box.

I open it.

"I have been waiting for this for a long time."

PART 2

Friend

Spring, Late '90s, Five Years Old, Kindergarten

BABUSHKA IS PEELING off the bark from a tree in a stranger's front lawn. The bark comes off easily, the tree moist and green underneath.

"In Russia our trees can withstand harsh winters. They don't peel so easily," she says, frowning at the tree. Now that Babushka is here, our favorite thing to do is take long walks after school where she explains to me how everything is better in Russia.

Babushka enjoys criticizing people's lawns too, not just their trees. She doesn't understand why there are no gardens filled with fruits and berries and so much unused space in front of the houses.

I get mad at the lawn too. How sad to have a useless tree growing in a lawn instead of useful fruits and vegetables.

"Do you know the name of such a sad twig? Is it an oak? Or a maple?" She asks, flicking the bark on the ground. "Whatever it is, it is too frail," she scoffs.

I shake my head no.

"Probably better you don't know. More room in your brain for *our* trees when you come back to us."

Babushka turns on her heel and takes my hand as we walk home.

Last week it was the grass, how it was too sharp, which made it impossible to walk barefoot. The week before it was how the flowers have too dull a color. America has too many problems, Babushka thinks. I agree with Babushka.

Babushka also doesn't understand what is wrong with American children. She asks me every day to invite my friends from school to play in the park with us, but I have to repeatedly tell her I don't have any. She tells me it's not healthy for a child not to have friends, even if they are American ones. She tells me I must make some, and I keep telling her no one wants to be my friend.

"A five-year-old girl with no friends? Only in this country!" Babushka says, very upset.

On our way home from school, she suggests different ways I can approach the kids in my class. Today she says I should draw them pictures to give as gifts.

"Pictures of what?" I ask, thinking about what the kids in my class would want with a drawing from me.

"Owls, elks, bears," she says. "Mice with hats."

I shake my head no. I do not want these friends anyway.

After Babushka came, I realized I didn't need friends.

When we get home, Jerry isn't there, which means we are safe to eat because he doesn't get mad at us for using too many ingredients that he will have to pay for. When Jerry is home, we go straight to my room. Babushka has to wait until Jerry is drunk, and she sneaks sandwiches for both of us. Mama isn't home either, but that has become normal.

Babushka starts making me some of my favorite foods. She makes me *blinis* with strawberry jam she brought from Russia. Dedushka, my grandfather, made it just for me, she said. Babushka hides the jam under her bed so Jerry doesn't see. She says Jerry doesn't deserve it.

Babushka has been here for several weeks, and I don't ever see Mama anymore. Babushka tells me Mama is making money in secret. Jerry takes only half her money now, instead of all of it, because he doesn't know how much time Mama is spending at the place where she gives massages.

Babushka tells me to get my homework out while she cleans the dishes. The house is tidy now that Babushka is here. She wipes down the table while I take a workbook out of my backpack and write my letters.

The only problem with having Babushka here is that I'm forgetting my English. My teacher called Mama and told her I was speaking Russian in school again. Mama told her that Babushka was visiting, and I was probably mixing up my languages, so Babushka makes me work extra hard on my homework now. Babushka is eagle-eyed as I write my letters over and over, making sure I finish each one.

"You need to be a good girl in school," Babushka says. Sometimes she talks to Dedushka on the phone when Jerry is gone, and she tells him what a good child I am. She hands me the phone, and I confirm what she says by telling him about how I always do my homework and I never argue with anyone.

"I love you, my Katyusha," he says to me, in Russian. I don't remember much about Dedushka, but my heart tells me I miss him when I hear his voice.

I will realize later that Babushka was preparing for me to live in this country without her. Even though Babushka hated everything about America, even though every ounce of her being wanted me to be home with her in Russia, she knew learning English would make me successful here in case Mom didn't come back.

We hear the familiar sound of Jerry's car door close, and Babushka grabs my workbook from the ground and an apple from the bowl on the table. We head to our room where we stay for the rest of the evening. We know not to be anywhere else in the house if Jerry is home. We are either outside or in this room.

Jerry clanks his way inside and sits down. We hear his decompression in the puffy leather chair in the living room like the air being let out from a balloon. I quietly finish the rest of my work, and Babushka watches me from the bed, which is the only place to sit other than the floor.

For furniture, we have a few cardboard boxes where I keep my toys and our closet. Babushka left her suitcase out so we have more space to organize things. She keeps her bras and underwear in it. When I am done, Babushka already has my favorite toys out, and we play that I am the teacher and she is the student until it is time for Mama to come home, which is when Jerry usually starts yelling.

Babushka likes to sing me songs, especially "Katyusha," which she says is her favorite song because it has my name in it. She sings very loudly when Jerry yells at Mama, and I don't hear them fight anymore. They disappear and it's just me, Babushka, and the lyrics of *"Rastsvetali yabloni i grushi, Poplyli tumany nad rekoy; Vykhodila na bereg Katyusha, Na vysokiy bereg, na krutoy,"* floating above us like angel wings.

Apple and pear trees blossomed, Mists flew over the river, Katyusha went out onto a riverbank, Onto a high and steep riverbank.

Summer is finally here and kindergarten is over. We are at the recycling plant, Mama giving her box of Jerry's beer bottles to the woman counting them. She gets ten cents a bottle. The most we've ever come back with is ten dollars. Mama is happy if it is over five. She used to save everything we made at the recycling plant, but now that she is making more money massaging people, she takes me and Babushka out for a treat.

When we are done exchanging the bottles for money, we go to the car, which Jerry lets Mama drive now. Mostly she drives it when he is drunk so she doesn't have to ask him if she can use it.

"Katulia, where do you want to go?" Mama asks me, when we close the car doors.

I've been excited for this all week, knowing we were going to go to the recycling plant. The bottles were stacking up. I haven't decided yet, even though it's been all I can think about.

Babushka's favorite is apple pies from McDonalds, and I like getting the vanilla cones from there, too. Sometimes we go to Baskin Robbins, but Mama says we can only afford one scoop, and Babushka and I have to share.

"McDonalds," I say.

On the way to McDonalds, Babushka and Mama argue. Ever since Jerry told us we are moving to Texas, Mama has started to argue with everyone.

"I don't know what to do!" Mama says, turning the car left. My body knocks into the window.

"Yuliya, please come home. It has gotten better. There are more jobs. There is more money."

Mama's eyes are shiny in the rearview mirror as she steers the car. She's not nervous, like she once was when she first started to drive. Now it's like she expects the car to listen to her.

"I can't go home," Mama says. My heart sinks. Babushka and Mama talk a lot about us going home with Babushka. Mama never gives good reasons why we don't. She just says that we can't.

"But I want to," Mama continues.

Mom didn't want to go to Texas. She had accumulated a bevy of loyal clients who tipped well and came to her for massages often, allowing her to build a secret nest egg. If we left, she would have to start over.

"But if you stay, you will have to get rid of the baby!" Babushka says. She slaps the glove compartment. I jump. I've never seen Babushka angry. I feel an invisible hand grip my stomach tight. Before Babushka came, I was afraid of everything. Now that Babushka is here, I am not afraid of anything except for her leaving. "Jerry has told you so many times he doesn't want it!"

Babushka was so happy when Mama told her that she had a baby inside of her that she cried, and Mama cried too, but different tears, telling her that Jerry wouldn't let her have it. The only thing a baby means to me is a way home with Babushka, so I want Mama to have it. If this baby means we will go back home, I will love it so much. Even if it cries all the time. I will take care of it. I will change diapers. I will give it my toys, except my Barbie horse, which Mama got me with the very first money she got from her job. I will be a good big sister.

When we stop in the McDonald's parking lot, Mama and Babushka are both crying. Mama turns towards Babushka, tears running down her face. Babushka is holding Mama's hands. "I want to go home, Mama," Mama says. "I want to go home so bad." I want to hold Mama's hands too.

"Then come home. We have the money for a plane ticket back."

My eyes start watering because I see Babushka crying so hard that she starts to hiccup. I don't remember Russia, but Babushka talks about it so much I feel like I remember it.

We are in the car for a long time until Mama says, "Let's go get apple pie," and we head inside. I hold Babushka's hand, like I always do, as we walk from the car to inside the McDonald's. Mama orders her the apple pie and me an ice cream. The total is around $2, which is almost half of what Mama made at the recycling plant today. When Babushka comes back we sit at the same booth as always, me eating my ice cream and Babushka eating her dessert. Mama eats nothing. She never eats. When we're done, Babushka and Mama watch me slide down the slide until I get tired, and it's time to go back home.

I will find out later that Mom was desperate to go home to Russia, that Jerry was beating her, that he was a raging alcoholic, but she knew that what she would face in Russia would be worse than staying with Jerry. So, we remained here.

In Russia, my mom was a waitress in a mafia-run casino. Casinos weren't legal, but after the Soviet Union fell, laws didn't matter. Russia was in anarchy. It was normal for people who weren't in the mafia to pay them weekly for protection. There were different mafias that formed, and they tried to kill each other over territory. Shootings in public places became normal. Car bombs became normal. One day, the casino my mother worked in was shot up. My mother was in the kitchen when she heard screaming and the noise of the bullets against the doors. She hid in a freezer for hours until she was brave enough to poke her head through the door to see what the damage was. Everyone in the casino was dead. It was a massacre.

Because casinos weren't legal, and no one wanted to report anything, it wasn't on the news. My mom realized that if the opposing mafia had found out that anyone survived the shooting, her whole family would be in danger. That was when she decided that we would leave.

My grandmother often tells me how she begged my mom to leave me with her, but my mother refused. I think regularly of what a life in Russia would have looked like for me, who I would have become had my mom left me. Would I be someone I like more? I also never got to know the version of my mom who grew up in her home country. I barely remember who my mom was before she was raped in America, before the United States repeatedly rejected her, before she had to fight for so much. I wonder which direction our relationship would have grown if she hadn't taken me with her to the United States.

Father

Spring 2020, Late Twenties

I STARE AT MY biological father's message.

I've been waiting for this for a long time.

I don't know how to answer. Waiting for *what*?

I respond, *I saw you on Facebook.*

My father's reply comes immediately.

I'm so glad. He says. I've tried over the years . . . I was always going to keep trying but I wanted to give you time.

I type *Time in Moscow*, into Google and see that it is four in the morning.

I frown.

Tried over the years?

I want to close my laptop, but I push through.

Can I have your number? It's much easier to message on WhatsApp than Facebook, my father asks.

"Liam?" I call.

He comes into the living room, cocking his head when he sees me on my laptop.

"My father wants my phone number," I say.

"Oh," he says, sitting down. "Wait, what? He messaged you? Didn't you just add him an hour ago?"

I nod, pulling my laptop over and showing him our correspondence.

Liam takes his time reading.

"What do I do?" I say, after what feels like twenty minutes.

Liam pauses, like he's chewing on a thought. "Let's go through what we know about your father."

I shrug. My mind is suddenly blank. I want Liam to do this work for me. I don't want to sift through my mind, uncovering my memories.

"OK . . ." he says. "Here's what Yuliya has told me about your birth father: He killed his sister to get her apartment. We're not sure how he did it but there was something about giving her poison? Yuliya wasn't clear."

"He beat Mom," I add.

"Right," Liam nods. "Yuliya said he beat her, and that's why they got a divorce."

"He also wouldn't give up custody of me so I could get more money for college. And he wouldn't pay child support," I say.

Liam frowns. "What else?"

"Mom said he chose having a career over me. That's why he let her take me to Mexico. He told her that he didn't care where she took me because he didn't want a kid."

Liam nods slowly.

"You know . . ." Liam says. "Your mom is not the most reliable."

"Yeah," I agree. I haven't talked to her in over three years. I don't plan on talking to her anytime soon. "I've never actually given him a shot. I've just taken her word for everything she said about him."

"I mean, there's a reason you don't talk to her anymore," Liam continues.

"I'm gonna give him my number," I say, my heart racing.

"Do it," Liam says.

Liam isn't usually impulsive, so maybe this is a sign. I write out my number in the text box and press "enter."

A minute later a text appears on my WhatsApp.

It's your father, Ivan.

"What do I respond?" I ask Liam.

"Tell him you have questions for him. You want to get to know him."

I have to ask you some stuff, I type.

Anything, Ivan says back.

Floating

Summer Late 90s, Five Years Old

We are in the car driving to the airport.

Babushka is sitting in the front seat with Mama, crying, her hand holding on to mine in the back. I squeeze Babushka's hand with everything I have.

Mama told me this morning that I can't go back to Russia with Babushka, and I cried so hard my eyes went black. Mama said if I didn't stop crying she would leave me home, and she would take Babushka to the airport alone.

Babushka sat next to me and rubbed my back while Mama cried and took my things out of Babushka's suitcase.

"Yuliya, are you sure?" Babushka asked, sniffling. "There is still time."

"I am sure," Mama said, zipping Babushka's suitcase back up.

"Let me take her. You can get her when you have the green card. She won't have to deal with all of this," Babushka said, opening her arms up to the little room.

"Katya, stop crying," Mama said angrily, instead of responding to Babushka. "It's time to go."

"Yuliya, she can't help it. Leave her alone."

"Don't be on her side! Especially when she is screaming like a baby."

Babushka squeezed my hand and kissed the top of my forehead, and I tried my best to stop the tears from falling.

"When will I be back next, Yuliya?" Babushka asked.

"I don't know," Mama said.

The car doesn't feel real. Nothing feels real.

I don't feel like I'm in my body. I feel like I'm on the roof of this vehicle, looking down at the top of my head. My thoughts swirl in my head until we park, and Babushka opens the door to the back seat. When I see her face I am in my body again. She gives me her hand, and Mama carries the suitcase inside the airport.

After Mama drops off Babushka's bags, we follow her to where her plane is and wait until they call her to board. Babushka kisses me, and Mama, and says she will call us and that she promises she will see us soon, and not to forget her.

I try not to cry out loud. I can't help but hold Babushka's hand as tight as I can.

"Why can't you stay, Babushka?" I ask her.

"*Maya lastichka*," she says, cupping my face in her hands. "I have to go home. I will see you soon, I swear."

She kisses me on the forehead and wipes her eyes, turns around, and gets in line for the plane. I look at Mama. Her face is like concrete, but there are tears streaming from her eyes. When Babushka disappears into the plane, Mama tries to take my hand but I don't hold it back. We both cry on the way home, but I don't want to look at Mama, so I turn towards the window.

The next week, we move to Texas.

Jerry's worst quality wasn't that he beat us. It wasn't that he was an alcoholic. It wasn't that he took what he thought was all the money Mom made from her job as a masseuse. It's not that he made Mom get rid of the baby. We didn't leave him for any of those reasons. We left him because he refused to submit Mom's green card application.

Mom would tell me that Jerry held the application for a green card too far over her head. He continuously told her he wasn't applying for it because she wasn't cleaning enough, or she was burning too many things when she made him dinner. Mom decided to put an ad in the Houston paper that said she was a Russian woman looking for a husband. I'm not sure how this ad worked, since I know it gave a number to call. Did Mom have a secret phone? Did she know Jerry wouldn't read the newspaper? She never explained the logistics, but suddenly we were meeting what would be our second husband in the United States at a restaurant in Texas, and Mom's only standard was that he'd get us a green card.

I'm supposed to be in school but Mom hasn't signed me up yet. It's September. We just moved from Idaho to Houston. We had to come here because Jerry got a new job. I'm not sure what he does. All I really know about Jerry is that he is very good at drinking beer. Maybe that's his job.

Mom parks at a restaurant in the middle of the day. She turns to me before she opens her door. She looks especially pretty today. Her hair is curly, and she has bright red lipstick on. Her eyes are so shiny and round they look like glittering marbles.

"We are going to meet a friend today," she says.

My only friend is Babushka, but she left a month ago. I want to tell Mom that I don't want any new friends.

"And we have to do whatever he says," she adds.

"Why? What do we have to do for him?" I ask.

She frowns. "Be nice to him."

"OK," I say. I watch her turn away from me and pop open her car door, so I do the same.

I'm glad I get to go inside instead of waiting in the car, so I won't argue Mom about being nice to this person.

At this point, Mom was looking to leave Jerry, but she needed a place to go first. Luckily, Jerry bought Mom a car. He said it was for her to find a job, but Mom wasn't looking for another job. Mom was looking for another husband.

I skip all the way to the door of the restaurant. When we enter, there is a big shark hanging from the ceiling.

"Welcome to Joe's Crab Shack!" A lady says. She's wearing a black apron and has her hair in a ponytail. "How many?"

I study the white underbelly of the shark. It's bigger than Mom. Its mouth is open and I can even see the little triangular teeth poking around inside. "Is the shark real?" I ask the lady.

Mom pushes my head forward so it's not bent back anymore. "You will break your neck," she says.

"We're meeting someone," Mom tells the lady. "He said he will be in the back. His name is Chris." Mom whispers this part to the hostess, like it's a secret.

The woman nods and says, "Right this way," pointing away from the shark. I grab Mom's hand so I don't have to look where I'm going. I want to keep looking at the shark.

"Here you are," the lady says, then walks past me.

"Katya!" Mom hisses.

I rip my eyes from the shark and turn around. We are in a closed off room. It's hidden away from the rest of the restaurant. Just a long table with a man at one end and no other people in the room.

The man has black hair that is cut close to his head. He is wearing a light blue shirt that reminds me of the Texas sky. He is much skinnier than Jerry. His skin is very smooth, like he polishes it. His nose is also very short. Almost like a button.

"Yuliya?" He asks, standing up and coming over to Mama to give her a hug and kiss on the cheek. I squeeze Mama's hand. "You look beautiful."

"Hi," Mom says, letting go of my hand to put it on his shoulder as she kisses his cheek back.

I want to stand in front of Mom, but I am pushed to the side.

After Mom is done kissing him, the man bends down to my level. "You must be Katya," he says. "Your Mother has told me how smart and beautiful you are, and she's right! Here, I got you a gift."

Chris takes a box from the top of the table. The box has a big white cat on it, and when the man opens the box, there is music that plays inside with another little cat wearing a tutu and spinning in the center of the box. He pushes the box towards me.

I am not sure if I should take the box or not, but I like it, so I do.

Chris wants to sit between me and Mom. I don't like this because I can't see Mom but Chris talks to me a lot. He shows me that you can draw on the table because it's all covered in paper so he draws shapes and asks me to teach him how to say them in Russian. Kvadrat. *Square.* Krug. *Circle.* Treugol'nik. *Triangle.*

It is strange to speak Russian to someone other than Babushka, because Jerry hates when we speak Russian and even Mom doesn't like to speak it to me.

When we're done eating Mom and Chris start whispering to each other, and then Chris says he wants to show us his house. Mama gets her purse from the chair, and I grab my jewelry box and run to the front of the restaurant to look at the shark some more.

"Katya!" Mom says, a few seconds later, pushing my head back up. "I told you not to look back like that! Your head will stay that way! And you know not to rush ahead of me!"

"Yuliya, it's OK," Chris says, taking Mom's hand. "She just wants to see the shark. She's probably never seen one before."

I can tell Mom wants to yell at me more but she smiles at Chris instead.

"Is it real?" I ask Chris.

"It is!" He says. "They got it right out of the ocean."

"Wow," I say. "I have never been so close to something so scary before."

Chris takes me and Mom to a small black car with only two seats. I have to sit in the trunk, Mom says, because I'm too big for her lap. Chris laughs and tells me his house is only a few minutes away and that he will drive really fast so it will be fun, and I won't even notice.

I crawl into the trunk, which has a window over it. It's slanted and I have to squish my legs to my chest to make myself fit. Mom takes my jewelry box since it doesn't fit back there.

Chris goes really fast. My stomach drops as we make sharp turns and speed up and down roads. I don't like going so fast. It makes me feel queasy.

When we get to Chris's house, Mom tells me to hurry up, so I unstick myself from the back of the car and follow them inside. I don't want to leave the jewelry box in the car, but Mom says we'll be back for it.

The outside of Chris' house is large. The bricks are white, the door is blue. There are dark blue shutters around windows. The lawn is neat and tidy. It is a perfectly square house. Chris closes the door behind me. He holds his arms out to his house like we've never been inside one before. I can tell he is proud of how big it is by the way he puffs out his chest.

Babushka's *dacha* is better.

The house is very clean. It smells like lemons. There is a black cat that rubs itself along my leg. It feels like the cat is trying to tickle me. "That's Sammy," Chris says. "He's very sweet. His sister, Veronica, is shy, but she's around here somewhere."

I bend down and scratch Sammy's head.

"I have a few more presents for you," Chris says, motioning for me to follow him. He leads us into the kitchen where there are all sorts of different crayon boxes and some blank sheets of paper. There is a box of crayons that is glittery. One that smells like fruits. One that has neon colors. One that has over 120 crayons.

"Your mommy says you like to draw. Can you draw us some pictures?"

I stare at all the crayons and paper. Something feels squirmy in my chest.

"Will you draw too?" I ask, looking at Mom and Chris.

"Your mommy and I are going to go upstairs. Why don't you color us some pictures?" He says again.

My shoulders drop. My heart speeds up. I don't like the idea of Mom being alone with anyone. I don't care how nice.

I will never forget the time in the closet.

"Can I come upstairs too?"

"Katya," Mom says, moving close to me. "Stay and color. I'll be down soon." Mom has her strict voice on. The voice she has on when I need to be a good girl. The voice that means not to ask any questions.

"But Mom—"

"Katya—" Mom says. "Enough. Stay here."

Mom takes Chris's hand. "Let's go," she says, smiling at him.

Chris looks at me, his eyebrows bent, like he thinks maybe they should wait.

I try to tell Chris with my eyes to stay.

"Just ignore her. She'll be fine," Mom says.

Mom turns around and pulls Chris behind her. I hear their shoes on the stairs, Mom's high heels clicking until I can't hear them anymore.

My heart flip flops. I know I'm supposed to sit still, to stay, to listen to Mom. I'm not supposed to move. I'm supposed to color a picture. But I can't. I want to know Mom is OK.

I start drawing circles on the paper in front of me. I can't think to draw anything else. Sammy the cat rubs himself against my leg, but I don't care. I just want to see Mom.

I get up from the table and find the stairs, taking them one by one, as quiet as I can, trying to listen for her. I want to make sure she's not screaming. My hands start shaking and I breathe slowly, stopping a lot on my way up. I want to cry but I know if Mom sees me crying I will be in even bigger trouble. Maybe she won't let Babushka come again, which is my second worst fear.

I wish I could be invisible.

I don't know what to do. I stay at the top of the stairs, listening for any noise that could tell me where Mom is. Finally, I hear a moan. My whole body stands still. It's Mom. It's coming from a room to my left. I follow the noise, pressing my ear to the door. I don't know if it is a bad noise. I don't know what to do. Mom will be upset if she knows I moved from downstairs. I don't know if Mom is safe. I wish all the doors were open.

The noise comes again. It's loud. It sounds like a scream. I start shaking. I know Mom is in there.

I don't know if she is OK.

I knock. "Mom?" I ask.

I hear movement, like when someone pulls their bed covers to the side.

"Katya?" I hear Chris ask.

"Yes," I answer.

"Should we go get her?" He whispers, but I know not to me.

"Katya! I told you to stay downstairs! Do not bother us!" Mom says. I can hear she is very, very, upset.

"I—I—I heard—I—Are you OK?" I ask.

"I'm fine! Go back downstairs and do not come up here again!" Mom yells.

Suddenly air comes back inside my body. I feel dizzy from how OK everything is now that I know Mom is safe.

I know she is mad by the sound of her words. They are sharp, like a pinch. Later, she is going to yell at me.

I start to head downstairs but as soon as my feet start moving down the steps I have to use the toilet. It's a pressing pain on my stomach. No one told me where the bathroom is. I go back upstairs, quietly, and open and close several doors, making sure to stay away from the door that I know Chris and Mom are in. Finally, I find a toilet, but it's too late, and I pee a little on the white rug in front of the toilet when I am taking off my underwear.

After I'm done, I walk out into the room that the bathroom is in. It has a computer in it. I touch the keyboard. I like the click of the keys. I have only played with a keyboard one other time and it was at the library with Babushka. There's nothing else on the desk next to the keyboard except tiny Ziploc bags. I've never seen Ziploc bags this tiny. They look like they are for Barbies. When Babushka packed my lunch last year, I asked Mama if we could buy Ziploc bags instead of the sandwich bags we got. The ones we bought didn't close like the Ziploc bags do, so whenever Babushka would pack me food it would spill all over my backpack. She said no. They were twice as expensive, just to be thrown away.

I wonder what Chris needs these tiny Ziploc bags for. They can maybe hold one single goldfish. There are several of them. I think about taking one. They must be for toys anyway, and he's a grown-up and grown-ups don't play with toys. But I don't. I don't want to get into trouble.

I go back downstairs and start drawing. I draw Babushka wearing her favorite hat with a jar of jam in her hand. It doesn't look anything like Babushka, so I get upset and put my head down on the table. I must have fallen asleep because Mom and Chris come downstairs, holding hands. Mom's face is red and so is Chris's. I am scared Mom is going to be mad at me but she says, "It's time for us to go," and we walk towards the door, get in Chris's car, and he drives us back to Joe's crab shack.

I am sad that no one asks about my drawings, but I am happy Mom doesn't yell at me.

Mom and Chris kiss for a long time by Mom's car. Chris gives me a hug, but I don't hug him back.

"What's on your neck?" I ask Chris, when he pulls away. He's wearing a gold chain with what looks like a triangle on it. I didn't notice it before, but now that we're outside and the sun is shining I do.

Chris looks down, like he forgot he had jewelry on. "Oh, this?" He pulls the necklace out of his shirt. He laughs. "I forget I wear this. It's a shark tooth covered in pure gold!"

He takes the necklace off and hands it to me. I take it. It looks like what I thought it was, a triangle.

"Why is it covered in gold?" I ask.

"To protect the tooth. It's very rare. The kind of shark it belongs to doesn't exist anymore. It's called a megalodon. It's the most dangerous creature to ever exist."

Chris bends down to my level as I examine the tooth. It's not big, and it doesn't look scary.

"I think if it were actually scary it wouldn't need gold to protect it."

He smiles. "It looks good in gold."

I give it back to Chris, unimpressed.

"The shark inside the restaurant is better."

He laughs. "Tough crowd."

I go inside the car. Mom and Chris kiss some more, and I fall asleep.

When Mom finally gets in the car she says, "Don't tell Jerry what we did today. Don't tell him about Chris. Don't tell him about the jewelry box."

Mom won't let me bring the jewelry box back home with us.

"OK," I say, even though I don't even remember the last time I said "Hi" to Jerry.

"We are going to get out of there soon, Katulia," Mama says. "Just give me some time, and you won't have to be afraid of Jerry anymore."

I don't tell her that I'm not afraid of Jerry. I am not afraid for myself. My greatest fear is that something bad will happen to her.

We move into Chris's house a month after meeting him, in October. Mom took our big red suitcase and sneaked us out of Jerry's apartment in the morning when he left for work. I like Chris a lot better. What I don't like is this new school.

Everyone else has been in kindergarten for a while when I arrive. Mom says it's fine that I've missed the first part of school because I went to kindergarten last year, and now I won't have to pretend to be the same age as everyone else.

In my first week, I decide I hate kindergarten in Texas. It's worse than in Idaho. I mostly hate it because of a girl named Sophia. Mrs. Sandy, my new teacher, tells Sophia to show me the school, but I don't need anyone to show me around. It's not that hard of a school to understand.

Sophia has socks that have tiny bells that jingle when she walks. She wears a new bow in her hair every day, and her sandwiches are always cut in different shapes.

Sophia is mad when I don't bring a snack for snack time because Mrs. Sandy says she has to share with me. She gives me one of her Oreos but takes it back when Mrs. Sandy's back is turned.

What is the point of Sophia? Probably it is so no one will kidnap us in their white van.

This seems to be a huge worry of every grown up at the school. I had to watch a whole video on why taking candy from adults means they will kidnap me and throw me in a van, and why I can't speak to anyone I don't know, and how I can never be alone ever.

I feel that kidnappers would not take me since Sophia is now my assigned "buddy." Her voice is too loud and whiney, and if someone did want to kidnap us, they would give us right back thanks to her.

Everyone in my class looks like Sophia, with pretty hair with clips and matching clothes and "I love you" notes from their mommies in their lunches.

No one in Idaho dressed very fancy and almost everyone ate lunches from the school cafeteria. I did too, until Babushka came and she packed my lunch.

When I get home from school Chris helps me with my homework. He helps me with my sentences. He wakes up early to watch Pokémon with me. Sometimes he comes home with a new Disney movie, and we watch it on the couch together. Mom doesn't like any cartoon movies, so me and Chris have lots of movie nights while Mom talks on the phone to her friends in Russia. Nights at home aren't scary like they were when we lived with Jerry.

We've been with Chris for a month now, and Mom is pregnant again. Mom and Chris told me today. I know not to prepare for the baby though, because Mom had to get rid of the last baby.

Chris and I are watching Aladdin, when I feel him turn to me.

"Katya, I want you to know that I consider you to be my daughter."

I don't understand what he is getting at so I keep my eyes on the screen and say, "OK."

"I want you to think of me as your father. Your dad. I promise you'll always be my daughter. I'll always treat you like my own. No matter what."

I move my eyes from the TV screen and to Chris's face. He looks like the other dads at school. His face has lots of lines in it. His hair is very thin. He looks a lot older than Mom. He wears glasses, and he always has money in his wallet.

Jerry told me to call him Jerry, not Dad. I have never had a dad before, and now I do.

This is the moment I become his.

English

Summer 2020, Late Twenties

"MY FATHER WANTS to call me," I say to Liam, when the alarm from his phone has woken him up enough to shut it off. He's blinking slowly and stretching his arms, hitting our headboard.

I'm already sitting up. I've been waiting for his alarm to go off all night.

It's seven in the morning. I haven't slept yet.

"What?" He mumbles.

A bit of brown hair has fallen into his eyes. He was supposed to get a haircut last month but with the COVID quarantine going on, the only time we've left our apartment other than to walk the dog was to look at houses.

"He says he wants to call. Me. Like on video," I say, again.

Liam lifts his eyebrows. "Have you slept?" He asks.

"No," I say, pointing to my phone. "I've been texting with my father all night."

"Wow," he responds, scooting up to a seated position next to me. He clears the sleep from his throat. "How are you feeling?

"I don't know," I say, turning my head to look out the window. "I don't know anything anymore. It feels like my life has been upended."

"What did you ask him?" Liam asks, indicating to my phone.

"I questioned him. It was more of an interrogation, really. He sent me evidence of stuff. Emails. There's a lot I didn't know." My eyes feel salty. I should close them.

"Like what?" Liam asks.

"Here," I say, handing him my phone. "You can read it. I'm too tired."

He takes my phone and opens up my conversation with my dad, scrolling up and up and up. He makes a whistling noise with his mouth. "Honestly, Katya, there's too much for me to read. I've got a meeting in ten minutes. You really did talk to him all night. Can you give me the highlights?"

I sit, sorting through all the bombs he dropped. I haven't downloaded all the information to my brain yet—there's so much to sort through, so much to decide. All the realities I believed about my life that weren't actually realities but were fabricated so my mom could take me with her to the United States and not give me back. I wonder if I believe him. My mom has repeatedly told me, over and over, never to believe my father. It's ingrained in every fiber of my being. Yet . . . there's evidence that supports his claims of innocence from what my mom has accused him of.

"Well," I say. "I have a whole-ass family on that side. Siblings. Cousins. Grandma. My grandpa died, but—" a little bit of my stomach dips at that, that I was never given the opportunity to have a relationship with him, but I'll deal with that later. "I had an aunt and an uncle but they also died."

"The poisoning of the aunt?" My husband questions.

"Cancer. She had breast and ovarian cancer. That's what made her sick. He doesn't have control over any of her property. She has a daughter, my cousin, who owns her apartment. My dad helped pay for my aunt's medical treatment. He took care of her daughter. My cousin thinks of him as her dad. My dad thinks of my cousin as his daughter."

Liam smiles, but it's sad.

"He said—he said he wanted me," I continue. "He said he didn't know she was taking me away. I had just gotten sick. I had pneumonia or something. The doctor recommended I go somewhere that was sunny, so she asked his permission to go to Mexico. He said yes. She said we'd only be gone for three weeks. He said he didn't hear from her again for almost five years. He didn't know where I was."

Liam looks up, like he is contemplating something. "Did he—did he search for you? I mean, what did he do to look for you?"

He has gotten out of bed now, probably looking for a shirt so he can hop on his morning sync with his team.

"He told me that back then there were no child abduction laws in Russia. You couldn't do anything if the other parent decided to take your kid. Also, there were basically no parental rights for fathers after a divorce. He asked everyone who knew my mom, and they wouldn't give her up. He said someone told him we were in America but not where."

"Wow," Liam says, finding the shirt he's looking for in our "clean clothes" pile on the floor. He slides it on. Another alarm goes off, and I recognize it as the alarm he sets to tell him he should log onto his computer.

"He wanted me," I repeat. "She always, always told me he didn't want anything to do with me."

Liam comes over to me, taking my hand. "You're cold," he says, cupping my hand in both of his.

"You're late to your meeting," I point out.

"How does he know English?" Liam asks, ignoring my comment.

I'm not crying, I don't feel like crying, but I feel like there are tears in me that are stuck.

"He said . . . he said that he never stopped learning English for me."

Liam kisses my hand and smiles. "That probably feels really good to hear."

"He studied English when he was in school but . . . when he found out I went to the US, he picked it back up again. He said he wanted to be able to talk to me when he saw me again because he didn't know if I knew Russian, since it had been such a long time. After he saw me for the first time, in the States, when I was eight, he said I refused to speak Russian to him. He said he knew he'd never stop learning English for me."

"That is definitely the opposite of how callous your mom described him as being," Liam observes.

"Yeah," I nod. "I feel guilty for how mean I was to him when I was a kid. I mean, I was a kid, I didn't know better, but I feel bad, especially after he forwarded me the emails he traded with Mom. He offered to pay for my college, he tried to call me every Sunday, and he tried to see me several times, but my mom emailed him and told him she wouldn't let him. It was shocking to see the emails she sent back. I mean, he offered to pay for my college. I wouldn't have had any school debt. Why would she take that from me?"

Liam shakes his head. "I don't know, sweetheart. That's . . . awful."

"It just feels like my mom didn't want me to have any connections to my family outside of herself. I can't understand it."

Liam's alarm is going off again. I look at the clock and see he is ten minutes late.

"Maybe she was afraid you'd leave her," he says, turning his alarm off.

"Well, her worst fear came true." I respond. "What gets me the most, I think, is that she maintained that he had never tried to get in touch, when he so clearly did. I guess maybe because she had both parents growing up, I don't know, but didn't she think about what it would do to me to think he didn't want me?"

Liam sighs. "Well, I mean, maybe she thought her loving you would be enough."

I scoff.

"It wasn't. Not the way she did it."

PART 3

Baby

Late '90s, Six Years Old, Summer after Kindergarten

I AM ON THE way to the mall to pick out a present for my new baby sister. I haven't met her yet, even though she's been born for a few days. I stayed with Dad's friends from work while Mom was pushing Masha out. As soon as Dad picked me up he said, "You have a beautiful baby sister. Her name is Masha."

Like mashed potatoes, I think, but I don't say that.

Mom got pregnant right after we left Jerry and moved in with Chris last October. We only met Chris at Joe's Crab Shack in September, so things moved pretty fast.

No one was happy about Mom and Chris getting married so quickly, especially not Chris's Mom, who calls Mom a "gold digger." When I ask Mom what this name means she says it means that Chris's mom thinks that my mom only cares about Chris being rich, but Mom says she cares about a citizenship for us too. Also, she didn't think Chris was that rich when she first met him. She only found that out later. Chris's best friend helped Mom get a divorce from Jerry. Mom said all she wanted from him was her ring.

Dad is more happy than I have ever seen him before. His smile stretches out his whole face. I feel a spark of sadness. I wonder if seeing me makes him this happy, or if it's because he has a real baby now.

We just got to the toy store in the mall. Chris tells me to get whatever I want because it's my first gift to my sister, so it has to be very special.

I very carefully look at everything the store has and pick out a mermaid Barbie doll. I am sure the baby will want to play with it too. She is my sister so I will make her like what I like.

"A Barbie?" Dad asks.

I nod my head. "So she can play with me."

He looks around the store, like he's wondering if there is something better, and then looks at the Barbie again.

"You're right. All little girls love Barbies," he says. When we get up to the counter to pay, I see a baby bottle pop, one of my favorite candies. I grab two. "Can I get these?" I ask him.

He nods.

"One for me, one for the baby," I say, carrying our gifts to the car.

When we get to the hospital room, Mom is asleep. Dad immediately goes to Mom and gives her a kiss. I want to see Mom too, but first I see a pink blob in what looks like a large carry-out container toward the back of the room. I walk closer to it and look inside.

The pink blob is a baby. I didn't know babies could be so ugly and fat. This one looks like the old used up pink play-dough my teacher gives us in school when we have to stay inside for recess because it's raining. The baby is wearing a white shirt that covers her whole body. It has rabbits on it.

I look at Dad, who is laughing with Mom. He's holding my bag with the ring pops in it, and I don't want to bother him to give it to me because I want to be alone with my sister. I am thinking about whether I should wake her up to introduce myself when she starts sucking the air. I think this means she is hungry. I dig around in my pocket and pull out nothing.

I put my finger in her mouth so maybe she feels like she's eating something.

We stay like that for a while until I hear Mom say, "Where's Katya?" She moves her head to look at me and immediately she puts her mean voice on. "Don't put your finger in her mouth! Your hands are dirty! Katya!"

Dad laughs and comes over and takes Masha out of the large food container. Masha starts crying. This makes me feel good because she wasn't crying when my finger was in her mouth. Dad hands Masha to Mom, and Mom tries to stick her boob in Masha's mouth, which Masha does not accept.

Masha is born really knowing how to cry. She is very loud. When Masha has finally calmed down and stuck Mom's boob in her mouth, I ask Dad if I should give Masha her toy.

Dad says to wait until we get home.

I wonder what the point of getting the toy was. I ask if I can give Masha the candy and Mom snaps at me and says no. Then she turns to Dad and asks why he would let me buy candy for a baby. Dad laughs.

I'm sitting in the corner of the hospital room, wishing I could watch TV. Masha seems like she is sleeping now, but Mom doesn't look like she wants to put her back in the takeout container. She keeps staring at her squishy face, like Masha has some sort of hypnotizing baby power. "You have the best sister in the world," I hear Mom whisper.

This surprises me. I didn't think Mom liked me very much. I wonder if she forgot I was in the room.

"You need to grow up to be just like her."

I decide this baby is a good thing.

Babushka

Fall, Late '90s, Six Years Old, First Grade

I AM SUPPOSED TO be in school, but Mom lets me miss it to pick up Babushka from the airport.

Tears spring to my eyes when I see Babushka come through the doors at the airport. I have not seen her since I was five, and now I'm almost seven. Babushka runs to me and squeezes me tight. I'm holding Masha in my arms, and she kisses both of our heads. She says that we are her loves, her life, her suns, her rabbits. She takes Masha out of my arms and holds her close to her chest. In three months, Masha had gone from looking like a used piece of pink chewing gum to how an actual baby is supposed to look, like a doll.

Masha doesn't like anyone she doesn't know holding her, but Masha must know that this is her Babushka because she doesn't even start crying. Mom is hugged last which I think annoys her. Everyone is crying, except Masha, who is looking at me like she doesn't know what's going on. I smile at her to let her know that this is not a moment for her to also cry, because she doesn't know how to cry in a happy way yet, and she will probably just make everyone anxious if she opens her mouth right now.

Babushka tells us that we are being ridiculous and that she is here and that we are all fine. She keeps crying and kissing our heads, even while we're picking up her bags and walking from the airport to Mom's small car.

"Do you realize I will now have to spend three months out of the year in America? Do you know how old I am? What do you expect me to do when I am even older?" Babushka says, when she closes the passenger side door to the car. Me and Masha are squished in between one of her suitcases. I'm glad Dad isn't here because there's no way he would fit in here too.

Babushka is wiping away tears. "Do you know how hard that trip is for someone as old as me? How bad the clouds are for my legs? It's going to take all three months to be able to sleep on a regular schedule, then when I get home it will take another three months to sleep normal again!"

"We will go back home, Mama," Mom says. "Soon. You won't have to keep making this trip. I promise," she says in Russian.

Does Mom plan on going back to Russia? Are we going to move back? Does Daddy know?

"When? Katya is already losing her Russian. Masha will not know any. Why aren't you speaking Russian with them?"

"I don't want Katya to get an accent. She's smart. She can do whatever she wants as long as she sounds like an American."

"You are making them forget their home! Where they came from!"

Masha didn't even ever go to Russia. I don't know how it's her home. But Babushka is right. I don't remember it. The only thing that makes it home, really, is Babushka.

"I am doing my best, Mama. I just have to wait on the documents."

"Uh-huh. The documents. Pew!" Babushka says, and spits over her shoulder. She crosses her arms and looks out the window. I wonder if this is why Mom has been talking to Babushka less on the phone.

When we get home, Babushka starts to unpack all her things in Masha's room.

"Babushka, what did you bring me?" I ask, peering in her suitcase. She swats me away.

"When did you become so greedy?" She laughs, but then grabs my head and kisses my ear. "Here," she says, giving me a bag with my favorite *krasna shapka* candy.

Masha is lying on the bed, and I bring a piece of candy to her face. “You can’t have any,” I say. “You can only have a bottle until the doctor says you can have food. But trust me when I say it’s the best chocolate.”

Masha looks at me with her wide eyes. I open a candy and eat one in front of her, pointing to my lips. “See? I love it. There probably won’t be any left for when you can finally try food.”

“In Russian!” Babushka scolds.

“You can’t have any chocolate,” I say to Masha, in Russian.

Stuck

Spring, Early 2000s, Seven Years Old, First Grade

Babushka was only supposed to stay for three months, but it's been seven months, and she's still here.

Babushka says we need a lot of help and doesn't know how we've been doing anything without her. I don't know how we did anything without Babushka either.

Mom is gone most of the time. I don't know where she is, and when I ask, Babushka says she is getting our documents so we can become American. Dad is at work a lot. He comes home late at night and sleeps most of the day.

Every day Babushka takes Masha in a stroller and picks me up from school. We walk home even when it's raining.

Today, I run out of class and start heading toward our favorite tree when I see Mom's angry face.

"Where's Babushka?" I ask her, looking around.

"I'm sending her back to Russia," Mom says, grabbing me by the arm and leading me to the parking lot.

"You can't do that!" I shout at her, pushing her off. "Why would you say that?"

Mom ignores me.

My whole body shakes as Mom drives us home. When I see the front door, I jump out of the car and run inside, looking for Babushka.

She's sitting on the couch while Masha is playing on a rug in the living room. Babushka's face is red and her head is in her hands. She looks like she's been crying.

"Babushka! What happened?" I run over to her.

Babushka's face crumbles, and she opens her arms for me. I start crying too even though I don't know why.

"Mashinka—" she says.

I turn to look at Masha. She's smiling and drooling all over herself, like she normally is. I notice there is a dark red mark next to her ear. Mom goes to pick up Masha and kisses where the mark is.

"What is going on?" I ask Babushka, who still has her head in her hands.

"Mama is trying to get us deported!" Mom says. "She is trying to get us sent to Russia!" Mom pauses. "I understand why Papa left you for another woman! This was so idiotic of you."

I feel my eyebrows start to bend in a frown, but I stop them. It's not a good idea to show how I feel right now but I don't like how Mom is talking to Babushka.

"No, Yuliya. It was a mistake! I promise. I was scared!" Babushka shouts. "It wasn't on purpose!"

"Ah-hah." Mom says, walking away. I can see the fear in her face. She looks like her fear is too big to hide under all her fire, and it's coming out, and she doesn't know how to handle it.

"What happened?" I whisper.

"Oh Katulia," Babushka says. "I was cooking *katleti*, and Masha was pulling herself up on the chairs. She pulled herself up and stuck her head through the rails in the chairs! I didn't even think she could do that! I turned around, and she was screaming. I ran over to her and started screaming and begging her to take her head out. She couldn't! Chris gave me the 911 number to call in case something terrible happened. Yuliya said to never call, no matter what, but I was not going to let Masha die!" I have never seen Babushka so frantic.

"Babushka, it's OK," I say. I don't know how else to make her feel better.

"By the time the police arrived, Masha pulled her head out," Babushka continues. "She was laughing, like nothing had happened. I can't speak English, so I couldn't explain to the police why I called. They stayed until Yuliya came."

My chest squeezes. That is why Mom is so angry. Because the police came. She's afraid they know we don't have our papers.

I sit back down next to Babushka and lean into her.

I am terrified Mom will send Babushka back to Russia. I want to disappear into her, so we can't ever be apart again.

"It's OK," Mom sighs, coming back into the room. She sits down next to us on the couch. "We're fine. Just—just keep a closer watch on her." Mom puts her head in her hands.

"She is slippery!" Babushka says. "She's not like Katya was. Katya was a quiet baby. You could leave her in the same spot for hours. Masha likes to crawl around. She likes to stand up. She likes to put her fingers in things! It makes it hard to cook!"

Mom doesn't move her head from her hands.

I feel Babushka sniff and wipe her eyes. "She's more like you were. You were so fast. I chased you around everywhere. You could walk at eight months!"

I think that Mom probably doesn't know what kind of baby Masha is because Mom doesn't spend time with her. She doesn't know what kind of baby I was either. But Babushka knows. Babushka will always know.

We're not supposed to celebrate birthdays early in Russia—it's bad luck—but Dad doesn't care. Dad decides to throw Masha's birthday almost a month early.

Dad calls it a "black tie event," which means everyone has to dress up in really nice clothes, including Masha. The problem is that most of the time we have trouble keeping a diaper on Masha.

"Katya, you hold her hands above her head," Babushka says to me. At this point, we have tried holding Masha's legs down, we have tried holding her arms at her sides, we have tried distracting her with cartoons, with Babushka dancing, me dancing, but nothing is working.

She refuses to wear this dress.

"Can't we put her in something else?" I ask Babushka. Masha is screaming like someone is trying to kill her.

"I wish, Katyusha, but Chris says it needs to be this dress." Babushka's face goes into a hard line when she mentions Dad's name.

"Let me try," I say to Babushka.

Babushka shrugs and gives me the dress. I sit in front of a wailing Masha. "Masha, listen. Can you please just wear this dress for a few hours? You'll really make everyone's life a lot easier if you stop yelling. I promise you'll get to take it off at some point in the middle of the party so you can eat cake. They always let you run around naked when you want to eat."

Masha's big blue eyes leak tears, but silently instead of at an annoying roar, so I take this to mean that I am allowed to put the dress on her.

"You're right. It's ugly," I say, when it's all the way over her head.

The dress is a pink, puffy, thing that looks like if Mom's shaving cream was clothes. Masha starts pulling at the collar, and I ask her to stop so she does.

"You got the dress on!" Babushka says, coming back into the room. "A sister bond is so important," she adds.

Babushka is wearing bright pink lipstick and a yellow dress dotted with blue flowers. Mom got it from the secondhand store for her. "Your great-aunt, Baba Alonya, is three years older than me, and we have never been apart this long. I don't remember my life without her, ever. I can't. My kids have always been her kids. Her friends have always been my friends. We have always done everything together. Sisters have an unbreakable bond."

I look at Masha. "You are going to have to do everything I tell you forever," I say to her. I give her a very strong look with my eyes, hoping she will understand the seriousness of what I am saying.

I pick out the prettiest dress I have, then go to Babushka's bathroom to put on her lipstick, so we match. I put some on Masha too.

Downstairs, Dad is in the kitchen. There are a lot of people here already. Dad has waiters walking around with trays in their hands delivering food and drinks. I don't know how any of this is for Masha when her favorite things are mud and me and Babushka, but I think grown-ups do a lot of things they say are for their kids but are really for themselves.

When Dad sees me, he is smiling, but I can tell he's upset about something. I spin around in my dress so he can tell me how pretty I am but all he says is, "Katya, can you get the birthday girl? All her friends are waiting to say hi to her."

Masha doesn't have any friends. She barely even knows my name.

"OK," I say, and go back upstairs. I am sad Dad didn't say I am pretty.

Babushka and Masha and I meet Dad in the kitchen, where he takes Masha out of Babushka's hands and starts showing her around the house. Masha starts crying, which makes Dad's face red.

"We should follow them so Masha stops crying," I tell Babushka.

Babushka doesn't budge. "Let him take care of his daughter for once," she says, quietly.

I feel confused. Babushka doesn't like Dad because he doesn't take care of Masha, but he is always working to make money for us. It's not like Mom takes care of us either. Why isn't she mad at her?

After some pulling of her arm, Babushka finally follows Dad with me, and when Masha sees our faces she stops crying. She even laughs when I make funny faces at her.

Dad asks one of the waiters to bring out Masha's birthday cake, and he puts her in her high chair and everyone sings "Happy Birthday" and Masha slams her face in the cake, which I told her to do because that got Dad to take off her dress.

Masha is very smart. After that Dad hands Masha to Babushka, and we go back upstairs.

After we finish washing Masha, her eyes start to close so we put her down for the night. Babushka and I go downstairs to get cake when we hear Masha's soft snores.

"Do you remember much about Russia, Katyusha?" Babushka asks me, placing a forkful of chocolate cake in her mouth. We're in the backyard, on a bench.

"Sometimes," I say, thinking of the time Dedushka gave me a lollipop that was actually a whistle. It's my first memory, when I was two. "Can you tell me more about when I was a baby?" I ask, leaning on her shoulder. I know not to talk about Dedushka with Babushka right now because they just got a divorce.

"Of course," Babushka says. "You were a funny baby. You didn't walk until almost two years old because your thighs were so big," she laughs. "Me and your—your—dedushka just thought you liked to be carried by us."

"I'll tell you one of my favorite stories," Babushka continues. "When you were little your mother brought a man to our dacha. He was some British man, a potential husband of course, and he spoke only a little bit of Russian. Enough to tell us that he thought we lived like pigs because the dacha didn't have plumbing. You asked me why he was stupid," Babushka says, her smile breaking her face open. "You were only three but you understood that he was terrible. You said, 'Babushka, that man doesn't know how to use the toilet, and he can't say anything right. Is he dumb?' You said that because he refused to use the toilet outside." Babushka takes my hand and squeezes it, tight. She looks at the people in front of us in their fancy clothes. "Your mother said you would have a better life in America, but you never cared about this kind of life," she says, nodding to the crowd. "You just wanted to be with us."

She's right. I would use the toilet outside if it meant I can be with my Babushka all the time.

It's our first night without Babushka.

It's just me and Masha now. Babushka stayed for a full eight months, but today she went home. Masha is a year and a month old. It's summer and almost time for the school year. I'll be turning eight soon.

Masha has not stopped crying since Babushka left. I at least understand that Babushka went back to Russia. For Masha, one second Babushka is here, changing her diapers, feeding her mashed potatoes, and the next she's gone. Now the only person Masha has is me.

Mom's here, but she's not really here. She did all the right things for Masha tonight. She put Masha in her crib, gave her a bottle, changed her diaper, gave her a kiss on the forehead, and then left. Masha kept looking around, confused. I know she was looking for Babushka. She cried a lot, but Mom didn't do any of the things that normally comforted Masha. She didn't sing any of her favorite songs, or make any of her favorite faces. She didn't tell Masha any stories from Babushka's time at the orphanage. She just left a crying Masha and me in her room.

I pick Masha up out of her crib and hold her tight. We can't even call Babushka to hear her voice because she's on the airplane. I open the shutters to the windows and look at the sky. A few airplanes go by, and I know they're not Babushka's because she left hours ago.

Masha opens her mouth to start crying again and I give her my "don't" look.

"I don't know when Babushka will be back. I know you want her here. So do I. Her documents said she had to go to Russia, or they wouldn't let her in America again. She promised she would be back here soon," I feel tears at the edges of my eyelids, but I look away from Masha so she doesn't see them fall because then she'll think it's OK to start screaming.

The Worst Day

Summer, Early 2000s, Seven Years Old, Second Grade

I DON'T KNOW WHAT to do.

Masha ran away from me and fell on the fire place poker. It cut through her lip. There is blood everywhere.

"Mom! Dad! Masha is bleeding! Please!" I call up the stairs. They're fighting again, and when they fight, they can't hear me. They have fought a lot since Babushka left.

I look at Masha, who is breaking my heart with her face. She looks like she is in so much pain.

I want to call Babushka but Daddy has started to get mad at Mom for using the phone so much. Mom told me to stop using it because he is blaming her for the bill. It feels like someone is ripping my heart outside of my body when I can't call her, but I don't want Mom to get in anymore trouble.

I run to the kitchen and get a towel and put it on Masha's lip. "Mom! Dad!" I shout. "Please! Masha is bleeding!"

I start crying because Masha is hurting so bad she's closing her eyes and leaning against me. Usually when she gets hurt she gets back up quickly and starts playing again. This time, she doesn't wiggle away, so I know she is in a lot of pain.

My heart runs miles in my chest. I need to do something but I can't leave her. I wish they would open their door.

"It's OK," I say to Masha, stroking her tiny blonde curls. She has bled through the towel.

"I need to get you another one," I say. I get up and get another towel and remember we have ice in the fridge and get some and put it in there. I put the ice to her lip and that seems to calm her down just a little bit.

Finally, I hear the door to the bedroom open. I feel both scared and better. Daddy will know what to do. I hear his feet clonk downstairs and when he reaches us he stops and frowns. "What happened here?" His face is red and looks angry already.

"Masha fell when she was running," I pointed to the fireplace poker. "On that thing."

Babushka told him to take it down. Why does he need it? We're in Texas and there is no use for fires. He stares at us for a moment and says, "Yuliya! Get your ass down here!" There is a power in his eyes that I don't recognize.

I hear Mom scamper downstairs, like she is afraid. When she gets down I see that there is dark makeup running from her eyes. Her white shirt is ripped at the neckline. She's wearing her sad shorts. The shorts she can wear for days and days and not shower. They are gray and striped with black lines.

"What?" Mom asks, sniffing. Mom squints her eyes, looking at me and Masha. She opens them wide and blinks.

"Do you see this? Do you see what happened to our kid? You're a terrible fucking mother. Your seven-year-old is her babysitter because you can't get your shit together enough to keep an eye on her." Dad is wearing blue exercise shorts and a white T-shirt. He looks like he just got back from the gym. I can see his muscles through his shirt. His hair is messy, like he just woke up, and his eyes are red, like Mom when she cries.

I squeeze Masha to my chest. She has started sucking on her thumb, and her body is getting heavier in my arms. She drops the ice pack that I made. I'm afraid to see if she's still bleeding but maybe not if she can put her thumb in her mouth and it not taste bad.

I look down slowly, scared to see that we're sitting in a pool of blood. I wince. It's pretty bloody but not as bad as I thought.

In a small voice, I say, "What do we do?" I look at Daddy, because Mom looks like a tiny mouse who wants to run, but doesn't know which direction.

He squints, and it looks like he's examining her, but he's not getting close to us. "She's fine. It's her lip. It'll bleed more than the rest of her body, so it looks a lot worse than it is."

I wonder if I should get up to show her to him but I don't want to move her. My legs are getting sleepy with her sitting on them but I don't want her to start crying again.

"What about—what about medicine? So there won't be an—an—infection?"

"She'll be OK," he waves his hand toward us, like he's shooing us away.

He turns toward Mom, who hasn't said anything. He looks like he's going to blow up.

"What do you have to say for yourself?" He says, getting close to her face. I squeeze Masha to my chest. I have a feeling in my stomach like I don't want Masha to see what is coming next, but also like if I'm not watching mom something terrible will happen.

"You're worthless as a mother. It was the worst day of my life meeting you," he pushes Mom into the wall, and I see her eyes close tight.

"I thought you were done," she says, quietly.

"Done?" he says. "Done? I won't ever be done. I have to take care of you, both of your kids, I mean, I'm fucking shackled aren't I?"

Mom turns her head so that she's not facing him anymore. I feel myself start to shake, but I tell my body to stop because if I am scared, Masha will start to be scared too.

"I asked you a question," Dad's voice says, I imagine his words slithering out of his mouth like a snake. Suddenly, he reaches his meaty hands out and grabs Mom around the neck. I don't understand what's going on. Is he going to kiss her? It takes me a minute to realize what he's doing. He's choking her.

My body feels like ice. There is no more air in my mouth or my lungs. I know I need to protect Masha. I also need to scream at him to stop, but if I do that Masha will cry and that might make him more mad. I don't want to direct his attention to her.

Mom coughs and slaps his arm.

"Oh, you don't like this?" He asks.

Mom hits him harder. I feel dizzy. I want to scream at him to get away from Mom. I want to tear at his back. What is he doing?

Finally, he lets go of Mom. She runs outside from the hall to the backyard. Dad follows after her, but he pauses when he sees her purse on the kitchen table. He picks it up and goes to her. I look at Masha, who is still sucking her thumb on my shoulder.

"We're going to move, OK? Just a little bit." I get up, holding Masha by the butt, and move us so that I have a better view of the backyard.

Through the open doors to the backyard, I see Dad reach into Mom's purse and pull out a small book. I recognize it as her address book. "You think I don't know where you've been going?" He says, throwing it at her.

The address book hits her face. I wince, feeling it too.

"You have an immigration lawyer. I found you one. Who is this?"

"You haven't paid the bill. They stopped taking my calls," Mom says, swallowing. She keeps backing up but Dad is coming towards her, closer and closer. "We need papers, Chris. I had to find my own."

"I'll be in charge of if you go or stay in this country, and lately I've been leaning towards getting your ass deported and keeping my daughter here, where she can grow up and not end up a whore like you," Dad says, looking into her purse again.

Mom backs into the garage. She looks up, like Babushka does when she prays. "Chris, please, I ask you to stop. I ask you to stop with the drugs. Let's lay down," Mom whispers, but she makes no move to get up. "Let's go to bed, please, Chris."

Dad pulls out a tube of Mom's lipstick and pelts it at her. It lands in her eye. She hisses, melting towards the ground.

"Please," she says.

"You know why I do it?" He asks. "You know why I take 'the drugs'?" He mimics the way Mom says the words, making fun of it because he knows she didn't say it right with her accent.

"To get away from the hell that you make of my life. All your crying. All your nagging. All your constant *wanting*. Figure it the fuck out!" He spits. Mom puts her head in her hands. She looks like she's accepted whatever he's going to do next. Like she won't fight back.

Dad sticks his hand in her purse and he pulls out Mom's red phone. It has twelve buttons on the front. Mom says I'm never, ever, allowed to make any phone calls on it because it's very expensive. I've never even seen Mom use it. Dad smiles at the phone like it said a joke.

"Remember when I gave this to you?" He asks. "I have literally given you fucking everything your heart desires, and you still fucking complain! You should be kissing the ground I walk on! You should be calling me king!" He slams the phone down next to him. At least he didn't throw it at her.

Mom doesn't look up from her buried hands. I think this upsets Dad because he grabs her by her hair and starts dragging her across the concrete patio of the backyard.

I get up, holding Masha tight to my chest, and scream, "Daddy! Don't hurt my mommy!" I can't help the shaking. I can't help the tears. "Please!" I add. I hold Masha's head protectively, praying she doesn't cry. I couldn't leave her inside by herself after the lip disaster. I didn't have any other choice. I brace myself for her screams.

Whatever happens, I'll protect her.

Dad lets go of Mom's hair and stares at me, and I pray we're not his next target. I think of where to put Masha in case I am. Mom gets up from the ground and races inside the house, and Dad, when he recognizes what's happening, follows after her.

I follow after them, Masha in my hands. The doors to the backyard lead directly into the kitchen.

When we're inside, I see that the cord of the phone has been ripped out of the wall. The phone is off the hook and on the ground.

"You can call the police, but they won't believe you!" Dad screams. He's standing next to the big white fridge. There's a smear of blood on it. Is Mom bleeding?

"Who would believe you!" he screams. "No one. You can't even speak English right!"

"Stop! Daddy! Stop!" We're next to the back door still. I hold on to a kitchen chair to help me balance since Masha is still in my arms.

Dad looks at me again but he closes his mouth. Masha, surprisingly, still hasn't started crying.

Dad walks past me and goes to the backyard. Mom is on the ground in the kitchen, picking up the pieces of the phone.

"Shit," she mutters.

"You tried to call the police," I say. I hear Daddy's words about them not believing her echoing in my ears.

I didn't even know that was an option, ever.

She nods. "I don't know what we're going to do now."

Suddenly, a large crash comes from outside. Mom stands up and goes to the back door to the kitchen. I stay where I am. Masha also hasn't lifted her head from my shoulder. I pray so hard she doesn't.

"Are you OK?" I whisper.

She baby babbles back to me, but her thumb is in her mouth.

"Just stay quiet," I whisper. "I won't put you down." Even though my arms are burning. Something inside of me won't let me put Masha down. I ignore every other feeling I have.

"What are you doing?" Mom asks Dad. She's in the backyard now, in front of the garage. I am still next to the backdoor, my hand gripping the kitchen chair, but I turn around so I know what's happening behind me.

Mom's voice is even. She isn't yelling but her voice is strong, like she isn't scared.

"I'm locking your fucking car." Dad is in front of Mom's car, which is parked in the garage.

"Why are you locking the car? I need to get Masha milk. She's out."

"Because you're going to try to leave the fucking country with my daughter. I know you are. You are going to take her and disappear."

"How will we get food?" Mom asks.

"Figure it out," he says. "You're smart. You roped a rich American into marrying you and having a kid with you."

When Dad is done locking her car with a big, black metal thing that looks like a stick, he storms out of the garage, to the backyard, and back into the kitchen. He rushes past me, stomping up the stairs.

I hope that he leaves. I hope we do leave the country. I want to leave him. I want to leave here.

Mom comes through the back door. She looks in the hallway, toward the stairs, like she's going to go up there too.

"Mom, don't," I say, running over to her. "Please. Stay down here. With us."

She looks at me until his stomping breaks her eye contact. It sounds like he's moving things around up there. Mom backs down. "OK," she says, nodding. "Let me hold her," she says, opening her arms for Masha.

I don't give Masha to her.

"What if he comes back?" I ask, looking upstairs.

"He won't hurt me when she's in my arms," Mom says.

Something heavy drops from my mouth to my stomach. Masha isn't a shield. She should want to protect Masha.

"Come on," Mom says, hurriedly.

I feel tears in my eyes. I can't give Masha to Mom.

"Come on," Mom says, angrier. "She's my daughter. Give her to me!"

I don't move. Mom takes Masha from me, and Masha starts screaming, holding her arms out to me, her little fingers wiggling like she's uncomfortable.

"Stop," Mom says, adjusting Masha so that her back is toward the stairs and Masha is on her shoulder. I won't let Masha out of my sight. I'll jump in front of her. I don't care.

We're all in front of the stairs now, staring, waiting. Dad's shoes make an appearance on the top step.

He makes his way down.

"Where are you going?" Mom yells. Masha was already screaming but now she's screaming even louder. I feel like I'm going to pass out from how nervous I am. If Mom could give Masha to me then I know how to make her stop screaming and there would be less noise and Dad won't be in danger of going more crazy. "Huh?" Mom asks.

With Masha in her arms Mom is less scared. She looks like she feels like she can stand up to Dad. She trusts Dad not to hurt them. I don't know why. Dad has a type of crazy in his eyes that I have never seen before.

"I'm getting the fuck away from you," Dad growls. He's downstairs now, shoving past us.

"How am I supposed to take care of these kids?"

"You don't take care of them anyway!" he roars, turning around. He's close to the front door. "I come downstairs to them bleeding and stained. When's the last time you had a bath?" Dad screams, turning to me.

I swallow. "I—I—I don't know," I answer.

"See? Horrible."

He puts his shoes on and Mom comes closer. I want to stand between Mom and Dad, to protect her, to protect Masha. It's even worse because Masha's screams are piercing. Even I want to cover my ears to hide from the noise.

"Daddy, please," I say. "We need food. Please don't take the car away."

Dad comes over to me. He looks like he was about to open the door but changed his mind. My whole body goes stiff. Mom follows him, bouncing Masha, as though that will make her stop screaming.

"I'm not your fucking daddy!" He screams into my face. "Your daddy is in Russia. You should ask her about him," he says, pointing to Mom. "She took you away from him."

I feel my whole face scrunch up in confusion. What does he mean?

"But—"

"Now, leave me the fuck alone! All of you!" Dad turns around and heads to the front door, opening it wide, and walking through. He slams it as hard as I've ever heard. I hear a key in the main lock.

Masha's screams sound like static after he leaves. Everything in my head is swirling and it is very hard to stand up straight and not fall in the direction that my head is spinning.

Mom tries the front door. "He locked us in," she mumbles. Then, as though it hit her again, "Shit. He locked us in. We can only get out if we have a key."

I get a grip on myself, straightening up. Mom needs me. So does Masha.

"I'll go through the window." Babushka taught me how to unlock them and remove the screens.

"Go," Mom says. "Go to the neighbors. Call the police. He'll be back."

I don't ask if she's sure.

After I leave through the window I run to Ms. Nancy's across the street. I tell her I need to call the police. She dials immediately, and I don't even tell her Dad had done something bad. She said, "There's been a domestic dispute." I'd never heard those words but by the way Ms. Nancy speaks she sounds like she knows what had happened. Had she seen everything?

When she is done calling the police, Ms. Nancy takes my hand, and we cross the street. I feel dizzy as I lead her to the window I just crawled out of. She gets through it with me and we see Mom together. She is sitting against the wall, her face bloodied, her body bruised. Mom is crying and holding Masha, who sits in between Mom's legs, sucking her thumb. She's leaning against Mom's body, her eyes sleepy.

Ms. Nancy bends down. "What happened, Yuliya?" She whispers.

Mom starts crying instead of talking. Ms. Nancy sits next to her with her arm around her shoulders. I almost slide to the ground next to them but notice that Masha doesn't have her pacifier, which I know she will want later. Her thumb had clearly been working overtime. I run upstairs and into our room to grab it. On my way out I notice something gold and shiny in the corner of the hallway.

Dad's shark tooth necklace. I walk over to it, staring at the glinting gold on the ground. The chain is broken. Dad must have yanked on it. I pick up the necklace. The shark tooth is small in my soft, pink, palm. Dad told me that he covered the tooth in gold so that it would always be protected.

What is he trying to protect it from anyway?

Suddenly, I want to scrape all the stupid gold off. I want to stomp on the tooth. I want to crack it.

I want Dad to see me do these things.

I hate Dad. I hate it here. I miss my Babushka.

When the police come they tell Mom she has to go to the hospital to get checked out.

Ms. Nancy says she'll watch me and Masha.

We go to Ms. Nancy's house. Ms. Nancy brings me a cup of water and I drink it, sitting by the door.

"You can sit on the couch," she says, gently. Her face is bent in concern. Her black hair is in a bun, and she is wearing slacks and a fancy, white, button up shirt. She works in the same building as Dad, but he never mentions her.

"It'll be more comfortable," she presses.

I don't want to stand up and unfurl my legs and stretch out my arms. I don't want to expose my stomach. I want to stay curled up, with Masha on me, in our little cocoon by the door. I think if I move my heart will start beating fast again, and I just got it to calm down.

I shake my head at Ms. Nancy. "I'm OK here," I say.

She takes my glass and walks away. I hear her put it in the metal sink.

I wonder when Mom is coming back.

Masha's lip is still cut, and she has some dried blood in her mouth, but she isn't crying so I don't think the police noticed her.

The phone rings, and Ms. Nancy walks to get it.

My ears perk up. Ms. Nancy says "Mhmm," and "yes," and "OK," a lot and then hangs up. She comes over to me and Masha and sits on the floor next to us.

"That was your Mom. She's coming home soon. The police are going to ask you some questions about what happened. She asked me to feed you. You haven't eaten," Ms. Nancy says. I remember Ms. Nancy has two boys. I don't remember how old they are. They go to private school. Right now, they're at summer camp.

Dad likes all his neighbors, but he always stays away from Ms. Nancy.

I wonder if she knows he's bad.

"Can I take you to McDonald's?" She asks, her eyebrows up. "Do you like hamburgers? Or chicken nuggets? Does she?" She looks down at Masha. Babushka wouldn't like us eating junk food.

I wish Babushka was here.

I nod. We don't have food at home. There's no milk for Masha. I don't know when Dad will be back with food and since the car doesn't work I don't know how we're supposed to get any.

Ms. Nancy smiles. I want to ask her if she thinks Daddy is a bad man. I want her to tell me if we are going to get kicked out of America now because we called the police. I want her to tell me when Babushka will come back. I know not to ask her any of these things, but I wish someone could tell me.

Waiting

Summer 2020, Late Twenties

I CAN'T STOP TAPPING my damned foot, which irritates me because any noise bothers the hell out of me when I'm anxious. What the hell is this new tic? Usually when I am anxious I want everything, including myself, to be still. I need to know every sound, every motion. Today, it's *tap tap tap tap*. Like I'm some broken toy.

We are in our new house. It's May in Seattle and the windows are open because it's nice.

I am on the uncomfortable futon couch that I hate. Liam is working. I haven't been able to work since this whole situation started. My brain feels like it's on one track. I am cracking open my life like an egg, and the yolk is both golden and opaque.

My WhatsApp starts ringing, my father's profile picture popping up on my screen. His picture is twenty years old. He told me he took it in front of a castle in Sweden.

I swallow. Normally I would have rescheduled a million times. I am very flakey. I feel like I'll say the wrong thing or upset someone unintentionally, so I back out of most social engagements. I don't like phone calls, especially not video calls, and especially not with long lost dads and families.

Today, I pick up, holding my breath. My dad's smiling face appears on the screen. It's very pixilated, but I am clear on my end. I wonder if he sees me in choppy squares or if he sees this clear version of me, his twenty-seven-year-old daughter. I look at my face to avoid his blurry image, wondering what his perception of me is. I wonder if he notices the line on my forehead. I wonder if he thinks I look like Mom, like everyone else seems to. I wonder if that makes him dislike me.

His image becomes clear. He looks soft, gentle, kind. He has no sharp edges. My heart hurts. I can't tell if it's from sadness or shock. Maybe both.

"Um, hi," I say.

"It's really you!" He says. "Look! It's Katya!" He says, in Russian.

There are a flurry of people around him. I see that he's sitting at a dinner table, and they all have a plate of food. He called me at dinner.

"It's Katya!" He says again. He sounds very excited. When I met him as a kid, did he sound like this? Excited to see me? If he did, how did I think he didn't want me?

My dad takes the phone and shows me each person. My brother. My sister. My cousin. My grandmother. My stepmother. My other cousin. The dog. Everyone seems confused by my presence, and I wonder what they think of me, his American daughter, randomly contacting him. I wonder if they think I want something from him.

My heart skips a beat when the phone lands on my brother and sister. He lets the phone linger for a minute. I say *Privet*, and smile, but I recognize this as my American training. I am acting fake to try to quell the awkwardness of the situation. My brother frowns. He looks confused.

"Hi," he says, in English. I can tell he's studying my face but I don't know what he's looking for. I take a screenshot. I am going to ask my friends if he looks like me later.

"OK," he says, to his, *our,* dad and gives him an annoyed look.

When my dad gets to my little sister my heart breaks in half. Half sad, half happy. Half healing, half broken. She doesn't smile. She doesn't say "*Privet*" back after I say it. I like that she doesn't. I like that she is saying what she wants to say even if that is nothing.

She squints her eyes and raises her eyebrows, and I realize she's making faces at the camera, watching herself, not me. "How are you?" I ask her in Russian. She continues to ignore me.

"Papa, I don't want the phone anymore," she says, looking up to him.

He puts the phone back onto his face and goes to sit on a bench. "We are having BBQ!" He says. "It's so nice here at the dacha."

I wonder if it's the same dacha I had visited with him when I was little, the one he told me about in our messages. I don't ask. I feel more relaxed with him now. "It's very beautiful," I comment.

He smiles, staring at me. "I can't believe I am seeing you. I can't believe you want to talk to me," he says.

I want to tell him that I'm shocked too, that I didn't think he wanted me, that I didn't think he searched or cared or wanted to be my dad. I don't say any of those things. I look back at him, suddenly scared that he's not my real dad. What if we're not actually related? What if Mom lied? Panic builds in my chest.

What if this is all a lie?

"I remember bringing you home," he says, pulling me out of my thoughts. He moves the phone closer to his face. "I remember it was just me and you. Your mother got sick—some sort of infection from the hospital. It was me and you for several months. I didn't know how to take care of a baby. Your grandmother and grandfather wanted to take care of you but I said of course not. You're my responsibility. You're my child. I learned how to boil cloths for diapers. We didn't have Pampers back then!" He laughs, like he's enjoying remembering this time that must have been very difficult for him. "There was no milk. I was in line for hours to get that powder. For your bottle. Your grandmother called it sugar water. It was all we had. Half the day I was feeding you and changing your diaper and the other half the day I was cleaning the diapers and boiling the bottles." He smiled at me.

I don't know how to respond. I don't think he needs me to. There's a sinking feeling in my chest. I recognize it as guilt. An all-too familiar feeling.

"I am so happy to see your face," he says. "I am so, so, happy."

I nod. "Me too," I say to him. "Thanks for waiting

PART 4

Spy

Fall, Early 2000s, Seven Years Old, Second Grade

Mom points to a big, white van, the kind that Sophia's Mom says is made for kidnapping. It's parked across the street from Dad's house. "That's his spies," Mom says. I know a lot about spies already because I checked out books from the library about them. I didn't read any of the books because they weren't my reading level but I flipped through the photos of walkie-talkies and all-black outfits. I also asked my teacher about spies, and she told me to watch James Bond. Me and Dad watched James Bond together. It was the last movie we saw before he got kicked out of the house by the police.

I never thought he'd send spies after us, but I see them every day now.

I look at the white van, with dirty brown and black marks scratching the outside. It's pretty obvious. If I was a spy I would not use this van. The whole point of spies is that they are supposed to be sneaky. Who has a kidnapper van parked for hours in the street? Not a great spy, that's who.

Every time we go outside Mom points the van out. It would be a fun game if Mom wasn't so scared. The van used to be parked further away, but now I guess the spy doesn't care that we know we're being watched. Maybe he wants us to know. Maybe he wants us to be scared. Maybe he's not just a spy but also a bully. Mom opens the door to Dad's house and lets us in, closing it quickly behind us. I put my backpack down next to the piano and sit on the stool, watching as Mom rushes over to the windows and looks out the shutters. Ever since Mom noticed the van, she started watching it back. They watch each other.

"When will he stop watching us?" I ask. Mom doesn't answer.

Sophia's mom and my mom have become best friends, which is really upsetting since I don't like Sophia still, but her mom is also going through a divorce. Sophia's mom, Lenora, approached my mom at school when she saw her crying while waiting to pick me up, and asked her what was wrong. Mom told her about getting a divorce, and they have been friends ever since. Mom says she is helping her a lot with the court case and custody battle.

"Why are you watching him?" I ask. "He just sits there."

She doesn't answer that either.

Masha is asleep in her car seat next to the door, so I don't have to worry about whether she's eaten. I give up on Mom talking to me and go to the kitchen and pour a cup of milk and get some white bread and put some stinky turkey on it. Mom doesn't like buying white bread but it's the only bread Masha will eat, and she says buying two kinds of bread is crazy, so white bread it is. I like white bread, though. I can squish it between my fingers and roll it into a ball with deli turkey and make turkey balls. I make four turkey balls and put them on a plate. I pretend Mom made them for me. They look American, and like something someone's Mom would make them.

It's September, and second grade has just started, but I already feel like I can graduate elementary school after what happened this summer. After The Worst Day, the police said me and Mom and Masha are allowed to stay in Dad's house while Mom and Dad fight for who gets to keep Masha full time in the courts. Dad got an apartment close by, but I've never been there. Dad is trying to take Masha away from us and send us back to Russia, even though he is the one that hit Mom.

I hurry and eat my turkey balls. *Powerpuff Girls* comes on in ten minutes. I can't eat and watch Cartoon Network at the same time anymore unless I take food in the living room, but Mom says we can't do that because we have an ant problem.

I will do my homework after my show. Mom says I have to make good grades now because Dad can take Masha away from us if I don't. Everything we do is about how we look to other people, even if it's not real.

After *Powerpuff Girls*, I read the chapter book we're working on and do my math. I'm not good at math, but I finish all the addition problems. I also color in a house from a coloring book that I try to make look pretty, but I'm really bad at coloring in the lines.

When I'm done, Mom is at the dinner table. I am surprised because there is some food there. Normally I make frozen chicken pot pies for me and Masha, out of the box.

Mom has made *katleti*—meat cutlets. Maybe Babushka got mad at her for not cooking enough. I sit down and eat the *katleti* while Masha plays on the red rug in the living room. Mom is speaking to Babushka and watching Masha. Ever since Dad and Mom had The Worst Day, Mom has been watching Masha more. I don't have to worry about her as much.

"It's not like at home, Mama," Mom says. I can hear Babushka's fast Russian on the other end of the line. "They won't just give her to me. It doesn't matter that I carried her!"

Babushka says something I can't figure out, and Mom responds with, "In the American courts, it's a competition. Who has more money. It doesn't matter that she is my blood! I am nothing here. I am no one without documents." Mom's face looks broken. The shapes of the bruises are gone but a hint of them is still there. Mom's eyes are trailing Masha, who is building a tower out of wooden blocks.

One of Mom's arms is wrapped around her stomach, like it is a bandage.

"I am scared!" She says, suddenly, in Russian.

Mom starts to cry. She moves both of her hands to her eyes.

There is sometimes a big, fat, forehead vein that bulges in her head when she starts to cry hard. I watch for it. When it pops out, I know I need to go to her. For now, I can finish my food.

"All his bastard friends. They are talking against me. They are saying I am a whore. That I do drugs. They are trying to take her away from me. They say they will even call Katya's father."

My ears move at this, like when Scooby hears there is a snack. I know not to ask about my father, my real father, because Mom is already upset enough. Mom told me that he didn't want me, that he didn't care, but I want to know what he looks like. What if he's ugly?

"You didn't tell him anything, did you? You didn't tell Ivan where we were?"

I hear Babushka say "no, of course not," in Russian.

"Good. I don't need that problem too."

I see it then. Mom's vein. It's bulging out. I'm always afraid it's going to pop, and that there will be blood everywhere. I leave my plate even though I'm still hungry and go to her.

Gently, I place my hand on Mom's temple and kiss her. I kiss the vein, hoping it will calm down. "It will be OK, Mommy," I say. "You're not alone."

"Thank you, Katulia," Mom says. She pulls me into her arms.

"My Katyusha," I hear Babushka say on the phone. Masha crawls over to me and Mom and climbs on top of my back. She starts playing with my hair. We're OK as a family of three. We don't need Daddy.

"I don't know how this can happen," Mom says, through tears. "The police reports, the pictures of my bruises, they found the drugs, how can they let him have her?"

It's October. The divorce has been getting really bad. First it was OK because Masha has only been able to see Dad at McDonald's with someone from the courts watching them, since he beat Mom so bad, but somehow, Dad is allowed to have Masha alone tonight. I wish I was with Masha. I miss her.

I miss Dad, too. But I know I shouldn't. I'm not even supposed to call him "Dad" anymore. I try not to think about it.

"It's not fair, I know it," Sophia's Mom, Lenora, says. She puts an arm around Mom's shoulders and pulls her close. Lenora has big brown hair, like if Dolly Parton was brunette. It always stays in the same place without moving, even in the morning. I know who Dolly Parton is because Lenora told me every woman should try to be like her. Lenora and Mom are sitting on the floor of Chris's office, their backs against the wall. Mom leans her head against Lenora. Her eyes are closed. Her face is crumbled up. Lenora is teaching Mom about the courts. Lenora also helped to get Mom a job as a secretary at her church, and she helped Mom get a good lawyer. Mom keeps telling me to be really nice to Sophia because without Lenora, we would have lost Masha to Chris already.

Lenora kisses Mom on the forehead like Babushka does to me before we go to sleep. I hate Sophia but I love Lenora. I want to scoot to the other side of her but I don't make any movements. I don't want to take any of Lenora's love away from Mom. She needs all of it.

I am on the opposite end of the room, watching them. It's like I am not here. Ever since Masha left it's like I also disappeared.

I miss Masha because she's Masha and mine, but also because she never lets me feel alone.

"I'm going to lose the case," Mom cries. "If they are letting him have her tonight—"

"Stop it!" Lenora says. She has a very strong Texas accent. I imagine if this was a hundred years ago, Lenora would be a cowgirl. "Don't say stupid shit. You're not going to lose her. You're not going to lose this case. That man beat you. He did horrible things to you. He threatened to kill you. He will not win. Men like him cannot and will not win."

Mom is crying like Masha cries when she can't find her bottle. She is hiccupping. Right now I am so thankful for Lenora that I could cry too. I am so thankful that Mom is not alone. That we are not alone.

"Your daughter needs you to be strong," Lenora says. Her hands are on both of Mom's arms, and she's shaking her like Babushka told me I couldn't do with Masha. "Do you hear me?"

"But—they're asking about my status—"

"You have a good lawyer. She has gotten you this far. Your lawyer got you a stipend so you can feed your daughters. She made it so you can stay in this house. You will be OK. You came to this country for a reason. You came to this country because justice works. It will work. It will!"

Lenora pushes Mom's head against her chest and Mom's back moves up and down. I am totally still. I know not to even breathe.

"Your daughter needs you," Lenora says, finally.

Mom pulls back and nods, wiping her nose, her eyes, her chin. "Thank you," Mom says, nodding. "Thank you. I need to hear that."

"Let's go downstairs and have something to drink. You need something strong," Lenora says to Mom, standing up. I can hear her knees creak. She pulls a hand out to Mom. Lenora is wearing blue jean shorts and a white shirt that has black polka dots on it. Her toes are hot pink.

Mom smiles and takes her hand.

"I know your Russian ass has the best vodka!"

Mom laughs. "I hid some from him. In my closet."

They file out of the room, not noticing me as they turn out the lights.

I sit in the dark and don't notice that I am crying until I see the light from the hall reflect on the small puddle my tears have made on my knee. I wish I was with Masha, but maybe I deserve to be alone, since I miss Dad. And Dad is bad.

Christmas Lights

Winter, Early 2000s, Seven Years Old, Second Grade

BABUSHKA IS COMING for Christmas. I'm very excited. Mom has told me a lot of times that we don't have money for presents, so not to expect anything this Christmas. I tell her Babushka coming is the best gift. I also mention that I want a scooter, just in case some money shows up and Mom doesn't know what to do with it.

"Can we do something nice for Babushka?" I ask Mom. "Something to surprise her?"

We are at Fiesta, Mom's favorite grocery store. It's the cheapest grocery store, Mom says, because it's where all the immigrants go. My pockets are filled with malted milk balls and sour belts from the candy bins. When I'm a grown up, I will pay for the candy. Right now I can't. I look at the kids with the clear plastic bags filled with their favorite gummy frogs or sour worms, and I imagine what their school lunches are like. They probably get Lunchables. Or maybe their parents give them money to get whatever they want out of the lunch line. One day, when I can make my own money, I will bring Lunchables and candy from the candy bins and expensive Juicy Juice.

"What do you want to do for her?" Mom asks me. We are in the canned food aisle, Mom stocking up on black beans because there is a sale.

I don't want to tell her my idea because it costs money, but it's such a good idea I tell her anyway.

"Can we get Christmas lights?" I ask. I bite my cheek as I say this. I know Mom wants them too. They're not just for

Babushka. The one fun thing Mom takes us to do is drive around Houston to all the best Christmas lights. We sit in front of the houses and watch them twinkle in front of us. I know Mom thinks the same thing about the Christmas lights as I do about the candy from the bins.

One day.

I'm afraid Mom is going to get angry at me for asking, but instead she looks sad. "The lights are so beautiful," she says.

We wheel the grocery cart into the aisle with Christmas lights. Fiesta has one aisle with just Christmas decorations. Mom picks up the cheapest box of lights. They're five dollars.

"I don't even know how to put them up," she says, flipping the box over and reading what's back there.

I think about it. How do people put their Christmas lights up? What's the strongest material I know? "With duct tape," I say.

She puts the box in the cart and my heart leaps from my chest. "Really?" I ask. I feel my eyes widen.

She nods. "We can have this."

Mom tells me to eat as much out of the bins as I can so she doesn't have to make dinner later.

When we finish unloading all of the groceries, Mom says, "Let's put up the lights," and I nearly jump from my socks. I can't believe we're going to have Christmas lights! Mom finds some of Chris's old duct tape in the garage, and we go to the front of the house. There's an outlet next to the front door where we plug in the lights. They immediately start blinking on and off. I am hypnotized at how beautiful they are.

Mom and I look at each other, excited. "How should we organize them?" She asks.

I look at the house. It's a rectangular house. There are four windows and then the door. "Maybe we'll just tape the lights around the windows and doors?" I ask.

Mom nods, and we get to work. We finish the downstairs, the string of lights making two perfectly neat squares around the windows. I hold the string and Mom tapes. She cuts three big pieces of glittering silver tape along the edge of each windowsill. Top, bottom, and both sides. They are beautiful. We had to get a ladder for the second floor, and Mom wouldn't let me help because she said there wasn't enough room.

In the end, we only had enough lights to wrap three windows. It's perfect anyway.

We watch the Christmas lights sparkle until bedtime.

Two days later the phone rings in the kitchen. When Mom gets off the phone her eyes are big and full of tears.

"Fuck!" Mom says.

I am doing my homework at the kitchen table and Masha is sitting next to me, coloring. She always gets crayon on the table, but Mom says not to worry about it.

"What?" I frown, immediately worried that Babushka can't come.

"The neighborhood association called and says we have to take lights down." Mom is wearing her exercise clothes—a big T-shirt over tight black bike shorts. She has her hair up in a ponytail. Mom has started running to make friends.

I feel madness boil inside of my belly. I worked hard for Mom to have happiness and now some stupid neighbors are going to try to take it away?

"Everyone else has lights up!" I argue. "There's nothing wrong with ours!"

"It's because we used the duct tape," she says, crying. "They say it looks cheap."

"Please, Mom," I say. "Leave them. Don't listen to this association." I don't know anything about the association she is talking about, but right now I am so angry I feel like if anyone tried to take our lights down I could scare them away by how mad I am.

Mom stares at me like she doesn't recognize me. Then she gets up from her spot at the table and brings me to her hip, holding me close to her. She squeezes me so tight I can't breathe. "You're right. Fuck them. How did I get so lucky with you, huh?" She asks, kissing my forehead. "We will leave the lights up."

At night, every night, when it becomes dark out, we go outside and sit in the grass in front of the house and watch our lights. It feels like they yell that we are here. This is our place too, and we will make our mark, even if it's messy.

Wishing

Fall 2020, Late Twenties

"I just feel so mad at him," I tell Liam. We're on a walk, the only thing we do since we have moved into the house. COVID has been ravaging the world for seven months and I have been talking to my father for five. It's summer and so beautiful outside it's piercing.

"What do you feel mad at him about?" Liam asks me, gently. One of the things that made me fall for Liam all those years ago is his way of never making me feel judged. I can tell him anything, even if it doesn't make sense, and his solution is always to get to the root of my feelings, not to question them.

"It doesn't make sense," I say, shaking my head. "I know Mom took me. I know Mom lied to him about how long we were going to be gone for. I just—I wanted a dad so bad." I'm crying now. We've sat down at a bench in a park. It's bright and sunny, the green of the trees a sharp contrast to the blue of the sky. Seattle in the fall is out of a storybook. Liam puts his arm around me. I lean into him.

"I know," he says. "He seems like a really good guy, though. He tried to pay for your college. He called you every Sunday that you were in middle and high school. He sent countless emails trying to get into contact with you, and when you did finally reach out, he just wanted to get to know you. Also, your siblings love him a lot. That's a good sign."

I nod, slowly.

"Why didn't I get to have him?" I ask Liam. "Why did my mom keep me from him?"

I lean into Liam's shoulder, hiding my face from the sun. I hate feeling ungrateful. Shouldn't I be happy I'm talking to my family now? Shouldn't I be happy we reconnected? Why am I so sad?

"I can't help my mom's voice. It always pops into my head when I'm talking to him. She tells me not to trust him, that he will use me, that he never wanted me. She's so loud, even after all these years of no contact, I still can't believe that he just wants a relationship and nothing else from me."

"What would he want from you? He has his life in Russia."

"An American citizenship?"

Liam waves his hand away. "When he came to visit you all those times, you didn't have that. He just wanted to visit you because he loved you. Katya, he's trying to convince us to move to Russia. He bought you an iPhone so you guys could FaceTime. He doesn't want anything from you."

I nod my head. The facts are there. They should make sense. But in my messed up mind, I still can't think of him as a good guy. My mom's ideas have screwed themselves tight inside my mind and no amount of evidence will get them out.

"I think . . . I think I just have to meet him in person, maybe. I don't know when that will happen, but I think I just need to see him with my own eyes. To see he's not using me."

"We will. We will meet him. I promise," Liam says, kissing my hand.

Lemonade

Winter, Early 2000s, Eight Years Old, Second Grade

Mom is gone most nights. I think the spy must be pretty bored by me and Babushka and Masha. We stay inside and do homework, and Babushka makes us food.

Mom says she can't have dinner with us because she is making copies for her lawyer so her lawyer doesn't charge her any more money. Alana, the lawyer, charges her ten cents per page, but only five if Mom makes all the copies herself. There is a lot of evidence needed in American courts, Mom says.

Babushka brought only a little money with her from Russia, and she and I have bought lemons and sugar with it. We have decided to start a lemonade business the weekend of the Martin Luther King, Jr. holiday to help mom with the legal fees so she can have dinner with us instead of spending all night making copies.

Today, we are at the kitchen counter squeezing lemons. We have squeezed over seventy lemons. It has only equaled one-half bucket of lemon juice, even though my fingers are shriveled and stinging.

"We will just add more water and sugar, and no one will notice it is not a lot of lemon juice," Babushka says, frowning at the very small amount of liquid we have.

"I don't understand how we can work so hard and nothing come from it," I say, sadly.

"Lemons are very flavorful. You don't need a lot of juice to make the whole drink taste like a lemon. It is plenty. People will buy," she says, smiling at me. Babushka runs her hand through my hair and brings me to her chest. She does this a lot now. When I am in Babushka's chest I feel better.

After a few seconds of Babushka's softness, I push myself off and get myself together. "Babushka, how should I get the lemonade to people? We don't have any disposable cups to give them."

Babushka pauses. "We can pour it in their mouths. It can be a dollar, and we will pour two drinks. They will get a deal."

I scrunch my face, remembering other kids' lemonade stands. Usually they have a big, clear glass container with a spout where the customers could get their own lemonade with a cup that the lemonaders give them.

All we have is an orange Home Depot bucket. I look inside the bucket and see little black dots. I bite my top lip. "Babushka, what are those?" I ask her.

"Maybe bugs or seeds," she shrugs. "It's good. From nature. I wiped it down already Katyusha, don't worry."

I don't think anyone is going to want to drink lemonade with stuff floating around in it, but I don't say this to Babushka because she will tell me how that is ridiculous because food is food. I add water to the lemonade and half the sugar bag. "We will add more if it is not selling," Babushka says. "Don't waste."

I search the kitchen for something to put the liquid in that is not the Home Depot bucket but can't find anything. It's the only thing big enough to sell to lots of people at once. The good news about it being orange is that people will not see everything floating around inside. "Let's go," Babushka says, taking my wagon and going outside with it. We go to the corner of the street. I put LEMONADE, 1 DOLLAR on a poster board that was in Dad's office with black Sharpie. I add a drawing of a lemon but I don't have yellow marker so it kind of looks like I don't know how to draw a circle.

After thirty minutes of sitting outside with no customers, I run inside and grab the Sharpie and put BRING YOUR OWN CUPS on the poster board.

Babushka and I sit outside for an hour. Seven people have passed us. Four of them have looked in my bucket, and all of them say they don't have any money on them. I don't believe them. I am upset because we need money so Mom stops spending her nights away from us.

"Babushka, I am going to knock on people's front doors and tell them to buy the lemonade to their face," I say, turning the wagon around. "Sitting on the street like rocks is not working."

Babushka falls into step beside me. "That's correct," she says. "Good. The more forceful you are, the better."

The lemonade sloshes as I pull the wagon to the first door. I am tired, but I knock. People already have cups in their homes, so it's a perfect plan. I don't have to provide anything. The house I have chosen belongs to the lady who has a granddaughter in college. Mom says she's rich. She doesn't ever come outside, but she paints all day, so she's probably home. I knock twice. When that doesn't work, I ring the doorbell. The lady, her hair like a gray bird's nest, opens the door with a big smile on her face.

"Do you want some lemonade?" I ask. I add a smile in there so she knows I am trustworthy. "It's homemade from me and Babushka."

The lady looks around me to my bucket. It would be nice if I knew her name but I don't. Mom has always complained that the neighbors don't like her. She went to a Christmas party with Chris once, and she heard one of the husbands from down the street make fun of how she talked. Only Ms. Nancy is nice around here. I would offer her free lemonade but her car isn't in the driveway.

"How much?" She asks.

"It's a dollar, but you can use whatever cup you have, even if it's a big cup," I say, to sweeten the deal.

She looks at my bucket, then at me, then at my bucket again.

"How about I just give you the dollar? I have a lot of lemonade already."

I pause, searching her face. Maybe she is giving me a dollar for free because she thinks I will keep bothering her. Maybe I will.

"OK," I nod.

"What is she saying?" Babushka asks, when the lady cracks the door open a little bit and leaves to go get the money.

"She is giving us money but she doesn't want the lemonade."

"Why?" Babushka asks, shocked. She puts a hand to her chest like she can't believe it.

"She says she has a lot of lemonade already." I shrug.

"She has to take the lemonade!" Babushka says. She looks upset but I don't know why because we are getting a free dollar from this, and we get to keep our lemonade.

When the woman comes back she hands me a five dollar bill.

"Are you sure you don't want any lemonade?" I ask, marveling at the big bill. I can't believe we made money from only asking.

She looks over at my bucket and smiles. "I'm sure," she says, then closes her door.

I look at Babushka, my eyebrows raised. "Five dollars!" I say, waving the money in front of her.

"She thinks we're charity," Babushka says, crossing her arms as I take my wagon to the next house. She looks mad. "Next time, tell them they have to take your lemonade, or you will refuse their money."

"Babushka, I'm not going to say no to free money if it brings Mom home," I say, giving her the five dollars to keep because we both know I will lose it.

Babushka huffs.

The next three houses don't open their doors. I check their windows too, just in case. We chose to do this business on a holiday weekend specifically so people will be home but Babushka says maybe the holiday means that people travel away, so we decide to go to only the houses with cars in the driveway.

The house that finally has a person open the door is my friend Stephanie's house. She's not really my friend, but I wish she was. Her mom doesn't let her play with me since the start of Mom and Dad's divorce. We used to sit in front of her house and play with our Barbies. Her mom never let me go inside because I don't wear shoes very often, and she said she's afraid I will get her house dirty.

"Hi," Stephanie says, opening her big, white door. She looks behind her, like she wants to make sure no one is watching.

"Hi," I say. "Do you want some lemonade? It's a dollar but you can use your own cup."

Stephanie looks around me at my bucket. "That bucket is for dirt. Or dirty water if your roof is leaking. You're not supposed to put drinks in it."

"I cleaned it," I say. Babushka wiped it down with a rag, but Stephanie doesn't need to know Babushka didn't use any soap. "Do you want some?"

Stephanie shakes her head and makes a face, like she would never have any ever.

My cheeks grow hot. Stephanie makes me feel like I am doing something wrong.

"OK, well, never mind," I say, turning around. I hear Stephanie shut the door.

"I want to go home now," I say to Babushka, looking down.

"Why?" Babushka asks. Her voice is suddenly gentle. "What did that ugly girl say to you?"

"She said our bucket is dirty." My eyes feel like a microwave, warming up tears I don't want them to have.

"Impossible," Babushka says. After a while of not saying anything, which isn't normal for Babushka, she adds, "Dirt is good for your immune system."

"Let's go home," I say. I want to curl up in a ball on the couch and listen to Babushka sing to me.

"We have all this lemonade! Let's try selling a little bit more. Don't give up now," Babushka says, rubbing her hand on my back. "If we drink all of it ourselves, we will get sick."

I take a deep breath in. I think of Mom. She cries so much now. I know she's tired. I can keep going too.

The next door I knock on is answered by an old man wearing a red, plaid shirt. He looks like he's a hundred. He's hunched over, like he needs a cane to walk.

"Lemonade?" I ask him. I put my body in front of my wagon with my bucket. "It's a dollar but you get your own cup so you can have as much as you want."

The old man blinks a couple of times like he doesn't understand what I'm saying.

"Do you have a dollar!" I yell, because maybe he can't hear. "I have some lemonade for you!"

The man smiles and nods, walking away. He kind of waddles. "Bring a cup!" I shout after him. I turn around to Babushka and shrug. Hopefully we get a dollar out of this.

"Make sure you give him lemonade this time," Babushka warns. "Don't just take money for no reason."

The man comes back with a coffee cup that has the Eiffel tower on the handle. I take it and scoop it in my bucket, filling it to the very top. I turn around and take a bit of bug out, hoping the man doesn't see. I hand the man his cup.

"This looks great," he says, smiling. His voice is crackly, like he's popping corn with his throat. He takes the coffee cup and puts it down on a small table next to the door. Some of it spills on the ground.

"One dollar please," I say. I smile back at him, but it's forced.

He hands me the five-dollar bill that is already in his hand.

"I don't have change," I say, but this time I put a real smile on my face.

"That's OK!" He waves me off. "You have a great work ethic!" he adds.

I don't know what this means, but I thank him again and take Babushka, walking away. He watches us until we knock on the next door. I think maybe this man is very bored and I also hope Babushka never loses her mind enough to hand out whole five-dollar bills to random kids when she gets that old.

Me and Babushka walk the street for another hour. We collect a total of fifteen dollars, which I think is a lot of papers Mom doesn't have to copy. I hope when Mom comes home and I give it to her, she can stay for dinner a couple of nights this week.

When we are finally done selling, Babushka and I decide to try the lemonade. She makes a face as soon as she takes a sip. "Oh! That is sour. Too much lemon juice," she says.

She hands the cup to me. The liquid pinches my throat all the way down. I squeeze my eyes shut.

"We should have tried it," I say.

"I will put it in the fridge and add more sugar. Tomorrow we will try to sell it again."

"Babushka, we can't fit the bucket in the fridge," I say.

"We'll leave it out," she says. "Lemons are used for preserving jam. It's fine. They won't go bad."

At night both of us have diarrhea, but Babushka doesn't think it's from the lemonade. "It's the bad weather," she says.

The Titanic

Spring, Early 2000s, Eight Years Old, Second Grade

IT'S SPRING BREAK, and Mom has made me invite a friend over. Her name is Rachel. The lawyer Alana says I need to look "very well developed in Yuliya's care."

I ask Mom what "very well developed" means, and she says, "I shouldn't have to explain these words to you because your English is supposed to be better than mine," so I think hard and decide that the lawyer Alana means that I have to pass as an American child to the court system so that they won't take Masha away from us. This is something we are in danger of because Masha is spending a lot more time with Dad than just one night here and there.

I overheard Lenora and Mom talking about the divorce when I was supposed to be sleeping.

Lenora is divorcing Sophia's dad, but Lenora is getting whatever she wants because Sophia's dad is mean. He isn't as mean as Dad though. He didn't even hit Lenora. He didn't cut any of Lenora's clothes or burn her family photos, like Dad did to Mom. He didn't call her any names. He just yelled a lot. Lenora told Mom that she doesn't understand how Dad is even seeing Masha after all the evidence against him. Mom says that Dad keeps asking for our documents, and Alana tells him that it's none of his business, and Dad's lawyer is telling the court that if Mom can't show legal citizenship documents then she shouldn't be in the country, and Dad should keep Masha.

I don't understand why we can't get our papers that let us stay in America. I don't know why keeping Masha is so much work. She's just a baby. It's not like she poops gold nuggets.

To look "well developed." I have to have more kids over to the house so their parents can tell the other parents in my class that we're a normal family, and Mom is a good mom even though she's single and has an accent.

I decide to ask Rachel if she wants to come over. I choose Rachel because she's the nicest girl in our class. We have only ever played tag at recess, but she agrees to come over because she never says no to anything.

On the first day of spring break, Rachel's Mom's car pulls into the driveway. It's blue and shiny and clean on the outside. It's big, like it can fit a lot of kids inside of it. Dad makes fun of big cars like that because he says they look fat and not sexy. Dad bought Mom a tiny convertible when they first met, which he says makes her look skinny. Me, Masha, and Babushka barely fit in it.

I press my face to the window and watch Rachel's Mom park in our driveway and get out of her unsexy car. Rachel's Mom and Rachel are both coming to the door, which is something I did not prepare for. Me and Babushka only have enough food for Rachel. Babushka boiled hot dogs and made mashed potatoes.

"Babushka!" I shout. "She's here! With her mom too!"

I hear shuffling coming from the kitchen. "I didn't make enough food for the mother! Why is the mother coming? Isn't she thankful I am feeding her daughter? How greedy of her to want my food too!"

I hear the doorbell ring and rush to open the door. At first, I don't smile. But then I see Rachel smile so I copy her because I need to look like Mom is a good mom and I am happy. Rachel is wearing a green T-shirt and matching shorts and pink jelly sandals. Her T-shirt has a picture of Barbie in a pink convertible, like the car Dad bought for Mom except Mom's car is red.

Her shorts have the name "Barbie" written what looks like a million times. Rachel is dressed like she could model for Barbie. Her mom is wearing long sleeves that go to her elbows and button up at the center, with jeans and brown leather sandals. Her clothes look like the type of clothes at the front of the store, not on the sales rack.

I feel squishy, seeing their clean clothes that fit their bodies perfectly. Mom always buys me clothes that are too big so I can grow into them. My clothes either show my bellybutton or go down to my knees. Today I am wearing a T-shirt that is pink but shows my stomach. It has holes in it from when the dryer overheated and almost burned down the house. It has no pictures on it. I am also wearing jean shorts that are too tight but Mom says denim is expensive, so I have to stop eating so many *blinis* and fit in them. They are from the Gap, so we have to try to make them last as long as we can.

Babushka says we need to save my nice clothes for school, so we don't have to wash them several times. I didn't dress up for Rachel, but maybe to look very well developed I should have convinced Babushka to let me wear my school clothes.

"Hello, Katya, how are you?" Rachel's Mom asks. Her blonde hair falls over her shoulders as she leans towards me and holds out her hand.

I reach for her hand, knowing exactly what to do. Dad says a good handshake means squeezing the life out of the other person's hand to tell them that you're a strong guy and not to mess with you. I do this with Rachel's mom.

She pulls her hand back and says, "Ow! That hurts!" She looks confused and surprised.

"I took karate!" I say proudly. I have a white belt with a yellow stripe from last year. Babushka is very proud of how strong I am.

When Rachel's mom does not smile back at me, I suddenly feel butterflies in my stomach and say, "Sorry."

We're quiet as she shakes her hand out.

"Where is your mother?" she asks, her head bobbing back and forth, searching our house.

"Mom's at work," I lie. Mom is actually at the lawyer's again. Not Alana. Her other lawyer. The one that is helping us get our documents to stay in America. Mom gets this week off since she works at the church and they're on spring break too. She said she is going to do as much work to get us our citizenships as she can. "But my Babushka is here. Babushka!" I yell.

Babushka rushes in from the kitchen wearing her *tapochkis*, slippers, that Mom got her. She is wearing one of Chris's big shirts. It's plain and white with sweat stains under the arm pits. Babushka smiles and says, "Hello! Valentina!" In English. That's really all Babushka can say. She can understand more but sometimes pretends not to.

Rachel's Mom does not stick out her hand. She puts the hand I squeezed on Rachel's shoulder, like maybe she doesn't want to let her go any further in our house.

"Well, hello," Rachel's Mom says. "I'm Cassandra, Rachel's Mom."

Babushka nods.

We are all quiet. I should do something to look very well developed, but I don't know what. I should maybe offer Rachel's Mom some food, but I don't think Babushka made enough, and I don't want to ask in Russian, because it makes Americans nervous when they can't understand us. Mom says they think we are talking about them. The truth is, sometimes we are.

"Well, OK then," Rachel's Mom says. "I'll be back in a few hours. Rachel, you know how to reach me, in case you need anything?" Cassandra asks, bending down to Rachel's level.

Rachel nods, smiling, and gives her Mom a kiss on the cheek.

Cassandra looks around, a line in between her eyebrows. She doesn't look like she wants to leave her daughter here. I look around too, trying to see what she sees. It's cleaner than normal. Me and Babushka put all of Masha's toys away in her cardboard box in the corner. There are none of Babushka's food experiments out. She was working on making sauerkraut, pickles, and pickled beets but we put everything away. Normally the kitchen looks a lot crazier. We also cleaned up the lines of ants that were on the ground. I don't know what she is seeing that looks like she needs to put on a sour face.

Rachel's mom smiles at me, pats Rachel's back, waves at Babushka, says "Thank you," then leaves through the door, closing it gently behind her. I feel instantly better when she's gone. Maybe I'll just repeat the words "well developed" a lot to Rachel and hopefully that's what she'll tell everyone about us.

"We have food," I tell Rachel, taking her hand and leading her to the kitchen. I sit Rachel down next to my normal seat, which is in the seat Mom sits at when she's here.

"Her mom was strange," Babushka tells me, in Russian she knows Rachel doesn't know. She's plating mashed potatoes and hot dogs.

"I think I upset her with my handshake," I respond. I am not as nervous about making Rachel uncomfortable as her mother.

"I speak a different language at home, with my grandmother," I tell Rachel, to explain to her why she doesn't understand me. "She doesn't know English. It makes me well developed and smart," I add.

Rachel smiles at me and I realize none of the other kids in my class know another language. "Say Da," I command.

"Da," Rachel repeats. She waits, and when I don't say anything she asks, "What did I just say?"

"You said 'yes' in Russian. Now you know another language. It feels like you have two brains, doesn't it?"

She shakes her head no. I don't ever remember not knowing Russian. I remember learning English, how I messed it up a lot, how everything sounded like gibberish, but I also remember slipping into it quickly, like wearing a shoe that was the perfect size. Suddenly I just knew what everyone was saying. When I speak Russian to Babushka, I am always shocked that it is our secret.

After me and Rachel are done eating, I tell her it's time to play Barbies. We walk into the living room where I have set up the Barbies, and I ask her what game is her favorite. I hope she says mermaids. I pick up my mermaid Barbie to give her a hint at what she should say.

"Do you want to play Pizza Hut?" Rachel asks, examining each one of my dolls. She has her hands behind her back, not picking any of them up or touching them.

I shrug. I went to a Pizza Hut a few times with Dad before the divorce. Mom and Babushka don't let me eat pizza, but we eat it at school sometimes for parties so it's not like I don't know what it tastes like. I can probably play this game.

"OK," I say, picking up my favorite non-mermaid Barbie. She's wearing a pink poofy dress. She looks like she's going to a ball. "How do we play?"

"Where's your Pizza Hut?" Rachel asks.

I frown. "Pizza Hut?"

"Yeah. Barbie Pizza Hut. Where is it?" She looks around, walking over to Masha's cardboard box of toys like there's supposed to be something in there. Mostly there's toys from McDonald's and Masha's favorite tools from the kitchen.

I follow her to the box, looking in it too, like I can find what she's searching for in there. "I have a Barbie house. Well, half of one. Sophia took the other half. And I have an orange Barbie car." I have a good collection of Barbies. Mom made Chris buy me a lot to make up for him giving me an electric pencil sharpener for one of my birthdays. They got in a big fight about that.

Rachel shakes her head. "No, it needs to be the actual Barbie Pizza Hut. With a check-out station and a counter to show the different types of pizza. Otherwise how can we point to what we want? If you don't have Barbie Pizza Hut, we can't play."

I feel like I've done something wrong. I feel my cheeks start to get hot.

"Do you want to play something else?" I ask quickly. It feels like I'm trying to keep a balloon in the air. I can't let the balloon touch the ground or Mom will be in trouble and we'll lose Masha.

Rachel looks around the living room, but her eyes get kind of droopy like it's nap time. It cannot be nap time right now. Rachel has to have fun.

Babushka walks in the room and has her hands on her hips. "Why is this girl upset?" She asks.

"How can you tell?" I say.

"Her voice sounds like she's whining. I've only ever heard it in American kids."

"She wants to play a game about pizza."

Babushka makes a face like she doesn't understand. "Pizza? How? How do you pretend to be a pizza?"

I realize the word pizza is the same in Russian as it is in English when Rachel looks at me with question marks in her eyes.

"I'm asking her if we have Pizza Hut," I lie.

Rachel nods, like this makes sense.

"I swear American kids are so spoiled. To pretend to play like food—"

"No she wants to play like at a restaurant, but we don't have the restaurant she wants."

"Ahhh," Babushka says, nodding, like she finally understands. Then she frowns again. "This is still stupid. Why would you pretend to work at a restaurant in America instead of pretending to be a mermaid? Does she not know what it is like to be poor?"

I don't answer Babushka because I don't know why Rachel wants to pretend to be poor in America. I bite my lip, thinking.

"All American kids love TV." Babushka says, walking back into the kitchen.

I breathe out, finally, because this is a good idea that Babushka has.

"Do you want to watch a movie?" I ask, quickly.

Rachel yawns. "What movies do you have?"

"We have to go upstairs in my mom's room," I say, and start going to where the TV is. Dad took the downstairs TV. Rachel follows me slowly, like she's dragging herself up. When we get to Mom's room, I show her inside and run over to where Mom keeps all the videos. There are maybe a hundred of them, all lined up neatly in her closet. They are really all of Dad's movies but I watch them all the time when the satellite goes out, which is a lot. Mom says Dad doesn't pay the bill for the TV on purpose, so she'll miss her shows.

Rachel scans all the movies. "You have *Titanic*?" She asks. Her eyes get big at this. She looks much more awake after looking to see what movies we have.

"Yeah," I say. "It's one of my favorite movies." Dad showed it to me when it first came out, and we also went to the museum exhibit where I got to see pieces of coal from the real ship.

"I've always wanted to see it. I read a lot of books on it but I haven't seen the movie."

"Let's watch it!" I say. "It's long though. Two whole videotapes!"

I feel good that *Titanic* is so long. This means I won't have to entertain Rachel.

"Can I use your phone to call my mom? I'll ask her to pick me up later, like around dinner time."

I smile so big I almost cry. I feel like I have done good. I am helping Mom. I am helping us keep Masha. Everything will be OK.

After Rachel is done calling her Mom we settle on the floor of Mom's room. Babushka makes us sit on pillows, and we lean against the bed and watch *Titanic*. I almost fall asleep. Rachel's eyes are big the whole time. When Rose is naked on the screen while Jack draws her, she starts laughing, and I don't understand what's so funny but I pretend to laugh too. When Jack turns blue and dies, Rachel cries, and I try to make tears come to my eyes too but I can't. I don't think Jack dying is sad, but I do wonder if that is really what a dead body looks like. Babushka comes upstairs when Rose throws her diamond necklace in the water, and she shakes her head. Babushka thinks Rose is an idiot for throwing real diamonds away. "She could have gotten something different if she didn't like it," Babushka says, sighing.

Thirty minutes after the movie is over our doorbell rings. Rachel has finished crying and we are eating *piroshkis* filled with leftovers and joking about how Jack was pretty dumb to give his door boat to a girl he met only a day ago when we hear the bell. "That's probably my mom," Rachel says, putting her napkin on her plate. "This was so much fun, thank you!"

I stand up and me and Babushka take Rachel to the door. When we open it, Rachel says, "Hi, Mom," to Cassandra and walks outside, taking her Mom's hand.

"Thanks a million!" Cassandra says to Babushka, waving. Me and Babushka close the door.

"Phew!" I say to Babushka. "That went better than expected."

"She was very strange. She wants to pretend to be poor and then acts like she's never seen a movie."

I shrug. "I don't care, as long as she tells everyone in my class that she had a good time."

For the rest of spring break, I tell Mom that all the kids at school were going to be on our side for getting custody of Masha. They may be Chris's friends, but they are going to think she is a great mom and that she is doing an amazing job raising us. Mom says a million times how proud of me she is and to keep up the good work.

I decide I will invite Catherine over next. She's not as nice as Rachel but her Mom works at the same place where Dad works. If Catherine reports back that I'm doing good then that would make Mom really happy.

My first day back from spring break, I'm wearing a green shirt Mom bought from Gap because of how much help I am being to her. It has a white poodle on it, and you can pet the poodle fur so it feels like a real dog. I am also wearing a blue skirt that Babushka says is only for church. I feel very pretty and fancy and like I do not stick out. I imagine myself with friends and feel light and bouncy, like a balloon.

Me and Babushka arrive at school early, before the bell rings, instead of right before, because I tell her I want time to ask Catherine to come over. Babushka waits on a bench with Masha, who is still in her stroller, as I approach Catherine.

Catherine is talking to Rachel next to a tree that is by my favorite slide. This is the perfect time.

"Hey," I say, walking over to them. I stand next to Rachel since I don't know Catherine that well yet. Rachel waves at me and gives me a small smile. Catherine doesn't say anything. Rachel must not have told her about what a great time she had watching *Titanic* at my house.

"Do you guys want to come over? My Babushka says she will make us *blinis*, which is actually really rare for her to make for strangers since jam is expensive and should only be used for family."

Rachel looks away from me.

"We can watch *Titanic*. Catherine, have you seen it?" I ask.

Catherine frowns at me. "I can't go over to your house because your grandma lets little kids watch PG-13 movies!"

"What's PG-13?" I ask Catherine, who has blonde highlights in her brown hair. I only learned what highlights were because it's so cool that Catherine's mom let her get them.

Catherine puts a hand to her mouth and points at me. "You don't know what PG-13 is?"

I look at my grandmother. She smiles and waves at me. I nod at her.

"It's where you can only see a movie if you are above thirteen years old," Catherine says, like she is a teacher. "*Titanic* is PG-13. It's against the law if you are under thirteen, and you've seen it. Your grandma can go to jail for showing movies like that to kids."

I look at Rachel. "How are you supposed to know if a movie is PG-13?"

She doesn't look at me or say anything. Catherine looks like she is going to tell on me.

"It says it on the video box in big letters. You have to be an idiot not to see it."

I feel my face scrunch up. I haven't ever cried in second grade, but right now, I feel the tears like rocks behind my eyes, pressing hard into my face, and I just want to go home.

I walk away as fast as I can, to Babushka. "Let's go," I say to her, taking her hand and pulling her off the bench.

"Katyusha! Where are you pulling me! You have school!"

"I am going to be sick!" I say. "I need to go home."

Babushka, who is normally filled with a million questions, doesn't ask anything. For some reason I feel like she knows. We walk home, and when we get home I lie on her lap on the couch, and she sings me songs in Russian. I don't want to go back to school. I should never have tried to help Mom.

Court

Spring, Early 2000s, Eight Years Old, Second Grade

TODAY IS THE first day of court. Mom and Chris have spent almost a year preparing for this day. Mom tried not to go to court, but Chris refused. Then Chris tried not to go to court and Mom refused. Now they are here. Mom did not sleep last night. I heard her crying to Babushka until the sun came up. Babushka sang to Mom like she sings to me when I can't sleep, but it didn't work. Mom still cried.

"Babushka, why is Mom so scared?" I ask her. It is morning, and we are on our usual walk to school. We are waiting at a stoplight, which always makes Babushka nervous. She says there are too many cars in America.

"Well," Babushka sighs. "I don't know how to answer you, Katyusha."

"We can't really actually be almost losing Masha, can we?" The little crosswalk person turns white, and me and Babushka and Masha in her stroller cross the road. We're the only ones walking today since we're late, and it's nice that it's quiet.

"I don't know. I don't know the language, only what your Mom tells me. From what she tells me," Babushka coughs, "maybe."

I know Babushka wouldn't lie to me. I don't know why, but I haven't thought of us actually losing Masha. I thought of us going to Russia together, I thought of us living here together, but never me not seeing Masha again. I just haven't pictured in my mind what it would look like without Masha in our life.

"So . . . will it be like when I have to say goodbye to you every time you leave but with Masha?"

I imagine how it feels like when I say bye to Babushka, and it hurts so bad I can't breathe.

Babushka swallows. I'm not watching the sidewalk and trip over a branch and land on my knee.

"Katyusha! You have to watch or you will fall!" She says, stopping the stroller to give me her hand. My hands are on the sidewalk where they have stopped my fall, but I already know my knee will be bloody. I don't care. I don't feel anything. I look over Babushka to where Masha's feet are sticking out of her stroller.

I can't lose them both. Instead of giving her my hand, I sit down on the sidewalk and start crying. "Katinka," Babushka says, patting my head. She leans my head against her hip, smoothing down my hair.

"It's OK," she says.

"I can't lose two of you!" I cry. I am sobbing so hard I feel like I can choke on my snot. "I'll die!"

"You won't lose anyone," Babushka says, handing me the handkerchief she always keeps in her pocket. I wipe the snot off my face but don't get up. No one is coming so it's OK. I don't want to get up. I don't want the world to keep moving, I don't want time to keep going. I just want to stay here on this broken sidewalk, with my sister and my Babushka, my two favorite people in the whole world, and no one else.

We're back home, and Chris has turned off the air conditioner. Mom says he's mad because she did good in court today. "Even with all his money he donated to the police station," Mom says, eating Babushka's chicken soup. "Even with them saying he's not a threat," she takes a bite of carrot from the soup. Mom never eats, so she must be really hungry. "The judge is still going to give Masha to us." Mom has her hair in a ponytail and her make up is smudged from spending twelve hours at the courthouse.

"What are all the different choices?" I ask, slurping my soup. I am sweating but Babushka says hot soup is a good idea because it will regulate our body temperature.

"He could take full custody," Mom says, holding her spoon up. "If he did that, we'd probably be deported too, because that's really the only way he could take full custody of her. He doesn't have anything else against me."

Mom picks up the soup bowl with both hands and drains it. I've never seen her eat so much. "The other option is we split custody. He gets her half the time, and I get her half the time."

"Like now?" I ask.

Babushka rushes over and picks Mom's soup bowl up and refills it quickly, setting it back down in front of her. Mom wipes her forehead. It looks like she's been on one of her runs.

"Yes, like now," she answers, taking a spoonful of chicken. "Except more strict. He'll get more time. Half the summer, I think. Although, the lawyer says she doesn't think he'll even get that. I had too many witnesses show up today. There was Chanel and Lenora. There was some friends from work." She looks down, this time taking a slow bite of chicken.

I want to ask if we'll ever see Chris again. I don't, I won't ever, because I know he's bad. He hit Mom. I saw it. He does drugs. He is trying to get me and Mom kicked out of the country. When I think of him in my head I have to stop myself from calling him Dad. Even though he wants to take Masha from us. Even though he wants to send us back so he can raise her all by himself.

I will find out later, when Masha is eighteen, that the court case for Masha's custody lasts seventeen years, Masha's entire childhood. Even when the judge makes his initial custody decision, Chris continues to tirelessly argue that because Mom is undocumented, she should not have rights over his daughter. Chris beating my mom didn't matter, evidence of Chris's drug use didn't matter; what mattered most was my mother's status in the United States, which was what Chris used to argue my mother's fitness as a parent against his own.

"What about the house?" Babushka asks, sitting down. She waits until everyone has cleared their bowls to eat. Sometimes I have finished my food and asked for more and didn't know that means Babushka wouldn't get any, but she gave it to me anyway. Now I know better.

"He gets the house and most of the furniture, because he had all that before our marriage, but he will have to pay child support. We're asking for one thousand a month."

"Only one thousand?" Babushka spits. "Doesn't he make forty thousand a month? Yuliya, an apartment here with one bedroom costs five-hundred dollars minimum!"

"And I have to have two bedrooms. The court requires for Masha to have her own room."

"So, what, you can maybe pay the rent for this thousand a month? What about bills? Doctors? Babysitters for when you go to work? How is that fair? You gave birth to his child!"

"I can't ask for a lot, Mama!" Mom says, shouting. "I just want my baby."

Mom's face breaks a little, like she's going to cry, but no tears come out. Babushka immediately grabs Mom by the shoulders. "If you win her, come back home. You won't need to stay here."

Mom looks away. "I need to get Katya's citizenship."

Babushka looks at me, her eyes shiny.

I shake my head. "I don't want to stay!" I blurt. "I decided. Let's take Masha and go back with Babushka. It's too hard here, Mom. Please. Let's go. I don't like it."

It hurts to say these words, but after court is over Babushka says she has to go home because her visa ran out, and I can't survive here without her. I will never see Chris again anyway. It doesn't matter. I can't be here alone without Babushka again. I have to go with her.

Mom looks down at her soup, this time her spoon swirling around the bowl. "We'll see what happens," she says. "But I don't want our time in America to be for nothing."

"So productive, all the time," Babushka says, upset. She picks up her bowl, slurping it. When we're all done drinking our soup, we get pillows and sheets from the upstairs and lie downstairs in the room where Chris keeps his grand piano because it's the coolest room in the house. Mom is too afraid of Chris to crack a window so we don't sleep, turning a fan on to cool ourselves off.

"How can he turn off the air conditioner on his own child?" Babushka says. It's the last thing I hear before I fall asleep.

I saw on TV how a lot of eight-year-old kids run away, so I decide this is a good option for me. I know there is a train close to the house, but I am not going to jump on it because I don't want to accidentally get trapped under the wheels and run over, which is what Babushka says will happen if I get too close to the train because I don't exercise enough to run fast.

Tomorrow we are moving out of Chris's house, and a week after that Babushka is leaving to go to Russia and I am not going with her. I can't think any further than that.

I have a small, red, briefcase that I found in Chris's stuff that I decide to keep. It doesn't hold much. I put in a doll Babushka brought for me from Russia and that's it. I thought about putting a Barbie, so that I could have something valuable to sell like the Pipi Longstocking show says to do if you run away, but I don't because there's not enough room. I don't know where I am going. I do know that if I run away, Babushka can't leave. She'll have to stay to find me and she'll miss her plane, and we can't afford another plane ticket for her so she'll be stuck here like us.

I wear shorts and short sleeves and no jacket because it is summer and hot.

The divorce also finished last week. The courts said that Chris gets Masha half of the time. Mom came home crying. She said Chris's lawyer tricked us so he wouldn't have to pay as much money in child support. Chris's neighbors, the ones who bought lemonade from me and Babushka, told the court they thought he was a good dad. Chris even got the parents of kids who went to school with me to say he was a good dad. Lenora came over with Mom and cried with her. She said it wasn't fair that rich men won. They said Mom wasn't a fit mom for full custody because she couldn't speak English without an accent, and that she was young and only cared about money.

"At least you have a path forward with your citizenship," Lenora said. But I don't know what that meant. All I know is we only get to see Masha half the time now, and also that it means we have to stay in America.

I find out as an adult that Mom would have been able to apply for a green card under VAWA, the Violence Against Women Act, that had been passed a year prior. Under the act, which is sometimes referred to as "the mail order bride law," if a person applying for their green card through marriage experiences abuse at the hands of their American partner, they can receive a green card without them. The act was passed as a result of a Russian woman. Her family said she was being abused but was too afraid to leave because of what it would mean for her immigration status in The United States. My mother also applied for us under VAWA, though it's not ultimately how we got our green cards.

Babushka is in the kitchen humming to a song on the radio. I can smell the *katleti* she is frying. My stomach grumbles. I think about leaving after they are made, so I'm not hungry, but I don't want to walk in the dark. I open and close the front door quietly.

With every step away from Babushka, I feel my throat closing up. It's like there is an invisible string between us, and the more I walk away from her, the tighter it gets until I can't breathe.

"Katyusha!" I hear from behind me.

I turn around and all the air comes back into my lungs. I feel better when I can see my grandmother.

"Katyusha, what adventure are you going on?" She yells, smiling.

Tears spring to my eyes. "I am running away, Babushka!" I have never been able to lie to her.

"Oh, is that right?" She says. She laughs a little bit. "Well, your *katletka* and *kartoshka* are ready! They are going to get cold if you run any further!"

"I have to learn to be hungry!" I shout, turning around and letting my tears fall. "There is no food for runaways."

I hear her laugh again. Her laugh always sounds like bells. "Well, why not just a little for the road? So it doesn't go to waste? I can't eat everything myself, or I will get fat!"

I wipe my eyes and listen to my Babushka. I won't ever not listen to her.

"OK," I say. "For the road."

Mom's Twenties

Early 2000s, Eight Years Old, Summer Before Third Grade

TODAY IS SUPPOSED to be my first time calling Babushka. I haven't been able to talk to her on the phone because Mom has to pay for everything herself now, and every minute calling Russia costs a lot of money. I have gone from talking to Babushka every second of every day to not hearing her voice for a whole month. Mom has already talked to her, but she has not let me have the phone because she said that I will waste so much time mispronouncing things with my bad Russian that the spy listening on the other line probably thinks I'm dumb.

Mom promised me if I was good and did not ask her to leave early from her parties this week that she would give me thirty minutes with Babushka this Sunday. Well, today is this Sunday, and I am waiting.

I have been sitting next to the phone since 11 AM. It's already 2 PM here in Houston, which means its 10 PM for Babushka in Moscow. I imagine her sitting by her phone, waiting for us to call. My thighs are sweaty and sticking to the kitchen floor. If Babushka were here, I know the kitchen floor wouldn't have chocolate chip cookie crumbs all over it, but I can't keep the apartment as clean as Babushka.

I am afraid to wake Mom up because I don't want her to get mad and not let me talk to Babushka today, so I will just wait. I know Babushka will also wait for me. I move the blinds to one side and let the sun slice through the floor. I wonder if me and Babushka ever look at the sun at the same time.

This has been the worst month of my life. It's the middle of the summer, so I don't have school, which I think is making everything worse. I would rather be at school then at home. Mom doesn't have work right now, because it's summer and no one needs her at the church, but she's looking for another job anyway.

Masha has been gone on her visitation from the courts with Chris, and I think if she were here, Mom wouldn't be acting this way. If Babushka and Masha were here, we would be a whole family. Instead we are half of a family, which I don't think makes a very good family at all.

We moved from Chris's house into an apartment close to where Mom's friend Chanel lives because it's cheap, and Mom got a deal. Chanel babysits for a girl who is a fifth grader at my school. Mom met Chanel when she was waiting to pick me up from school last year. She has big, curly black hair with blonde stripes in it and big eyebrows that Mom says she wishes she had. Chanel isn't as skinny as Mom, but Mom says Chanel is fat in all the best ways. In her boobs and butt, two things Mom wishes were much bigger on herself. Chanel is an immigrant too, but she came here with the right papers. Mom tells Chanel that she wishes her skin was as dark as hers so she wouldn't have to go to the tanning bed every week, but Chanel says they wouldn't have let Mom and me through Mexico if she wasn't as white as paper.

The longer we live in these apartments, the more I think we moved here so Mom can be in her twenties and not because it's cheap. The apartment has two bedrooms. If the courts ever ask, Masha is supposed to have one of the rooms and Mom has the other one. I guess the courts don't care about me because that would mean I don't get anything, but in reality the room that Mom tells the courts is Masha's is actually both mine and Masha's. I don't sleep there though. I sleep on the couch in the living room.

I stay in the living room a lot. I watch TV, which Babushka wouldn't like, but Mom won't take me to the library. Not even to return the books I checked out with Babushka.

Ever since court ended, I feel like Mom doesn't want to be a mom. Maybe not my mom. Maybe only Masha's mom. Mom has never felt like my mom, but now, with Masha gone on her visitation, it's even worse.

I feel like I don't have a mom. Moms are supposed to feed you and wake you up and give you medicine and protect you. My mom is sometimes not even at home when I wake up. She makes me food but not at the same time every day like Babushka did. Babushka knew everything about me. Mom doesn't even know what my favorite game is. Life without Chris and Babushka reminds me of when we first got to America, and I was alone in that motel room while Mom went to find a husband.

When we first moved into the apartment, Mom would leave me alone a lot. Then Chanel said she was doing child abuse. Now we have a situation that I really don't like.

"It's not child abuse!" Mom said to Chanel. She sounded like Chanel had slapped her in the face. They were in the living room, sharing a bottle of alcohol. I know it's alcohol because it smelled really bad and was clear. Chanel had come over to help us unpack even though we were already unpacked. "In Russia I went to the grocery store alone at six years old!" Mom shouted.

"Trust me, Hon, I'm a professional babysitter. It's against the law. They have to be over twelve. Just imagine if he found out." Chanel bent her head in the direction of a picture of Masha.

"This is idiotic," Mom said, angrily, looking away.

Now, thanks to Chanel, I have to go to a lot of places with Mom. She still leaves me alone, but not as often. The people Mom meets are Chanel's age, which is Mom's age, and they all smell bad because they smoke a lot. Mom is young, which I didn't know until noticing that most people say something about it when she introduces me as her kid. "You have an eight-year-old? Did you have her when you were sixteen or something? You look twenty!"

Mom smiles when people talk about how she looks too young to have a child. Mom looks like a grown up to me, but I guess she is actually more of a kid since she needs her Mom a lot too. I don't think Mom wants to be a mom anymore, too, because she tells everyone that she is so happy to not be on her best behavior for a divorce anymore. She tells all of Chanel's friends that she can finally party and "be in her twenties."

Except I am in my eights and not in my twenties, and I don't want to party with Mom. Ever since Chanel said she is child abusing me, Mom takes me to a different party every night. They are always in an apartment or a small house and the music is loud and the people are annoying and ask me too many questions about what I am doing there. I try to find a spot on a couch or bed and hug my knees until I get too upset, and then I ask Mom if we can go home a million times until she finally yells at me and we go.

After I said goodbye to Babushka at the airport, I started doing this thing where I count each letter in the words that I think, and I haven't been able to stop. Every time I get scared, I think of the last word I thought. If the letters that make up the word don't end on my pinky when I count them, that means something bad is going to happen. If they do end on my pinky, we are going to be OK. The only exception is if the letters add up to seven or three, then it's OK because Babushka says seven and three are God's favorite numbers. I started with just one of my hands, but added my second hand in when not enough words ended on my pinky.

I feel sleepy. I've been sitting against this wall next to this phone for a long time. If I don't get to talk to Babushka today, I don't know what I will do. It's the only thing that is keeping me from exploding.

I close my eyes. I would rather go to sleep than cry.

"Katya?" My eyes shoot open. Mom is standing where the oven is. Her hair is in a clip, and she is wearing her black and white striped shorts and a black shirt that shows her belly, but it's not too small, it's on purpose.

"Can we call Babushka?" I ask. It comes out in a whisper. I look at the time. It's 3 PM Houston time. 11 PM Russia time.

"It's too late," Mom says.

"I know she's waiting," I say, feeling the sadness in my throat.

"She'll be fine. So will you. Have better Russian, and then you can call her. When I feel like you won't waste my minutes." There is no way for me to work on my Russian unless she teaches me. I don't say this.

Mom walks toward the refrigerator and opens it, pulling out a carton of cottage cheese.

"You promised," I say. "I was good. I didn't say anything. I didn't ask to leave the party," I swallow, hard.

She doesn't say anything as she lifts the lid off the cottage cheese and dips her spoon in, taking a big white chunk and shoving it in her mouth. She closes the fridge with her foot and walks away, sitting at the kitchen table and pulling out the newspaper Chanel gave to her so she could circle jobs. The jobs she can get are jobs where they don't ask for her documents, so she doesn't have a lot of options.

"Please," I whisper. I can't stop the tears from falling.

Mom's face is hard, like stone. She ignores me. When she is with me and only me, she gets lines in her cheeks that make her look mad all the time. I watch her circle the newspaper. Her hair in the bright light of the daytime is thin like hay. She says it's because she has dyed it too much. She used to have red hair but now it is blonde. She said she did that to match Masha.

I touch my hair. I have blonde hair too. But she never cared about matching me.

9/11

Fall, Early 2000s, Eight Years Old, Third Grade

My third-grade teacher, Mr. Clark, rolls the TV into the room and tells us that we're done learning for the day. "A tragedy has happened," he explains. His eyes are red, like he has been crying.

Mr. Clark clicks the button to change the channel until the TV is not black and white anymore, but it's still fuzzy. I can make out two buildings on the screen, one of them covered in gray smoke.

"Damn it," he says, hitting the back of the TV.

"Did downtown explode?" Lia asks, from her seat next to me. "That looks bad."

I guess that is downtown, but I can't be sure because the picture still isn't very clear.

"Do you have a cable cord?" I ask Mr. Clark. "Sometimes when I wiggle the cord that connects the TV to the cable, it makes all the static disappear."

Mr. Clark turns around. He told us on our first day of school that this was his first year teaching. He has been my favorite teacher I've ever had because he hasn't yelled at us yet. Except right now he looks like he is about to yell at us.

"Students, we are in the midst of a tragedy, and I need you to just trust me and be quiet, OK?" He holds his hands up, like he is trying to push us back.

Mrs. Barr, the principal, comes on the speaker and tells everyone that school is dismissed for the rest of the day and for teachers to let students call their parents from the classroom phone and ask to be picked up.

Mr. Clark puts a hand to his mouth and closes his eyes. I want to ask him to explain what is going on but instead he takes a deep breath and goes to sit at his desk. "I will call you up alphabetically, and we will phone your parents together," he says.

Suddenly I see the other building on the TV screen start crumbling down. A girl who I don't like starts screaming behind me. I turn around to stare at her. If my mom had her as a kid, she would be very thankful for me. I am not as noisy.

"What is happening?!" Someone else asks. "Why is everything getting blown up?"

I don't know why Mr. Clark would turn on the TV and not say what is happening. I think Lia is wrong, though. I don't think those buildings are in Houston. I think they are in New York. I know because of the Statue of Liberty that keeps popping up on the screen.

Finally, Mr. Clark gets up and turns on the volume. "No more questions!" He hisses.

He continues calling us up to his desk. For the first time since I've met my class, we're mostly quiet and listening. When it's my turn to call my mom, I tell Mr. Clark her cell number. He calls her twice but the phone goes to voicemail both times.

"Do you want to give me your home phone number?" He asks.

I shrug. I know she's not home. Chanel got her a fancy new job that she loves, and she's always at work. She works in a brand new building that is shiny and black on the outside, and she can't pick me up from school until 6 PM on most days. She doesn't make much money, but she says to have an American company on her resumé is worth working for free. Chanel turned the job down to go to law school in Boston but said Mom would do it if they hired her without asking questions but for half the pay, and the American company agreed. She sells things over the phone, which she is very proud of, but it means she probably can't answer the phone all the time.

I give Mr. Clark our home phone number, and it goes to voicemail like I knew it would. "We'll try later," he says.

"Did your Mom pick up?" Lia asks me when I get back to my seat.

I shake my head.

"Mine did. She's coming to get me right now. She works for the government. She says they are closing everything downtown because the government is worried about an attack on Houston, since it's so big," Lia's eyes get wide.

"But this is in New York," I say, pointing to the screen. "That's not even close to Houston."

"Yeah, but they're everywhere," Lia says, her eyes moving around like she's looking for someone.

My heart starts to speed up. I turn around to look at Mr. Clark, but he's with Jared, whose cheeks are red like he's been crying. It wouldn't be normal for Mom to pick up the phone but today is different. Everyone else's parents in my class are picking up the phone, why isn't my mom?

I start to feel dizzy and get up. Mr. Clark created a reading corner for us, and I go to lie down on the little couch that is there. I am supposed to ask permission, but I feel like I'm going to fall down so I don't. What if Mom isn't OK? I count my words, starting from my thumb. "What" has four letters, which doesn't reach my pinky when I'm counting, which means it's a bad word, which means something bad will happen. Maybe something bad has happened. I shouldn't think of bad words. I should only think of good words. Is "good" a good word? No, because it has four letters and four doesn't end on my pinky. Something bad has definitely happened to Mom. I keep my eyes closed, even when I hear parents start to enter the room and pick up their kids. I want to know whose parent looks like who, but I can't open my eyes right now. I have to find a good word. I can't think of the word good cause it's bad. Maybe the word "maybe." Maybe is five letters. It ends on my pinky, which is great! I breathe slower. That was two bad words and one good word, but that was three counted words and the third one was the best word and God's number is three, so everything will be OK. I breathe in and out on the couch. Everything will be OK. I am OK.

After a little while, I sit up and notice that most of the class is gone. It's just me, Mr. Clark, and Jared. Jared's mom comes ten minutes later. She is a doctor and has to get the day off to pick Jared up. Now it's just me and Mr. Clark. There are still two more hours until school is normally over, and then my usual four hours I wait on top of that, but Mr. Clark doesn't know about those hours. No one does except the people at the grocery store who I ask to use their phone sometimes when Mom is running late.

"You OK over there?" Mr. Clark asks me.

I nod.

"Do you want to try your Mom again?"

I shake my head.

"OK, well, let me know if you need anything," he says, flipping through a magazine. He puts his feet up on one of the desks belonging to a student who isn't here. I think I'm keeping him from leaving too.

I look out the window. The TV is still playing how there are no more twin towers. If my mom had been in one of those buildings, what would happen to me? What would happen to Masha? Masha has Chris. He's not my dad. I don't have anyone here. I don't even have any telephone cards to call Babushka in Russia. If I did have a phone card, what could Babushka do to bring me to her? How could I leave Masha? I don't have any documents here. How can I stay?

When the bell finally rings, I say bye to Mr. Clark and pack up all my stuff and head to the grocery store, where I sit on a bench outside. I pray that Mom comes at six. I pray so hard that by the time I see her tiny car pull up, I almost fall down when I stand up to get inside.

"Why didn't you answer the phone when I called?" I ask, as soon as I open the door. "There was an emergency at school and everyone's parents came to pick them up."

"It's an emergency for Americans. It's not an emergency if you're an immigrant. The rest of us have to work," Mom says, speeding up.

I put my backpack in the backseat of the car. Next we head to Masha, who is with one of Mom's friends.

"It's sad, what happened in New York," I say to Mom. "I was scared that something would happen to you since you work downtown."

The sun is going down. I hate it when the sun goes down because it reminds me of The Worst Day.

"I'm fine," she says. Her voice is irritated. She rolls her eyes, and I know not to bring it up again.

Greece

Summer 2021, Late Twenties

We just received our second COVID vaccine. My husband and I take a selfie in the car and send it to my father. For some reason, I never thought this day would come. I didn't think we'd see a vaccine for COVID for a long time.

"Now we can finally meet," my dad writes back, along with a smiley face.

The tickets are booked. The hotel is booked. We're meeting my dad, stepmom, and little sister and brother in three months, in August, in Crete. We decided on Greece because it's in Europe, which seemed like a good middle ground between Russia and the United States.

We thought about going to Russia, but my Russian passport expired, and my mom's warnings about my birth country being dangerous for American citizens still ring in my ears, preventing me from going. Russia was a lot safer for US citizens before the annexation of Crimea. Now no US citizen, especially a dual Russian citizen, is advised to go.

"I can't imagine it—meeting him. Meeting my siblings. It doesn't feel real," I say to Liam, who is driving us home. "What if this is all fake?"

Liam smiles wide and laughs. "This would be one hell of a scam," he says.

I laugh too. "And sad."

"And sad," he agrees, nodding his head.

"If this goes well, then next summer I'm going to go to Russia," I announce. "We're going to go and see my family."

"Of course," Liam says, without hesitation.

"Your parents won't like it," I add, looking at him. He's looking at the road. We're five minutes from the house.

He shrugs. "They don't understand."

When we told Liam's parents that I reconnected with my dad their response was to be careful, as though all Russian people had an agenda, even though I have never talked about my dad to them. They had never asked.

I am used to this reaction, the idea that all foreigners want something from the person with an American citizenship. That their intentions aren't good. I feel angry that their response wasn't happiness and support, but when shows like *90 Day Fiancé* exist, how can I expect any different? The idea that an American citizenship is golden and the best in the world was an idea I also grew up with. The idea that Americans get taken advantage of by deceitful foreigners looking for a way out of their poverty-stricken country was a stereotype my mom perpetuated.

We park our car in the driveway and go inside our house, our left arms sore.

"I guess now it's time to prepare. We're really going to meet them in Greece," I say, as Liam unlocks the door.

"We really are," he answers.

Real Dad

Winter, Early 2000s, Nine Years Old, Third Grade

"JUST REMEMBER THAT your real dad is evil," Mom says. "Remember that he beat me. He only cares about himself. He only cares about his job and making money." Mom is in the bathroom, coloring her lips in with the red lipstick she only uses for dates. We're going to meet my real dad today. He will be here for my ninth birthday. I hope he knows how special a ninth birthday is because I feel very grown up, being almost ten.

"Why didn't he just send the documents in the mail?" I ask her, taking a brush to my hair. Maybe I can try to look more like Mom and less like him. "Why do I have to see him?"

Mom rolls her eyes. "Because he is a man and needs power over me. It's all a game."

I look at myself in the mirror. I put on a pink long-sleeve T-shirt and black pants. I have bangs that I don't like but Mom says I have to have because they make me look skinnier. If my real dad is evil, does that mean I am also evil?

"After he gives me documents, you know what to do," Mom adds, smiling. Mom called my real dad because she needs documents from him. That's the only reason she told him where I was. Otherwise she was protecting us.

Mom has been nice since she found out my real dad was coming. Normally I feel like she doesn't like me, but I notice that she likes to spend time with me if I tell her how I'm going to be mean to my dad for her.

"I'm going to break the TV in his hotel room," I say.

Mom laughs. "What else?"

"I am going to break all the lamps in his hotel room. And steal them!"

Mom's eyes get really big, like I'm giving her a present. This makes me want to continue, so I do.

"I will go to the store and make him buy me everything I want!" I say. "And be really difficult."

"Good," she says. "Let's see how he likes raising a child on his own." Mom kisses a piece of toilet paper and drops it in the trash which means it's time to go. Mom decides to wear one of her suits that she wears to work and her fanciest business shoes, even though she doesn't wear nice clothes on the weekends.

We go to the airport, which makes me sad because going to the airport reminds me of Babushka. Mom arrives late on purpose because she wants Dad to wait for us. Somehow, when we open the doors to the international arrivals, I know the man sitting on the bench is my dad without seeing his face.

"Ivan!" My mom says. I turn to her, surprised by her voice. She doesn't sound angry. She sounds happy. She recognizes my dad from his back too. The man stands up and smiles big when he sees her, and then looks like he sees a ghost when he looks at me.

His mouth goes from a smile to an "O." I have not wanted to hide behind Mom since I was a kid, but right now I want to hide behind her. Mom turns to look at me and then she looks at him.

We walk towards him. I don't smile. I don't forget that Mom told me he hurt her just like Chris did. I have to be strong for Mom.

"Hello," he says. He looks at me for a very long time. His eyes are the same color as my eyes. "I am—I am—I am your father. Ivan."

He has a little book in his hand and he shows it to me. "It's a—a pocket dictionary. For English. I am learning it. Do you know Russian?"

I look at Mom. She doesn't look happy anymore. I can tell she is mad again.

"She doesn't know any Russian," Mom says. "She is completely an American girl. You will have to speak only English."

My real dad looks at his dictionary, then at me. I look at Mom. I wish I could read in her mind what I am supposed to say right now that would make her happy.

My real dad doesn't seem like a mean person. He just looks sad and tired.

"Are you hungry?" he asks me. "Shall we go?"

I realize Mom hasn't asked me if I am hungry today. I don't know if I can say if I'm hungry or not because if I say yes then what if that makes her look like a bad Mom? I stare at him instead of saying anything.

"Is my English that bad?" He asks Mom, in Russian. "She isn't answering."

"She doesn't like you," Mom responds in Russian. "We can go," Mom says to him, in English, pointing to the door. "She will eat."

Mom doesn't tell me ahead of time that she's leaving me with my real dad for the next weekend. That was never part of the plan. I am crying on her bed as she is packing a suitcase. Masha has also left for the weekend. I am going to be alone with another man that has hit my mother.

"Mom, I don't know him. I'm scared," I cry to her.

"Stop crying. You're acting like a baby," she says. "You're going to make yourself more sick. It's the perfect time for me to leave anyway. You're sick so you won't remember anything bad, and you will make his life hell because no one likes sick kids. Win-win."

"I would rather be by myself!" I say. I fall back into her pillow and get snot all over her pillowcase. "You got the documents from him. Just leave me alone for the weekend!"

"No. He wants kids? He can see how difficult they are then," Mom is smiling like she just told herself a joke.

"I thought you said he didn't want me," I say. I blow my nose into my shirt, which I realize is a bad thing to do since that means we will have to go to the laundromat sooner.

"He doesn't," she says. "He just thinks he does."

"I don't understand you!" I say. When she doesn't respond I add, "Where are you even going?"

"Austin. My friends from work have a big house there. It will be fun," she says. "He has jacuzzi!"

"You're supposed to be a good mom," I say, too tired to filter my words.

She stops packing and looks at me. "I am a good mom. I do everything for you. I am allowed to have a break."

There is a knock on the door. I groan. Mom hops up to go answer it like she is excited.

"Ivan, privet!" She says. Her voice sounds like it's in a tunnel.

I hear my real dad's deep voice at the front door of our apartment, and Mom explaining to him in Russian that I'm sick.

"What do I do in case of an emergency?" He asks her. "My English isn't good for a child with such a high fever. What do I say to a doctor?"

"She doesn't need to go to a doctor. She will be fine. Just go buy some Nyquil, and it will put her to sleep."

Mom comes back in her room and zips up her suitcase. She kisses me on the head and leaves. I hear them talking but don't hear what they are saying.

I wake up to my real dad sticking a thermometer under my tongue. I spit it out.

"What are you doing?" I ask him.

"I—I—This will help me see if you have temperature. Please open your mouth again."

I do as he says because I am too tired to argue.

"You still have a very high temperature. It has not lowered. Have you had food?"

I shake my head.

"Will you eat?"

I don't answer him because I don't know the answer.

"What do you like?"

It hurts to blink. It hurts to swallow.

"Mashed potatoes? Do you like it?"

I nod.

"OK. What else?"

I think about the things Mom won't ever buy me because they are too expensive but they are my favorite foods.

"Fruit Roll-Ups," I say.

"Fruit. Roll?"

"Fruit Roll-Ups." I repeat.

He puts something to my lips and says, "Drink."

I drink what he gives me, thinking it's water. I spit it out and scrunch up my face when I can taste that it's medicine.

I can hear a smile in his voice when he says, "Katyusha. It is this NyQuil. It is very important you drink it."

I open my mouth wider and finish the spoonful. I am not sure that I am supposed to be drinking NyQuil for whatever I have, but I take the water he gives me and lie back down in Mom's bed.

I wake up to my real dad's hand on my forehead. "You are still very hot. Please open your mouth."

I open my mouth. He sticks a thermometer under my tongue until it beeps.

"Your temperature has gone away by three degrees!" He says, excitedly. "This NyQuil is working well. You will have some more. But you need to eat. I made you mashed potatoes. Eat. Please."

I open my eyes to a bowl of mashed potatoes next to my arm. It looks like how Babushka makes them. Mom makes mashed potatoes sometimes, but she makes them very creamy, like potato soup. Babushka leaves big chunk of potatoes in hers. That's how my real dad's mashed potatoes look.

I shake my head no and push the bowl away.

"Katya, you need to eat. You haven't had food all day."

"It looks horrible," I say, turning my head away. I know I should eat but Mom said I have to be mean and so far I have just done everything he has said, which isn't very mean of me.

I hear my real dad sigh and take the potatoes back. "Oh, wait!" He says.

He rushes out of the room and comes back with a big, red box. "Your fruits!"

He's holding a box of Fruit Loops.

"Those are Fruit Loops," I say. "Not Fruit Roll Ups."

"I ask them for what you tell me. The fruit rolls. They say they don't have them. They give me this."

"I don't like Fruit Loops. They taste fake. They are bad for you. I want Fruit Roll-Ups. I'm sick. I can't eat fake fruit!"

I sigh and lie back down. When he doesn't leave, I put a pillow over my head.

I pretend to fall asleep and only then do I hear him leave. He calls Mom and tells her that he is worried about me because I'm not eating. Whatever Mom says to him makes him sigh and hang up. I hear him open the Fruit Loops and pour some into a bowl with milk. Babushka would be happy he is not wasting food, even if Fruit Loops really do taste bad.

I woke up without a fever and my real dad says he wants to take me to my favorite store to celebrate. He is leaving the day after tomorrow. Mom comes home tomorrow. I told him we should wait for Mom, but he says he wants to spend time with just me.

I am too tired to be mean to him or ask to go to the jewelry store Mom told me to. She said for me to get him to buy me diamonds. I don't know how to do that, so I am honest and tell him my favorite store is the Discovery Channel store.

"What is your . . . favorite movie?" He asks. He has both hands on the steering wheel, his eyes forward. His Russian accent is thick, but I understand him.

I shrug. "I like all movies," I say.

He nods.

"What is your . . . favorite book?" He asks.

I don't know how to answer him. I like all the books I read when Babushka was here. They are picture books and for kids, but they are my favorite.

"Junie B. Jones books," I lie. I do like Junie B. Jones, but Sophia kind of ruined her for me because she told me the reason Junie is funny is because she is dumb, and I would think she was funny because I act like her. I told Sophia that she was dumb but not funny, and that's worse.

"What is it . . . about?" He asks.

I turn my head to look at him and feel myself frown. I've read all the Junie B. Jones books, but no one has ever asked me what they are about.

"I mean . . . why do you like these books?" He asks, turning to me when we're at a stop light.

No one but Babushka has asked me what I like. I don't know what I like.

"It's funny," I say, after a while. "The books are funny. That's why I like them, I think." I get the impulse to tell him more because I like that he wants to know about me, but I squash it down because Mom won't like that.

My real dad pulls into a parking garage in the Galleria, where the Discovery Channel store is. We both get out. He reaches for my hand. I stare at his hand like it's a pinching crab.

"It's very busy here," He says, shaking his hand a little. "Please hold my hand, so I don't lose you."

Mom never holds my hand. The last person to hold my hand was Masha. His eyes look intense, and I still don't have enough energy to argue, so I let him hold my hand. After a while, I decide I don't hate it because he leads me around, and I don't have to think about where we are.

We make it to the Discovery Channel store after what feels like ten stops. My real dad keeps stopping in front of different places and asking me if I wanted to go inside. He seemed disappointed when I said "no" to the ice cream place, but I reminded him that I still didn't feel good and he nodded.

Inside the store, I go to where the lava lamps are. My father trails behind me, looking around in amazement.

"This is a very . . . awesome store," he says.

I look at a hot pink lava lamp. It has glitter inside. I love glitter.

"You want it?" My real dad asks, pointing to the lava lamp. "I'll buy you whatever you want." I do want it, but I don't get the box. Sophia says lava lamps are for kids who are afraid of the dark, and I don't want her to come over and see it and make fun of me. Lenora drops Sophia off with Mom when she has a date, and Mom does the same thing to me with Lenora. They call them "play dates," but play dates are for friends, and me and Sophia don't like each other. Other than Sophia being a jerk all the time, she doesn't like Masha because Lenora spent a lot of time helping Mom with the custody battle for Masha. She even testified in court for Mom. Sophia was upset because this meant her Mom didn't pay as much attention to her. She called Masha a "Mom stealer" and made Masha cry, so I hate Sophia forever now.

My real dad picks up the lava lamp box.

I shake my head. "No, I don't want that," I say. I look around, at something Sophia will think is cool and not for little kids. My eyes land on a light stick that changes colors when you turn it on. I walk over to it and pick it up. I know Sophia does not have this, but I don't know what she'll say about it.

"I'll get it for you," my real dad says.

I nod, "OK."

My real dad smiles. "What else do you want, Katyusha?"

I freeze. The only people who call me Katyusha are my Babushka and my mom sometimes. I've never heard anyone else call me Katyusha.

"That's it," I say. "I want to go home now," I tell my dad. I don't tell him his being Russian makes me miss my babushka even more, and I just want to curl up in a ball until the pain of missing her goes away.

My real dad bends down to my level. "Do you want to . . . get a movie?" He asks me. "We can get a funny one . . . and watch it . . . if you don't feel good."

I think he said "funny" movie, because I told him I like Junie B. Jones because she is funny. I think about the movies that are out right now. I've wanted the *Rugrats in Paris* movie on video but haven't asked Mom for it because it costs money.

I nod, "OK," I say. "I want to watch the *Rugrats in Paris* movie."

My real dad smiles, like I've said something to make him happy.

"What is it about?" He asks.

"It's about a little boy who tries to find a Mom in a different country," I say. "His died."

"Sounds sad."

I shrug. "He finds one, so not really."

Flight

Summer 2021, Late Twenties

WE'RE ON THE flight to Crete, and it doesn't feel real. It feels like I'm moving in a dream. My doctor had to prescribe me fast-release anti-anxiety medication because I stopped breathing from panic again. I was diagnosed with panic disorder and OCD when I was in college, and I had done a lot of therapy to ease my worry, but the panic has come back, especially when I think about meeting my family in person.

"What if they don't like me?" I ask Liam. "What if they think I'm fat?"

"It's impossible not to like you. You're hilarious," he says, and kisses my forehead. "And you're not fat."

"Yeah, but to Russians I am," I say, looking down at my bumpy thighs. "I'm scared they'll think I'm ugly."

"They've seen you from photos," Liam laughs. "No one thinks you're ugly. You're great. They know that."

Years of my mom emphasizing that men only care about appearance have me scared that my own dad will leave me if he thinks I'm ugly. I think back to the first time my mom met Liam, when we were eighteen, and she pinched my stomach and told me I needed to lose weight to keep him.

I shake my head, trying to push away the memory. Reconnecting with my dad has caused a lot of memories to crash into my mind like waves, dousing my brain in insecurities. At the root of it all, I'm afraid of being left again. I know it. My life has revolved around the fear of being alone, like I'm the small girl in that California hotel room all over again.

I lean my head on Liam's shoulder. We had a rough start to our relationship. Three years of me constantly breaking up with him until he proposed and I took him seriously. He never left me, not once. No matter how many times I thought I had pushed him over the edge, he was always there, patiently waiting, telling me I was worth it.

He's the only reason I believe that my dad can love me, and maybe he does.

I feel the plane start to descend. The pilot talks about the weather in Crete. He tells us he hopes we have a good time.

I pray that my dad doesn't let me down.

PART 5

Lobby

Summer 2021, Late Twenties

We've been in Crete for twelve hours. My dad's flight just landed. I orchestrated our arrival so that we got here first. His flight was late, thankfully. It's three in the morning.

"We're here," Dad texts. With it comes a picture of what I recognize as the lobby my husband and I were just in. As soon as we landed we took naps and woke up a little while ago. I popped more Xanax because I need to calm down. If I don't get my breathing under control my family is going to think I'm unwell. Who am I kidding? I *am* unwell.

Layla, my best friend from high school, texts me and asks how it's going. I can't bring myself to text her back because I don't want to acknowledge that I'm not doing well. I should be. This is an amazing opportunity. We're in Greece, meeting my family. How many people get to have a reunion?

"They're here," I tell Liam. He's on his phone.

He drops it and turns to me. "Are you ready?" He asks.

"I guess," I say. I put my phone in my pocket and head to the lobby, my hands shaking.

"Hey, wait," Liam says, grabbing my wrist. "Can you take a breath in and out?"

I look at him. I breathe in. I breathe out.

Liam does this with me a lot when he knows I'm nervous.

I calm down, a little.

It's going to be OK. I'm not alone. Whatever happens, I'm safe.

Liam and I hold hands and walk to the lobby.

I see my brother first. He's on his phone, a hand to his head. My little sister is on the opposite couch from him, asleep.

My dad and stepmom are at the front desk, checking in.

The butterflies in my chest disappear. Maybe the Xanax is finally working. I walk over to my brother and touch his hand, gently. He looks up at me, and his face cracks into a huge smile.

My heart explodes. Seeing him smile at me fills my whole body up with light. His smile takes away my darkness instantly, like it was never even there in the first place.

My brother.

I hug him, tightly. He buries his head in my shoulder.

"Katya?" I recognize my little sister's voice. She's seven. I turn around, and she's waving at me, sleepily. I go to her and take her hands and kiss them. My sister. She gives me a big smile, and I feel like nothing bad will ever happen again. I feel whole, I feel safe. I feel complete in a way I've never experienced. I have a *family.*

"Oh!" I hear from behind my sister. My dad has turned around.

He has gotten old. He reminds me of Winnie the Pooh, his face squished but soft. He comes to me and hugs me tighter than I've ever been hugged in my life. He kisses my forehead, hard. I fold into him.

"It's you!" He says. "Finally."

There are tears in his eyes. They aren't you're-my-golden-ticket tears. They are the tears of a father who had had his daughter taken away from him.

I hug him back, tight.

"It's been so long," I hear him say into my hair. "I didn't know if this day would come."

"I am so glad it did," I say.

Moving

Early 2000s, Nine Years Old, Summer After Third Grade

I HAVEN'T BEEN TO school since March. Me skipping school all started because I got lice. My teacher told Mom I could come back when the lice were gone, but Mom didn't try to get rid of the lice because it meant I could stay home and watch Masha while she was at work. We would save money, she said. School is out now, but the only problem with Mom's plan is that next year is the fourth grade, and in the fourth grade they expect you to know your multiplication tables, which I don't.

We are driving to Chris's house to drop Masha off. Mom says I am allowed to come this time. Mom has a plan. Mom has lost her job, and she says we will lose our apartment soon. If we lose our apartment, we could lose Masha. We could lose everything. She says she has made progress on our visa, but if we don't have a way to pay for our lawyer, we will lose the progress.

The drive to Chris's house is quiet. The last time I was inside Chris's house was with Babushka. Going inside his house without her feels bad. The last time I was in Chris's house with him inside of it, he was hitting Mom. I close my eyes because I can't think of that. That. *Four letters.* It doesn't land on my pinky. I shouldn't have thought of The Worst Day. Shouldn't. Nine letters, including the apostrophe.

Bad luck. Again.

Mom pulls into the driveway. She looks pretty, like she is going on a date. I wish Lenora was here, but she moved an hour away to a different neighborhood. If she knew we were going to Chris's house, she would stop Mom. I think to call and tell her, but I'm not allowed to use Mom's phone because I'll waste her minutes.

We are alone.

Mom knocks on the door. Chris opens it and looks surprised to see all of us. He smiles big. He is wearing his shark tooth necklace. It is glittering. The sun is setting, reflecting on the necklace. Mom tells Chris she needs to do something on his computer. He says "Of course, come on in."

We go inside the house. Chris got new couches because Mom's lawyer said that she should get his old ones in the divorce. His new ones look comfier. Masha wakes up and starts crying. Chris and Mom don't move to take care of her. I get her out of her car seat. She stands up and stretches.

"Hungy, Kaka!" she says. "I'm hungy!"

"I know," I say. "What do you want to eat?"

She walks over to the kitchen, and I follow after her. I remember what it felt like when this place was my home.

I feel bad being here again. It feels like we're going backwards.

Masha opens the fridge and points up, like she wants the fridge to hold her. I look up and see that she's pointing at a Go-GURT tube. I take one out for her and one for me too. We sit at the kitchen table and eat the yogurt tubes. Mom and Chris go upstairs to use the computer.

We don't leave until the next morning.

We have started sleeping at Chris's house every night. Chris still thinks Mom has a job, so we have to find somewhere to be during the day.

"Don't tell Chris we're moving out of our apartment," Mom repeats. She has told me this a lot, like she is trying to drill a hole in my head with her words and put the thought in there permanently.

We watch two men pull Masha's and my pee-stained mattress down the stairs and into a moving truck. Mom found these men at Home Depot. She said Home Depot is where all the undocumented immigrants who aren't white get their jobs. She tells me American companies like white people for desk jobs, so we're lucky.

Mom tells me every day that I am not allowed to tell Chris we are moving because he will take her to court again and get custody of Masha and have me and her sent to Russia. She says she got back together with him to distract him. I guess it's worked.

"Where are we moving?" I ask Mom. We haven't looked for any apartments.

Mom sighs.

Masha is at daycare since today is moving day, which she likes a lot better than me watching her, since the last time I watched her we got into a fight, and I pushed her off the couch, and her head hit the glass coffee table, and she got a big bruise.

"We moving into storage place for now. I don't have job or documents so no one will rent to me. I will be looking. We just will live with Chris for now. But he doesn't know. Don't say anything!" she says again, screwing the thought tighter. Mom bites her thumb. She has gotten into the habit of doing this a lot.

"Miss? The dishes in the sink?" One of the movers has come back upstairs and is pointing to the pile of dishes that has been there for several weeks, since that first night we spent with Chris and never left.

The dishes are covered in food from weeks ago and mold that smells like orange peels.

Mom stares at the sink. She doesn't blink. The man says, "Miss?" I realize it has been a long time since he has asked Mom what to do. There is not even soap to wash the dishes with.

"I will throw them away," Mom says, like she has just woken up from a dream. "Katya, go throw the dishes away. Just put them in a trash bag." Mom points to the trash bags on the floor next to the front door. We have packed almost everything in these trash bags because Mom says boxes are too expensive. I take one and walk over to the dishes and start putting them in the trash.

The man shrugs and walks away, saying something in Spanish to his partner. They start lifting our small kitchen table where I tried and failed to feed me and Masha sandwiches for so many months of me not going to school. We mostly ate Little Debbie Cosmic Brownies and watched Sponge Bob. Masha doesn't like the smell of turkey. I tried to have us on a schedule, but putting a toddler on a schedule is impossible, I learned.

When the dishes are all in the trash, I look inside the sink and see there is something green growing in spots. If I could talk to Babushka on the phone I would tell her we were throwing all these dishes away. She would be shocked and mad. She would tell us to scrub them with our hands and water. I scrunch up my face. I don't want to touch these dishes more than I have to. I'm glad Mom is lazy.

When the apartment is all packed up we go to the storage unit and the movers fit everything inside. There's a little bit of space for us to still walk around in. It's air-conditioned in here, and there's a bathroom downstairs. We could live here. Mom says it's a hundred and fifty dollars a month. The apartment she was paying eight hundred a month. The only problem is we can't watch TV because there is nowhere to plug anything in, but all that matters is that we're not sleeping in the car because Mom could get into trouble if someone finds us.

If Chris kicks us out, we have this storage unit at least.

At 2 PM, Mom drops the workers off at Home Depot. We now have nowhere to go except Chris's house but we can't go there until after five because he doesn't know Mom was fired. Mom doesn't even have a key. She drives to her favorite grocery store, Fiesta. We park but don't go inside. Instead, Mom leans the seat back and closes her eyes. It is boiling inside the car, but Mom doesn't care.

I do the same with my seat.

"Are you going to marry Chris again?" I ask Mom, after an hour in the car. I know she's awake because her eyes are open and staring at the roof of the car. I wish I had a book with me. I'm too afraid to go to the library to check out any books because we never returned the last ones Babushka and I checked out together, and I'm worried about what the fines are.

"No," Mom says. "He won't get citizenship for us."

"What kind of job are you looking for?" I ask. I stare at the side of Mom's face. Her nose. Her fake blonde hair. The hair she dyed for Masha. I think to ask Mom if she could get a job outside Home Depot in the morning, like the other undocumented immigrants like us, but I don't ask her this because I feel like she will get mad at me for suggesting something she has probably already thought of.

"I don't know," she says. "It's hard to have a job here. I didn't fuck the boss, so he fired me and threatened me because I don't have papers. I don't want to do this again," she says, turning her body towards the handle of the car.

"What are we going to do?" I ask her. I try to keep my voice normal, but it cracks at the end. There's a big, dark puddle of sweat coloring her neon green spaghetti strap a darker, forest green.

She doesn't answer.

"Why can't Babushka come?" I try again. Babushka always knows what to do.

"Fucking 9/11. They stopped giving visas. It's bullshit. I don't know. Stop asking so many questions."

The air in the car is sticky, and it is hard to breathe. It feels like someone is sitting on my chest. At least I can count. I am thankful for my fingers. I think of the word fingers. *Seven letters.* A God number. Mom's back rises and falls quickly, like she is crying.

I turn away from her, because I don't want to see her sad. It will make me sad, but that only lasts a few minutes because I don't like the idea of not being able to see her, so I turn back around. I scrunch my knees to my chest. After a while I hear Mom snoring softly, but I don't let myself fall asleep, because someone needs to have their eyes open in this country.

Fourth Grade

Fall, Early 2000s, Nine Years Old, Fourth Grade

"DON'T ITCH YOUR head. You're always itching," Mom says to me, slapping my hand away from my hair. She has one hand on the wheel of her car and the other hand on the top of my head, so I don't touch my hair. It's the first day of fourth grade. I have stopped counting so much. I play a new game now where I pick the lice from my head and pop them between two fingernails. The popping sound reminds me of bubble wrap. Also, it's one way to get rid of the lice.

"I can't help it," I say. I've mostly gotten used to the itching, but sometimes, when I am not paying attention, I itch my head so much the skin of my scalp comes off on my nail, and I start to bleed.

"I don't know why lice shampoo doesn't work. Or lice bomb. They was expensive," Mom says, removing her hand.

"You're supposed to pick the eggs out with the comb after the shampoo," I say, because I read the directions.

"I don't have time to sit with you and pick out all these eggs," Mom snaps. "And your hair has too many knots. You need to brush it. I am not your babysitter."

Mom pulls up to the school. We are late. I know my class is in the little houses instead of inside the main building this year, but I don't know who I have for a teacher. I wish we had gone to meet my teacher before school started but Mom says she didn't have time. Mom is out looking for jobs most days, and Chris leaves me and Masha with a babysitter who we don't really know, but at least I am not alone with Masha like I was last year.

"Will you pick me up?" I ask Mom, my hand on the handle of the car.

She thinks about it. "Fuck, I don't know." She looks at the clock. "I'll ask the maid."

She means Carolina, who does everything for us in Chris's house. She calls her "the maid," like it's a bad word.

"Will anyone be here when I get out?" I say. My voice cracks. It sounds like I am going to cry, but I don't feel the tears behind my eyes anymore. Now they fall down my cheeks without any warning. I wonder if I don't know they are coming because I am in fourth grade, and I am too big to cry and my body is punishing me.

"The maid will be here for you," Mom says. "Don't worry. Now go," she moves her hands off the steering wheel and makes a motion like she is pushing me out of the car. I sigh and take my backpack from the backseat. I don't want to be back in school. I don't know my multiplication tables at all. Sophia says that fourth grade teachers are way more mean than in third grade. What if there is a test and I fail it?

"Bye," I say, getting out of Mom's car. I close the door behind me. She drives away immediately. I wish she was one of those Moms that would walk into school with me, like Lenora does for Sophia, but she's not.

I take a deep breath and walk to the front doors. Before I go inside, I look around. I could just run away. I could just tell Mom I went to school. She would believe me. Maybe I can sit in the park that Babushka and I used to play in.

It has been more than a year since I've even talked to Babushka. I try not to think of her because when I let myself think about her too much, I have to sit down and squish my body so my knees are pressed to my stomach. It's the only way I know how to hold myself together so I don't break apart.

"Late on the first day of school?" The lady at the front office says to me. She is new. I don't remember her from last year. I guess she is also mean.

"My sister wouldn't let me leave the house," I say. Masha sat on my foot this morning so I wouldn't leave. I think she got really used to me staying with her all the time since I didn't go to the end of school last year.

The lady makes a "tsk" sound. "What's your name?"

"My name is Katya Suvorova," I say. I used to not know my last name, but since Mom got divorced, I know it is Suvorova because me and Mom and Masha have different last names. "I'm in the fourth grade this year."

The lady moves some papers around her desk. She looks down at one, moving her finger down a list. Her blonde ponytail doesn't move as she shakes her head. She looks older than Mom, but then again every grown up looks older than Mom.

"You're in the T-buildings. Ms. Lopez, Room 3."

"Thanks," I say.

"Don't be late again!" She responds, like it is my fault.

I don't say anything and leave to go to Ms. Lopez's room. I hope she is nice and not mean. I walk outside and across the blacktop. Before going towards the fourth grade buildings, I let myself pick my hair once. I run my fingers through my strands and find what feels like a pimple and grab it. Sometimes the lice run away from me but today I get lucky. I take the pimple lice between my thumb and finger and slide my thumb gently off the bug. Then I bring my other hand to where the lice is and use a finger to squish it until I hear a pop. I don't know why, but it feels good to hear the pop. It's even better than counting. I move my hand to my head again, ready to find another one, when I hear a door open behind me. I put my hands in my pockets and rush to Room 3, knocking on the door. It takes a few minutes for someone to answer. I turn around to see who opened the door, but there is no one there. I could have probably gotten another lice but now it is too late. Late. Four letters. I need one more letter to make five. Today will be a bad day. I'm counting again. I guess I'm nervous.

"Welcome!" A woman opens the door. She has big, brown, curly hair and bright pink lipstick. "Are you Katya?"

I nod.

"Welcome to fourth grade! I've been so excited to meet you."

I raise my eyebrows in surprise but bring them down quickly. Why would she want to meet me? Grown-ups don't like reactions so I have been training my face not to move.

I don't say anything, stepping into Ms. Lopez's room and looking around. There is no piece of furniture that is the same color as the furniture next to it. The chairs go: red, yellow, blue, green, and then red again. I wonder why she didn't put all the red chairs together? Everything feels frazzled. I push my fingernails against the palms of my hands until I know they will leave a mark to avoid picking my hair.

"Your chair is in the corner, the yellow one," she says, pointing to a desk next to a window. I don't like yellow, but I decide not to tell her that since all the other chairs are taken. I feel everyone's eyes on me as I walk to my chair.

"We were just talking about what we will learn in the fourth grade!" Ms. Lopez says. I still haven't said anything to her, not even thank you. I take a seat and look at her.

"Sorry for being late," I say. Grown-ups like when you say sorry.

Her smile drops a little. "It's OK," she says, gently. She looks at me for what feels like a hundred minutes and then says, "OK class, what else do we want to learn?"

I breathe out when she peels her eyes from me. I'm glad she hasn't asked me directly what I want to learn. I don't want to learn anything. I just don't want to be asked about my multiplication tables.

Birthday

Winter, Early 2000s, Ten Years Old, Fourth Grade

I WAKE UP SAD, not excited it is my birthday today. I am afraid Dad forgot. We have reservations at The Flying Pig, because they have flying pigs hanging from the ceiling made out of paper and they give you one if you spend your birthday with them. I invited my best friend, Dream, and Chris invited her parents.

Dream has been my best friend since the start of fourth grade. I have been too afraid to invite her over because of how drunk Chris gets, but I love going to her house. She has a big family and her mom calls me "baby," and there is always good, warm food. Her mom and dad never leave us home alone, and before her mom drops me back off at Chris's house, she always asks me if I'm OK. I feel safe with Dream. I would go over to her house more, but I don't like leaving Masha alone with Chris. I almost ask if Masha can come, but I don't want Dream to stop inviting me over, so I only go to Dream's house when I know Carolina is home with Masha, and it's not just Masha and Chris alone.

I wasn't sure about having a birthday party, but I felt better that Chris invited Dream's Mom. After we eat at The Flying Pig, we're supposed to go to the movies. I have reminded Chris every day this week about my birthday. What if Dream and her parents show up and we're not there because he's too drunk to drive? The only thing I'm scared of is if Dream's mom sees Chris behaving bad and won't let me come over to Dream's house anymore.

"Katya? You awake?"

It's Mom. I shoot out of bed. Chris and Masha are already up since they are not next to me. Is everyone downstairs?

Mom has been gone for a week. She does this a lot now. She disappears when she and Chris get in a fight. Last week she called once to check on Masha. I heard noises in the background, like she was at a party. I think she's been with her friends in Austin again, but I'm not sure. I know her friends have a boat.

"Mom?" I ask, rubbing my eyes.

"Happy birthday, my big girl!" Mom grabs my head and squeezes it tight, giving me a kiss. "I've missed you so much."

My whole body tightens up. I don't hug her back even though I know I should. Mom has a huge smile on her face. I look her up and down, trying to see if she is drunk. Her eyes aren't clumsy. She's not tripping. Her breathe smells like the mint gum she is always chewing.

"I . . . missed you too," I say. I follow her downstairs and look around her to the breakfast table where Masha is sitting, playing with a fork. I go to take it from her but she pulls away. "You'll poke your eye out," I say to her.

Chris is making bacon. He has a big smile on too. I guess he is happy Mom is home.

"Breakfast is almost ready," Chris says. "Made special for the birthday girl."

I sit down next to Masha. She has set down the fork and is now hitting a spoon on the table, talking to herself. I think to take the spoon away from her because too much noise upsets Mom, but I don't because I feel like maybe I am dreaming.

Chris comes over with a plate of bacon and eggs, and Mom puts down a cup of orange juice. She never lets me drink orange juice because it is too many calories.

"What about me?!" Masha frowns, banging the spoon against the table.

"You're next, sweetheart," Chris says. "But today is Katya's birthday so she gets to eat first."

"Thanks Dad," I smile at him, so he doesn't know that I feel weird. I started calling him Dad again after we moved out of our apartment because Mom said I should keep him happy, since we have nowhere else to live right now. Chris sets down a plate in front of Masha. He also gives her a pink baba, which is just a bottle with strawberry milk. Masha is three and a half, too old for a bottle, but she screams if she doesn't have one, so Dad gives her bottles all the time.

Mom sits across from me. I know not to ask her where she has been, but I want to know, badly. Last time I asked she said it was a business trip, but I know she doesn't have a job. I know this is the answer she gives everyone when they ask.

"Eat," Mom says, pushing the plate towards me. I pick up a piece of bacon with my hands and put it in my mouth. Chris doesn't make good food, but I like whatever he makes because he cooked it for me.

"Daddy, this is really good!" I say to him.

He smiles, making another plate. I know this plate is for himself because Mom never eats. She says she's allergic to bacon, but I think she might be allergic to every food. When Chris has filled his plate, he sits down next to Mom. We are all sitting at the table, eating, like a happy family. I don't remember the last time we sat down and no one fought.

"Should we get her present?" Dad asks Mom.

Mom eyes my plate. "I will get it," she says. "She is almost done."

Mom gets up and goes to the dining room. She comes back with a cardboard box. It isn't wrapped, so I know it's a present for me. Mom says using wrapping paper on family is a waste of money.

Mom hands me the box and a pair of scissors. I break open the tape holding the two cardboard flaps together. Inside is a small, blue machine. It has a black and white screen with buttons that have arrows on them.

"What is it?" I ask, pulling it out.

"It's an MP3 player!" Dad says. "There are headphones in the box too. Plug them in and hear it work its magic!"

I find the pair of headphones he was talking about and plug them into the tiny hole in the MP3 player, then put the headphones over my ears. I look at Dad. "Nothing is happening," I say.

He rolls his eyes. "Did you turn it on and press play?"

I look at the machine and find the power button, and then another button with a sideways triangle that is the same as on my CD player. Britney Spears'"Toxic," blasts through my headphones.

"Whoa!" I say, smiling. I hold the MP3 player up. On the screen it says "Toxic."

"It knows which song it's playing!" I say, excitedly. Dad says something I can't hear, so I take the headphones off.

"What?" I ask.

"You can put any song you want on your MP3 player. You just have to hook it up to the computer. There is a program called LimeWire you can get songs from. That little thing can hold up to three hundred songs!"

I look at the little device in my hand. "Wow," I say.

"I think it can also record too, but I'm not sure."

"Thank you, Dad!" I say, running over to him and throwing my arms around his neck. "This is so cool!"

"Your mother helped pick it out," he said.

I turn to Mom, who is also smiling. I am surprised. Mom usually gets me clothes for my birthday.

"Thanks, Mom!" I say, going to hug her too.

Me, Dad, and Masha download songs onto my MP3 player while Mom cleans the kitchen. I have ten songs total. My favorite song is "Dancing Queen." Me and Masha take turns with the headphones, listening to the songs, until it's time to go to The Flying Pig. I am just so happy that everyone is together.

We are the first ones to the restaurant, which makes me relieved. When me and Dad are getting ready without Mom, we are always late. When me and Mom are going somewhere, we are also always late. But when we are together as a family, we're on time. Maybe this means everything is going to be OK from now on. Maybe my tenth birthday is a fresh start.

There are seven people total for my birthday. Mom, Chris, Me, Masha, and Dream and her mom and dad.

The Flying Pig lets everyone make their own mini pizza and even gives us dough to play with while we wait for our pizzas to bake. When they come out, everyone but Mom eats quickly, like we haven't ever eaten anything in our lives.

Mom crosses her arms over her chest, like she's mad, and my blood feels like electricity in my body. Dad has done something to make Mom mad, I can tell, because she is looking at him while he is stuffing his face.

"It's too bad this place doesn't even have a good salad," I hear Mom saying to Dad. "I haven't eaten all day."

I understand why she is mad now. She wants Dad to worry about if she's hungry, and he hasn't asked her. Dad doesn't know that, though. Sometimes I think Dad is dumb even though he makes a lot of money.

"Mom, do you want some dough?" I ask. Pizza dough isn't cooked so maybe it doesn't have calories. They gave it to us to play with.

Mom shakes her head. She's still looking at Dad, like she's waiting for him to care about her.

My hands start to shake because I know she is going to start a fight. I can feel it. I look around at the table. Most people aren't even halfway through their pizza. Dream's dad hasn't even started his. He keeps nibbling at Dream's Mom's pizza.

I wish I didn't choose The Flying Pig, even if they did give me a paper flying pig to hang in mine and Masha's room. I wish we ate at the movies instead because Mom can't fight with Dad in the middle of a movie.

When Dad doesn't say anything to Mom, her eyes move over to me. She frowns, like she just remembered something.

"Dream," Mom says. Her accent makes Dream's name sound sharp, like it will hurt me. "Where do you sleep?"

I stop eating. I know where this is going. Mom is going to tell Dream my secret. My stomach starts to vibrate, and it hurts to breathe.

Dream pauses eating. I want to tell Dream not to answer, but Mom has a look on her face that is scary, like she wants to hurt someone. I'm worried Mom will say something mean to Dream because Dream is Black and Mom does not like Black people. She is mad at me for being friends with Dream. I would not have had this birthday party if I knew Mom would come. Mom says things like, "You go to white school. Why you make friends with Black people?" I want to tell Mom that the white kids are always the meanest, like Sophia. They make fun of me the most. I don't know why Mom wants me to be friends with white kids so bad when white people have treated us the worst.

I am quiet, waiting for the blow.

"Um . . . in my room?" Dream says. She has just swallowed a big gulp of Pepsi.

"Inside your room?" Mom continues.

I know my cheeks are red, I can feel it.

"Yeah?" Dream says, looking confused.

"Do you sleep in your own bed?" Mom asks. The reveal is coming, and I bite my lip to brace for it. I look up and try to beg my tears not to fall because that will make everything worse.

"Oh, well maybe you can teach Katya. She sleeps outside of our door," Mom says, pointing to Dad. "Like she is a baby. She says she is scared." Mom smiles, like what she said is funny.

Dream looks at me like she doesn't know what to say. "Do you not sleep in your room?"

I smile, but this makes my tears fall. When we moved back in with Dad I started to sleep outside Mom and Chris's door because I was afraid he was hurting her again. When Mom isn't home, I sleep in Chris's bed with him and Masha because he says he doesn't like to sleep alone, but when Mom is home I make a pallet outside of the door so I can make sure Mom isn't screaming.

Dream's mom and dad look at each other. Her mom's eyebrows are bent, like she's worried. I hope we can still go to the movies after this.

"Now, why would you embarrass her like that?" Dad asks. I look at him. He's wiping his lips with a napkin. There is no more pizza on his plate. His face is red too, but an angry red, like he is about to yell.

"What embarrassment?" Mom asks, her hands in the air, like she is shocked. "What are you talking about?"

"You know damned well what you're doing," Chris says, his eyes like knives. My stomach feels warm. I feel good that Dad is yelling at Mom for being mean, but I feel bad because I can tell this is going to be a bad fight. Especially because my friend is here.

"I don't know what you talking about!" Mom shouts. She stands up, pulling her purse on her shoulder. "I am not embarrassing anyone. It was just a question, and you attack me!"

The tears are rolling down my cheeks fast, like they are in a race. I beg my eyes to stop.

"Mommy, wait!" I say.

"No, fuck you," she says, looking at me. Her fire has fallen on me, again, but now she is doubly mad. I wish Dad hadn't said anything. "Happy birthday!" Mom says, in a voice like she is making fun of me.

Mom slams her chair into the table and walks out. I look at her, wondering if I should follow her. Dream is here so I know I need to stay, but I don't want to look at her. I look at my shoes instead.

"Sorry everyone," Dad says. He raises his hand to the waiter. We were supposed to have cake but I guess we won't anymore.

I feel a hand on my back. "It's OK, baby," Dream's Mom says in my ear. "You're OK."

I want to lean into her, but I don't because I don't want to be a burden.

Instead I nod and say, "I'm OK." I want to go home with Dream and her family. I wish her mom was my mom. I want to take Masha and run away and live with them.

I look for Masha, who is playing with the dough I tried to give Mom. My scalp is burning with itches but I know not to touch it. Not until I get home.

Job

Winter, Early 2000s, Ten Years Old, Fourth Grade

Mom and Chris have broken up because Mom caught him in a VIP room at his favorite strip club. Chris still thinks Mom has her own apartment, but she hasn't had an apartment since last year.

Mom has locked me outside her friend Lena's apartment, where we have been staying. I can't stop crying, which has made a woman I don't know ask me if I'm locked out.

"I'm OK," I respond to her. I add a smile. "I'm just playing."

I can't let anyone know Mom kicked me out because it makes her look like a bad mom.

Mom met Lena at Russian church. Lena is also Russian. We have been living with Lena for a week now. I don't like living with Lena because I have to sleep in the corner on the floor. Masha and Mom get Lena's bedroom, and Lena sleeps on the couch.

Mom said she locked me out because I was annoying everyone, except I think she locked me out because she didn't want me to hear what her and Lena are talking about. I don't like being out here. I want to run away. What if I ran away and Mom never found me? I wonder what Mom will feel then. Except I won't run away because of Masha.

"Why are you crying?" The lady asks. She has a Spanish accent. She is wrinkly, like maybe she is good with kids. I don't need someone who is good with kids to pay attention to me.

"It's a . . . sad game," I say. I don't know what else to say. "Whoever cries the most wins."

The lady frowns, like she doesn't believe me.

I smile, so maybe she will understand that I am OK and her talking to me is only going to make it worse.

"Are you hungry?" She asks.

I am. I wonder if she can hear my empty stomach from where she is standing.

I shake my head. "My mom just fed me."

Suddenly, the front door cracks open. "Katya, Mom is smoking on the balcony. Hurry!" Masha whispers.

I turn around to the lady, who eyes Masha. Masha doesn't notice her.

"I won! Don't worry!" I say, hurrying inside. I close the door lightly, so Mom doesn't hear that I'm inside. Masha sneaks me to the closet, where we're not allowed to go since it's Lena's clothes and not ours. I scoot back against her shoes and lean my head against the wall.

I hope when Mom opens the front door and sees I'm not there, she will panic and feel bad for locking me out. I hope it makes her never lock me out again. I hope I scare her. I hope she thinks she lost me. I hope she thinks someone kidnapped me.

I can't hear what Mom is saying to Lena on the balcony, but she is laughing. I fall asleep and wake up when it's dark outside. I crawl out of the closet. It's quiet. I wonder if they are looking for me. Did Masha forget where I was hiding?

In the living room, Mom is curled on the couch, asleep. Masha is on my spot on the floor, playing with some cars she brought from Chris's house. Lena is gone.

Masha looks up and runs over to me, hugging my stomach.

"Did Mom forget about me?" I whisper to her.

Masha is only three and a half, but she's smart. She knows the truth will hurt my feelings. "Hungry?" she asks, instead of answering.

I nod.

"I got you cookies," she responds. She tiptoes to where her cars are and pulls out two chocolate chip cookies from behind something I can't see.

"Have you eaten?" I ask her.

She nods. "Baba Strawberry."

I take the cookies.

"Let's go to sleep," I say to her, pointing to the bed she normally shares with Mom.

Masha looks at Mom, then me, like she's trying to choose. She nods, taking my hand.

Lena kicked us out. We're in the house of someone I don't know.

I am watching Masha sleep from the floor because I don't sleep anymore. There are too many things on my mind. She's on the couch, and her arm is hanging off the side. She keeps twitching. I think to wake her up, but I don't because when she is awake she wants to play, and I feel too stuck to play.

Moving any part of my body feels bad. I just want to stay still. I want to hear every breath. I want to see every movement. I put Masha's hand back on her chest.

Mom says I need to keep Chris happy so he doesn't take her to court. He can easily get custody of Masha, since we don't have a place to live and Mom doesn't have a job. If Chris can prove Mom doesn't have those two things, he can take Masha away forever. Mom says the best way to keep Chris happy is if I act like his wife.

When me and Masha are not with Chris, we sleep in different places. Mom says it is hard to get an apartment without a job because you have to prove you can pay the rent, and no one will hire Mom because she has an accent and her documents aren't American. When I asked how we were supposed to get an apartment, she said she is figuring out how to lie about it but she needs someone to fake our documents. Faking documents takes time, so until we have the papers Mom needs, we have to keep asking people if they will take us in.

Right now, we're staying with a man I've never met. His house is so dark I can barely see Masha and count her twitches.

Mom says we are safe from this man because he sits on his computer upstairs all day and won't come down to bother us, but sometimes she goes up there and closes the door for a long time.

This man's couch is uncomfortable for three people, so I sleep on the floor, right next to Masha's side of the couch.

This man also doesn't have channel 41 or 22 or 43, which are mine and Masha's favorite channels.

To keep ourselves busy in his house, me and Masha have invented a game where the light reflection from my watch screen is a pet, and we have to catch it because it keeps running away from us. This game makes Masha run around the living room until she is tired enough to close her eyes.

I hear Mom creep down the stairs. I close my eyes so she thinks I'm asleep when she gets close to the couch. When she lies down, I hear her sniffling, like she is crying. Hearing Mom's sniffles makes me want to cry too.

Tomorrow is Thursday, which means Carolina, Chris's housekeeper and now babysitter for me and Masha, will pick me up from school. It is also Chris's weekend so I will get to sleep in a bed. I don't know if Mom will be in this man's house by herself, but I can't stay to protect her because I have a job to do for Chris.

Spring Break

Spring, Early 2000s, Ten Years Old. Fourth Grade

It's Easter tomorrow, and Masha is too young not to believe in the Easter bunny, so I have to plan the egg hunt so she still thinks the rabbit cares about her.

Being a good wife means that you have to keep everyone happy, not just the kids. It's three in the morning, and I am making bacon. I am still awake because Chris has to go into work early, so I'm preparing breakfast for him so he will want to come back home to us and not the strip clubs.

The bacon is popping in the pan, and I frown, studying it. I don't know how to tell when bacon is done but I am getting tired so I decide to put it on a plate. The bacon is still a little pink but the edges look crispy so I think it's OK.

I have been having a hard time keeping everyone happy, but I think I am getting the hang of it now. For Masha, all I have to do is give her a toy or turn on the TV. For Chris, he likes vodka and food. His breakfast will have bacon, eggs, and also a cup of vodka because that is his favorite drink. I open the freezer and find a bottle that has already been opened and pour him a cup.

The vodka smells like my nose is being slapped. Chris has offered me some before, but I never took any because I needed to act normal to watch Masha and keep him happy. I know vodka makes people sleepy and talk weird.

I bring the cup to my lips and take a small sip because I wonder why Chris needs so much of it. I spit it out immediately. It tastes like scissors.

I clean the mess up and put the drink next to Chris's breakfast with a note that says " Happy Easter Daddy" on top of the eggs. I go upstairs to Chris's room, where he is snoring. I had put a pillow between him and Masha, and I remove it to put myself in the pillow's place.

I make sure I am in between Chris and Masha, just in case his hands get touchy. Sometimes they do. This is part of being a wife, I've learned.

"Get your ass up!" Chris whisper yells.

I sit straight up, like he didn't wake me up, even though he did. My body feels like cardboard. I ask it to be steel.

"What's wrong?" I ask, opening my eyes to his red face next to the bed. He has already changed into his clothing for work. He hasn't left yet, which means it's before six in the morning.

"Why the fuck are there toy soldiers all over the back yard?" I don't think he has had the vodka I left out for him or he wouldn't be this angry.

"For Easter," I say, swallowing.

"Easter?" He says, narrowing his eyes. "You're supposed to hide eggs, not throw toy soldiers the same color as the grass all over the place."

"The store was out of eggs, remember?" He took us to the store yesterday to get Masha supplies for the Easter egg hunt, but there were no eggs, so we just got the stuff that goes inside the eggs. I didn't think the egg part mattered that much. Just the candy and toys part.

I look to Masha sleeping next to me. She hasn't woken up yet, so I move the covers off of me and slide off the bed so Chris knows we need to leave the room to have this discussion. He is only concentrating his yelling at me right now, but I don't want him to switch his anger to her.

I walk past him and out of the room, to the stairs. It takes him a second, like he is shocked I moved, but he follows me.

"Did you see the breakfast I made you?" I ask, on my way down.

"You left bacon and eggs out for God knows how long. Now I have to buy more bacon." His words hurt. "You need to clean up the mess you made outside. It needs to be gone before I get home. I was going to mow the lawn today, and now I can't because of all the stupid shit in it."

"Masha has to have Easter first," I say. My voice sounds weak. Maybe clearing my throat will help, so I cough.

"Fuck Easter. This is my lawn that you messed up!"

I look at the clock on the microwave. It's six. He should be gone by now.

"What time will you be home?" I ask him, picking up the plate I made and dumping the food in the trash. I also throw away the Happy Easter sign.

"In the afternoon. The backyard needs to be clear or I'll make you mow the damned lawn." Chris grabs his keys from the hook next to the fridge and walks towards the front door.

"Happy Easter," I mumble.

He slams the door behind him.

I go outside, where it's still dark. The foil of the chocolate makes the lawn look like it has gems in it. The bag of toy soldiers is on the patio table across from the lawn. If I had put it up, maybe he wouldn't have seen that I sprinkled them all over the lawn too. They blend in so well I can't even see them.

I wish I could call Babushka. I wish Mom was here. I go toward the lawn and pick a small foiled candy up and sit down on the concrete. The foil is hard to get off. I had to get whatever stuff was left. Luckily, Masha saw *Saving Private Ryan* and has been obsessed with guns and soldiers, so it was a perfect Easter toy. I pop the chocolate into my mouth and cringe. It has orange filling. I hate orange, but I swallow, because I don't want to make more of a mess. I wipe my hands on my white spaghetti strap shirt, one I chose because it was tight on me and Chris likes when women wear tight clothes.

I will wake Masha up in an hour so she can do her hunt, and we still have enough time to clean up before Chris gets home.

I don't like being a wife.

Crete

Summer 2021, Late Twenties

MY LITTLE SISTER Kristina and I fit perfectly together, like two pieces of a puzzle. We build sandcastles and she writes "I love you," in Russian on the beach. Her favorite thing to do is draw, and she is very good at it.

My father takes a million pictures of us. My brother and I talk as though we've grown up together. We argue about politics. We laugh at my father for being nerdy. My husband and my father have a bond I didn't realize would also help heal me. My father loves my husband, and my husband loves my father. My stepmom is kind and reasonable. I was afraid she would hate me, but she talks to me like I am part of the family too. Not her kid, but a sister. I think she knows that I love my siblings like they are my kids.

I stop taking Xanax. I don't need it. The butterflies in my stomach disappear.

My father drives us around Crete in a white kidnapper van that is the only car that can fit all of us, while my husband sits in the front and navigates. My husband tells my father about mortgages in America, and my father doesn't understand why anyone would put themselves in debt. My father talks about all the places he's traveled, all the adventures he and my stepmom have had.

In the car, I fall asleep on my brother's shoulder while I hold my sister's hand. I am happier than I've ever felt in my life. I can't believe I am so lucky.

Standardized Test

Spring, Early 2000s, Ten Years Old, Fourth Grade

"SO YOU IDIOT," Mom says, when we get into her car. There are tears dripping from my nose to my hands. I am looking down because I can't look at her face. I wish I could turn off my tears. "I knew you not bright but not so dumb that you fail American tests. It's good I take you out of Russia. You too dumb for school there."

Mom's car is parked in front of my school. I have one month until the fourth grade is over. Mom finally forged documents good enough to get us an apartment, but everything is still in trash bags at home. Today was supposed to be an unpacking day, but instead she had to go talk to my teacher, so she is extra mad at me.

"Ms. Lopez said that most of the stuff on the standardized test was from the third grade and—"

"It doesn't matter. You should have studied better. What were you doing when I let you stay home? Watching TV?" Mom backs out of the spot. I knew I needed to study math last summer.

"You know now I can't get a job because I will be taking you to summer school in the morning and picking you up in the middle of the day? That means I can't do any interviews."

If I could hang my head lower, I would, but my neck doesn't go that far. "I'm sorry," I say.

She makes a sound with her mouth like she is annoyed. "Chris can't know you fail test. He will use it against me. He will say I'm a bad mom because you fail," she adds.

I shoot my head up. "I'm just bad at math," I say. "I got a perfect score on reading."

"No one cares about reading in this country," Mom says, putting her blinker on. Our new apartment is over forty-five minutes away from the school. This will be a long drive of Mom being mad at me. She is in a mood where nothing I say will make her feel better so I just have to take it.

"Where's Masha?" I ask.

"I have to pay for daycare to go to this meeting for you," Mom says. "Twenty dollars a day. I should make you pay for it."

I want to tell her that I would work if I could, so she doesn't have to use all of Masha's child support money on the apartment, and we have some left over for good food instead of mashed potatoes all the time, but I know not to. I don't pay attention anymore because what she is saying is mean, and I know if I listen I will cry more, so I think of other ways to get money for us. If Mom doesn't have a job because of me, I need to get money somehow.

The only way I know how to get money fast is if I steal from Chris. I know every Thursday night his wallet has a lot of hundreds in it because Friday is his strip club day. Mom talks about him liking Friday night amateur night. If I wait until I hear him snore, I can sneak some hundreds out and he won't know. I'll give them to Mom so she can buy us food and not be mad at me anymore that she has to take me to summer school instead of looking for a job. I have one month to get as much money as I can from Chris because Mom gets me and Masha for all of June, and he gets Masha and me for July, so when school lets out, I won't see him until July. I feel excited about my plan. I want to tell Mom but she needs some more time to be upset, so I keep my mouth shut. She will be proud of me when I start bringing money back to her.

My first night stealing money is easy. Chris is in bed by midnight. He snores so loud he shakes the house. I crawl out of our bed and creep into his clothes closet, where he keeps his wallet. I have watched him put it on top of his pajama bottoms every night before I go to bed for as long as I've been sleeping in the same room with him. I open the cabinet up and there is his wallet. He has so much money, it creates a thick green band that I can see without opening it up. I take the wallet and unstretch its leather flaps, flipping through the money. There is a huge stack of hundred dollar bills, like I knew there would be. Every Thursday night after he picks me and Masha up, he goes inside the ATM and comes out with an envelope of money for the weekend. I know Chris' favorite strip club is called "Paradise" because that's where Mom caught him a few months ago, which caused them to break up.

I take out four hundreds from the middle of his wallet, my heart bouncing like a rubber ball in my chest. His snores have always calmed me down. I pray he does not wake up randomly, like he does sometimes when his snoring chokes him.

I slide the wallet back quickly where I found it, then stuff the money in my underwear. I know I have to find a better spot for the bills in case Chris feels me up, so I unzip my backpack and stuff the money in a tiny pocket in my pencil bag. I take my pencil bag and put it in the center of my binder, so it's harder to get to. I need to find a better hiding place. I think Mom is right about me being dumb. I have been thinking of my plan for a long time and didn't even think of a good place to put the money other than my underwear, which would definitely get me caught.

When I am done hiding the money, I crawl back in to bed. It's hard for me to breathe. Breathe. Seven letters. A God number. Maybe I'm spelling breathe wrong? I don't remember how to spell "breathe." I run my fingers through my hair, looking for a lice to pop because counting isn't helping. I find a bunch of tiny ones that aren't as satisfying because they don't make a squish sound.

My throat feels tighter and tighter. I wish I could find a big lice. Or maybe I wish all my lice were gone. There are no lice checks in the fourth grade. I don't know why, since the lice situation was so bad last year, but maybe they don't want anyone else missing school.

I wish I knew a good word. I turn my body to look at Masha, who doesn't twitch at Chris's house. Good. I hold her hand. She is the only good thing in my world.

Mom says I can keep half of the money I steal from Chris, but I am now in charge of food and clothes for me and Masha. Mom says this will teach me how to be responsible for money.

The first thing I do with my half is buy a hamster for me and Masha. We name him Max.

Today me and Masha decide to take the hamster to play outside with us. Mom has been in the bathroom all day and isn't paying attention to us. I feel like this hamster is our babysitter.

Masha is downstairs, waiting for me and Max. When I peek my head outside I see that she's playing hopscotch with our neighbors.

I cradle Max as I step outside, making sure I slowly take him down the stairs, step by step, petting his small head with two fingers in case he is scared. He's so warm, as though he has just popped out of the oven.

I skip a step and accidentally drop Max.

He tumbles on the steps, falling down one by one until he gets to the very bottom. I don't know how, but he gets up and limps to a nearby bush.

I start searching for him.

Suddenly, I feel something crack underneath my feet. When I lift my shoe, Max is there, his feet jerking up and down, his body bloody.

My mouth flops open, and my arms lock up.

I look to see where Masha is. She is still hopping around on the sidewalk. She hasn't seen what has happened yet.

I race upstairs and to the bathroom door. I bang on it, screaming, "Please open up!" Mom opens the door. Her eyes are smudged with black mascara rivulets, her cheeks flushed.

"What?" She asks, sniffling. I can smell the mint ice cream I was saving for later on her breath. Mom does this sometimes. She spends all day throwing up. Maybe it's like the counting thing I do.

I point outside. "The—the hamster," I yell and then pause.

I know if I tell her I took him downstairs to play with him, I'll get into trouble.

"Masha threw it out the window," I say instead.

"She *what*?" Mom asks, frowning, moving her head to the side like she doesn't hear me right. If she wasn't throwing up all day she'd probably say something like "Fuck, didn't we tell her hamster wasn't same as bat? Bat has wings! Clearly she got brains from her dad." And then she'd roll her eyes. But after a day of throwing up she acts like she only has air in her brain.

"She threw it out the window," I repeat, because Masha never gets in trouble for anything. "She thought it could fly."

Mom squints her eyes like she is trying to comprehend what I'm saying.

"Why . . . ?" she asks, dazed. I take her hand and lead her downstairs to where the hamster is squirming. There is a little pool of blood surrounding him, his eyes darting back and forth.

Mom stares at the hamster for a while. She doesn't move; she doesn't say anything. We just stand there, watching it die.

I pull at her arm a little bit, trying to wake her up. "Mom?" I ask.

"M—M—Max!" Masha cries. She has stopped hopping and has come over to us, looking at him.

This is Masha's first time seeing a squished Max. Mom clicks back on when she notices my screaming sister, her small face red and pinched, like a deflated balloon. Masha turns to Mom and me, but her finger remains pointing at our pet.

I should have maybe told Masha to pretend she threw him out the window, but Mom doesn't seem to notice that it's Masha's first time seeing Max like this too.

"Hold on," Mom says, clearing her throat. Her voice is suddenly stern. Alive. She is fully awake now, a vein twitching at her jaw, her hands fisted at her sides. Masha's cries woke her up, something my cries are not able to do. She runs upstairs and comes back with the car keys and a plastic bag. She scoops the hamster up with her bare hands and stuffs it in the bag, the lump still shaking. "Come on," she says, and leads us to the car. "Here," Mom says, and hands me the bag as I slide into the front seat.

I hold him away from me as we drive. Mom looks straight ahead; the tears silent as they slide down her cheeks. I didn't even think Mom liked the hamster that much. I don't understand why she is crying.

"Where are we going?" I ask, a little scared. Vets are expensive. Maybe we are going to a cemetery since the hamster is barely hanging on.

Mom doesn't answer, speeding between cars.

Finally, we pull into the Petco parking lot. When we park, Mom closes her eyes and rests her head on the steering wheel. The hamster is moving in the bag, making a muffled scratching sound. After a few moments, she sits up and wipes her face, opening the car door.

When I catch up to her, I try to hand the squirming bag back, but she says, "It's better if you take it," under her breath.

As soon as we're inside, Mom sets her eyes on a cashier and marches up to them, standing on the other side of the empty register. "I need to exchange this," she says, pointing to my bag.

The cashier frowns, peeking at my hand. "What is it that you need to exchange, ma'am?"

"This," Mom says, grabbing the bag in my hand and opening it up, showing what is inside.

The lady steps back, her hands in front of her face. "What *is* that?" She squeaks.

"Our animal," Mom responds calmly. "It's stupid, and I want new one."

The lady cocks her head to the side as though she didn't hear her right. "Uhh . . . I don't—I don't think—I don't know. . . ."

Mom shakes the bag towards the cashier, one eyebrow up.

The cashier calls the manager. Mom probably believes the hamster is defective and that they gave her a bad one on purpose.

Mom puffs out her chest.

The manager comes, a smile on his face as he approaches us. "How can I be of assistance?"

"They . . . um . . . they want to make an exchange . . ." The cashier says, stepping back.

"An . . . exchange?" The manager asks, his eyebrows lifting in question.

"Yes, I want to exchange this," Mom says, handing the manager the bag. The manager looks at the cashier and then opens the bag, his eyebrows shooting up.

My attention strays to the line forming behind us, but no one seems to care that they aren't being helped. Everyone's eyes are on the grocery bag that is still moving.

"Um . . . Ma'am . . . um . . . ?" The manager asks, pulling his head back and scrunching up his face.

"It's idiot," Mom says, matter-of-factly.

"I don't think we can—I mean—I just—how did this . . . ?" the manager stutters.

By this point, the cashier has left to move to a different register, but the people in line don't move over to her.

"I don't know. The hamster was idiot. That's how it happened. You gave me a dumbfuck hamster, and now I want better one."

The manager opens his eyes wide, biting his bottom lip. "I don't know if . . . you can exchange this . . . do you have a . . . uh. . . . do you have a receipt?" He leans his head back a little.

Mom pulls the hamster out of the bag, holding its squirming body up to his face. "See?" she says. "It's fucking idiot. I want new one." It is bleeding down her hand, the little face broken and twisted.

The manager moves away from her, stepping back. "I can't . . . I can't . . . exchange this."

Mom raises her eyebrow.

"OK, OK," he says, after thirty seconds, putting his hands up and sighing. "We can make an exchange. We'll exchange it."

I don't know if I believe this guy.

"What if we get another idiot one?" I ask.

"That's true," Mom says, narrowing her eyes. "What if we get another idiot one?" She is still holding our bleeding, dying, pet.

"I can um . . . I can't guarantee this won't happen again? But um . . ."

"I want a mouse instead!" I say. "Maybe they'll be smarter."

"She wants a mouse instead," Mom nods her head toward me.

"Uh . . . We can do a mouse." The manager nods, getting out from behind the register. We follow him as he fast walks to the back of the store.

"Which one do you want?" The manager asks us when we arrive at the rodent section of the store. We look at the different glass boxes housing dozens of mice, divided by color.

"Go for most expensive one," Mom whispers. "It's best quality."

I look at the prices of all the mice and chose the costliest one—a ten-dollar black and white mouse that looks like it is wearing a tuxedo. That's probably why it is the most expensive.

"Masha is this OK?" I ask her. She's sucking her thumb, her eyes tired.

She nods, like she doesn't care.

"This one," I point. Max is definitely dead now, since the bag has stopped squirming.

The manager opens the back door and retrieves the mouse, coming out a moment later with a little cardboard box. "Here you go," he says, handing it to Mom. Mom hands the bloody bag filled with our hamster to the manager for the exchange.

"Is this good?" She asks softly, bending down to my level and handing me our new pet.

I feel the little mouse scurrying back and forth in the box, so clearly *alive*.

"Yes," I respond. "What should we name it?"

Mom smiles as she ruffles my hair back. "Let's call it Max," she says. "So I don't have to remember new name."

Masha takes Mom's hand and then my hand, and we walk towards the entrance together.

"Thank you!" Mom calls before we get to the doors. No one says anything back.

When we get home, we put the mouse in Max's cage, like nothing happened.

A hamster was a terrible babysitter. Maybe a mouse will be better.

Fifth Grade

Fall, Early 2000s, Ten Years Old

I AM STARTING FIFTH grade today, on Mom's first day of college. Mom says she stopped looking for a job and decided she needed to get an American degree instead because all the good jobs make you have a degree. She already has a Russian degree but she says that's the same as a "Special Achievement" award.

"How will we have money?" I ask Mom, while I comb my hair into a pony tail. I am looking at the bathroom mirror. It's dirty with Mom's makeup and there are diapers in the trash next to the toilet. Still, I am happy we have our own bathroom, and we don't have to share with anyone else.

"Masha's child support pays for the apartment and bills and the money you bring in will buy us food and gas," Mom says. My cheeks get hot, and I look down. Mom is playing with her bangs to make them spread across her forehead. She looks nice today, like she is going to work.

I don't want to stay up all night and steal money anymore. Now that I'm in fifth grade, I have to wake up at six in the morning to get to school. I don't want to be tired all day. Plus, it feels bad to steal from Chris. Babushka told me that stealing was bad. I wanted to get some money and stop, but Mom says I can't now.

I walk out of the bathroom without saying anything. I can't cry, especially not in front of Mom, but my tears are already gathering up inside my eyes like they're waiting in line to fall.

I look at the clock. It's seven in the morning, which means we're already running late. "Mom, we're late," I say.

"Don't rush me," she answers, but she turns the light off in the bathroom. Masha is fast asleep on the couch. I am glad Mom doesn't want to leave her alone yet. Mom pushes kisses onto Masha's forehead until she wakes up. Her eyes blink, slowly. Her hand starts grabbing at something. I know it's her baba. Masha is four now, but she still needs her baba. I think this is OK since the real Babushka isn't here to take care of us, so for Masha her baba is the next best thing. I hold up a fresh baba. The milk inside is green because the Hulk movie just came out and they made chocolate syrup green, so now Masha will only drink green baba. Masha smiles at me and yawns, then gets up. She puts her thumb in her mouth and takes my hand, pulling me down. I pick her up, and she leans on my shoulder.

"Mom, can you grab my backpack?" I ask. "Masha is getting too big."

Mom laughs and snags my backpack off the kitchen chair. The jingling of her purse means she's ready to go, so I know I can open the front door. We all walk out to the car, where I put Masha in the back seat. I give her her baba and put a blanket over her. She immediately closes her eyes and curls up.

I sit up front with Mom, who itches her hair. Then she remembers it's bad to itch, so she hits her head. The lice haven't gone away even though we moved. It's been a year and a half. I have learned when and where I can scratch my head. Otherwise, I just sit with the itching. I'm praying there are no lice checks in the fifth grade.

"What time are you picking me up today?" I ask Mom.

"When school gets out," she says. "I make sure all my classes end at twelve."

My chest feels warm after she says this. It feels good to have Mom think about me.

"What will you do with Masha while you are going to class?"

"She's coming too," Mom says. "We can't afford daycare since I'm not working."

"Masha is going to college?"

Mom smiles. "Yes. She will sleep on the floor next to me. She will be fine."

I guess we will all be in school this year.

It's October. Mom came to my school at lunch today to tell me good news. She never comes to my lunch. I feel embarrassed when I first see her because she is wearing tight leather pants and a lingerie corset. Most of the moms in my class cover their shoulders, but Mom keeps pulling up her chest like she wants everyone to think she has big boobs.

"I'm engaged," Mom says, sitting with me. When parents visit for lunch, my school puts us at a table separate from everyone. I'm glad because Mom cusses a lot, and I don't need another reason for the kids at school to hate me.

My eyebrows go up. "To who?" I ask. Mom just started using a dating website to find men to marry a month ago. She says we need to get our citizenships faster than it will take for her to get a job through getting a degree, but she's still getting a degree.

"Ronnie and Adam," she says, taking a bite out of the apple I packed for myself.

"You can't be engaged to two people," I say to her. I know I should be nice to her since she is visiting me at school but I can't help but feel annoyed. The other kids' parents bring them special food and games.

"Well, I haven't said yes to anyone yet. I say I think about it. I told them each they have to show my smart and beautiful daughters how man should treat them right. Ronnie has a big ring for me. Four carats, but he makes less money than Adam, who says he will give me three carats." Mom takes another bite of the apple, so there's nothing left but the core, but I know she will eat that too. I only have Cosmic Brownies and a sandwich left. I stayed with Mom last night so my food for lunch isn't as good as if I stayed with Chris. Even though I have money to buy my own food, Mom barely takes me to the grocery store. She's always on a date.

"Doesn't Ronnie live in California?" I ask. "How are we supposed to take Masha to California?"

Mom chomps down on the core of the apple, like I knew she would. "They both do," she says. "Whoever wants to marry me has to pay for custody battle too," Mom answers. "You're right. Diamonds are good but custody battle will take bigger salary. I will go with Adam."

"Will I meet Adam before you marry him?" I ask. Mom is looking at the rest of my food with disgust on her face. It makes me feel bad, like I don't know how to feed myself.

She takes the brownie, playing with the wrapper. "This is too many calories. I will throw it away," she comments. "You don't need it."

"Will I meet Adam?" I ask, again. I ignore what she said about the calories. I will buy a cookie from the lunch line when she leaves.

"Yes. Next time he comes to town he wants to take you to dinner. I think next weekend."

"Will you have said yes to him by then?"

Mom shrugs, squishing the brownie with her thumb and finger. "Maybe," she says. "If I don't get a better offer."

"So will we be moving?" I ask. I can't let Mom know I am about to cry or she'll be mad, so I don't look at her. I will pretend she is a friend and not a Mom.

"That's the plan," Mom says. "OK, I have to go. Throw this away." She stands up and kisses me on the forehead. I look at the sandwich left on my napkin but the inside of my stomach feels like a hurricane. I'm not supposed to throw away food—Babushka would be mad at me—but I walk to the trash and throw it away.

Seatbelt

Summer 2021, Late Twenties

WE'RE ON A tour of Crete's best historical sights. Liam and I are standing outside of a stunning monastery while my family explores the interior. My father found this tour guide on the side of the road and "got a deal," which is his favorite thing to do. We have that in common. I love a good deal.

We've been in Greece for almost two weeks, and they've been the best two weeks of my entire life. Standing in front of the monastery, I'm crying. Our time here is almost over, and maybe I'm emotional because I know that, or maybe because I am holding back my big feelings. I can't stop the tears from falling. They fall hard and fast, and they are not familiar.

"What's the matter?" Liam asks, his face bent in concern.

I shake my head. "I don't know," I mouth. "I don't know. I just can't stop crying."

"What are you thinking about?" He asks me.

I close my eyes and try to sit my racing thoughts down. What is causing this grief?

Suddenly, I hear my father's voice. Not close, but he's outside the monastery again. I need to suck my tears in. "Smile, little one," he says in Russian. I know he's talking to my sister.

"I'll—I'll never have that," I choke out, looking at Liam's concerned face. "I'll never have the nicknames, you know? I'll always be an adult. We'll always have an adult relationship first. We never got the kid part."

I bite down on my lip. I don't want my father to see me crying. I don't want to explain this to him. It's not his fault he can't love me like he loves them. It's not his fault that I'll never get the sweet nicknames or the concern.

"He—he made sure she had that seat belt. But mine was broken," I say to Liam's chest.

"Ah," he says, nodding his head.

In the rental car, everyone's seatbelt was broken. He demanded they fix my sister's seat belt, but he was OK with me having a broken seatbelt. He doesn't carry that same concern. I'm not his kid like they are. I never will be.

"Everyone's seatbelt was broken," Liam says.

"I know, but, but I'm a grown up to him," I say.

Liam holds my head, stroking my hair.

"I'm so sorry," he says.

PART 6

Married

Spring, Early 2000s, Eleven Years Old, Fifth Grade

Mom picks me and Masha up from Chris's house with a big smile on her face. She normally is annoyed that we take forever to get our stuff and get ready.

Chris does not do the drop off. It's Catalina who does it.

Adam is in the car picking us up as well. He has been following us everywhere even though he lives in California. When he's at his house in California, Mom and Adam are on the phone all the time. It's nice to have Mom home, so I'm not upset she's not paying that much attention to us.

"We have a surprise," Mom says, when me and Masha close the door to Adam's rental car.

"Buckle up," Adam reminds us. He looks at me in the rearview mirror, making sure I am actually buckling up. Adam is younger than Chris, his hair brown, with no gray yet. Chris has gray stripes in his black hair like he's the opposite of a zebra. His face is big and round like a plate. He's big, but not in a scary way. He's big like a bear.

Masha doesn't like putting on her seatbelt because it squeezes too hard on her chest, but I like that Adam is protective so I give her a look when she starts whining. "You need to listen better," I whisper.

Masha pouts, but she buckles up.

"What's the surprise?" I ask. My hands feel squishy and wet. I don't like Mom's surprises.

"You'll see," Mom says, turning around to face the front.

"You can't just say we have a surprise and not tell us what it is," I say. I notice the whine in my voice.

"I can because I'm your Mom," she answers. She and Adam are holding hands, while he is driving with one hand on the wheel.

I roll my eyes. Masha leans against my shoulder and closes her eyes. We had a rough night last night. I am still stealing money from Chris, and Masha and I got in a fight because she wasn't going to bed when I needed her to. I told her she was grounded, and she started to cry, which made me want to cry too. We watched *Hercules* until she finally fell asleep. Chris was passed out drunk on the bed the whole night, so he didn't even know that we were mad at each other.

I look out the window of the car. I hope Mom isn't taking us to sleep in another hotel. Every time Adam visits he stays at a nice hotel and Mom wants to sleep there instead of our apartment, but I don't like the hotels because me and Masha don't have a room. We sleep on the floor.

After thirty minutes and me almost asleep, we pull up to the museum district. I like it here because I love the Houston art museum. I recognize we're only a few minutes away from it. We're in front of a garden that has a big, white gazebo in the center of it.

"Surprise!" Mom says.

Adam parks and turns around to look at us too, his smile is even bigger than Mom's. "We're getting married!" He says.

I turn my head to the side, not understanding. Mom is wearing shorts and a white corset, her normal clothes. Adam is wearing cargo pants and a button down shirt. That's what he always wears. I look around. Aren't weddings supposed to be in churches? With flowers? We're the only ones here.

Adam's phone rings, and he answers immediately. "Yeah, we're here, one minute," he looks at Mom. "That was Lenora. She and Sophia and Chanel are in the garden house waiting for you."

I know not to frown, even though my face is bending like I'm upset. Maybe I am upset. I don't like surprises. I don't know how we're supposed to get married. I thought I had more time.

I get out of the backseat, Masha following after me. She is blinking her eyes slowly, also not understanding what is going on. She grabs on to my hand.

Mom and Adam hold hands in front of us. Mom turns around occasionally to make sure we are following them as they lead us to the garden house. After five minutes, we're in front of a tiny white house that looks like someone could live there. Adam kisses Mom and says, "see you soon, future Mrs. Maxwell," and then he walks away.

Mom bends down to Masha's level and kisses her on the forehead. "We're getting married today!" She says.

"Why?" I ask.

"Adam is applying for our green cards. It will be easier to win in court when we have green cards," she says. I have to school my face not to react but this news swirls in my stomach like a tornado. Mom plans on having another custody battle for Masha so we can move to California.

I nod at Mom, hoping that will be enough. She lets go of my hand. "Adam is going to adopt you," she adds, as we walk up the steps to the house. "It will make everything easier."

My stomach clenches. I don't want Adam to adopt me. I think of my real father. I will let Adam be my dad, I will let him take care of me and Masha and Mom, but him adopting me doesn't feel good. I think Mom wants me to feel happy. Her face is so open and excited, her teeth shiny and white, like a row of little awards in her mouth.

She opens the front door to Lenora saying, "There she is!"

Sophia is sitting in a chair, playing her Game Boy. She looks up at me and rolls her eyes. I wish I'd brought my Game Boy, but I left it at Chris's house. I wish Mom chose someone else's Mom who was going through a divorce to be friends with.

I grab Mom's hand before she goes further inside and whisper, "Can we still see Chris?"

Mom looks at me like I've said something stupid.

"Of course not," she says, taking her arm out of my hand. "You have a new dad now."

She walks in front of me, taking Masha with her.

Confession

Summer After Fifth Grade, Eleven Years Old

"You slept with him every night in the same bed?" Adam asks.

I nod. I could tell him more things that could get Dad in trouble. I look at Mom's face, which is eager for me to go on. We are at dinner to celebrate me graduating fifth grade, but we haven't talked about me graduating. We have only talked about what I will tell the lawyers in the new custody case for Masha. Mom mentioned me sleeping in the bed. I didn't bring it up. I was hoping we would talk about my new school or California or anything else.

"He's in his fifties!" Adam says, a squeezed look on his face, like he is grossed out. I feel shameful and dirty for sleeping in his bed with him. "Did anything happen?" Adam's face looks more entertained than grossed out by me, so that's good. He looks like he is enjoying listening to the bad things Chris did.

My chest is vibrating. I'm not supposed to talk about being naked with Chris. It's a secret between us. I told him I wasn't Mommy when he touched me because I thought it was an accident. He said that no one would believe me if I talked about the bad things he does to me because me and Mom aren't supposed to be in America.

I nod, looking down. Adam says Babushka will come next year, but only if I am good and help get Chris in trouble with the courts.

"Yes. He touched me sometimes," I say. "In—in my underwear." I feel Adam's eyes on me and I have to look at him to see what his reaction is. Does he think I'm bad now?

Adam has already turned around, looking at Mom. She is saying something in her quiet voice. A voice she rarely uses but I can still understand what she is saying. They do this sometimes, where they talk about me in front of me, like I don't understand English.

"It would make you look bad, that you left her there," Adam responds to whatever Mom just said.

"You don't think I could say that I was worried about her younger sister? That I sent her to protect her—that's why she was spending the night with him?"

Adam shakes his head. "No, I mean, I understand what you were doing, but the court will see you as being negligent. She shouldn't mention that."

I don't know why, but I feel like I'm falling. The bones holding me up feel like they're made of paper. I lose air inside my lungs. I don't pick my hair in front of Adam—Mom made me promise I wouldn't—so I'm back to counting. Lose. *Four letters.* I have one finger left. I feel dizzy.

"Don't say you slept in the same bed as him to the lawyers," Mom says to me in her normal voice.

The waiter comes with our food. He brings me steak, even though I don't like steak. Mom says to always order the most expensive thing on the menu when someone else is paying, so I did. Filet mignon.

I nod, looking at the meat. Mom answered for me when the waiter asked how I wanted it. She said well done, except I know from going to eat with Chris that medium rare is my favorite.

"Anything else?" The waiter asks.

Mom shakes her head and starts eating her salad. Adam starts eating his steak. I don't think I can put anything in my stomach without it coming back out.

"Eat," Mom says. I can't look at her anymore. Or Adam.

Mom and Adam know what happened to me was wrong, but they're OK with it. They're not even mad. I betrayed Chris, and I didn't have to. It won't win us anything. Part of me is relieved I don't have to talk to the lawyers about how me and Chris slept in the same bed. The other part feels like I have died.

No one cares. They know it was wrong, they said it was wrong, but they don't care.

"Eat," Mom says again.

I cut the steak and put a bite in my mouth. I pretend to swallow, even though I have the chewy piece of meat in my cheek. I tell Mom I need to go to the bathroom. I put the meat in a piece of toilet paper and flush it. I don't want anything inside me. I want to fade away. Have I already faded away? Does my mom even think of me as a person?

I go back to the table. There is a present waiting in my seat. I look at Adam, who smiles. "We didn't know if you would pass the fifth grade this year, but you did, and we're so proud," he says. He looks at the silver wrapped package in my seat.

I lift it up and put it in my lap, unfolding and tearing the pieces of paper covering the gift. "It's sterling silver," he says, proudly.

"He picked it out by himself," Mom says, smiling up at him.

It's a comb set. There is a brush, a comb, a mirror, a ring holder, and a silver tray to put it all on. It looks old-timey, like someone on the Titanic would have it.

"Thank you," I say, forcing a smile.

"You're a young lady now. I thought you should have something valuable."

Maybe they don't care because I am not a child. Maybe they don't care because I am eleven and a woman. This must be it.

Dreams

Summer 2021, Late Twenties

"I HAVE A GIFT for you," my little sister Kristina says, when we finish dinner. "Come with me to get it."

Kristina and I walk to our dad's hotel room, which is right next to mine and Liam's. We left Liam downstairs with my dad, who is giving him a lecture on cars.

Kristina slides the room key into the door and runs inside, to where her bed in the other room is. I sit on her bed, waiting for her while she digs in her suitcase.

Kristina brings me a notebook that has "Katya" written in Russian on the cover. She looks embarrassed as she gives it to me.

I open the notebook. Inside are pages and pages of drawings.

"I made this for you," she says. "They are my drawings from since Dad started talking to you. And then I started talking to you." There are drawings of ducks, of fairies, of the beach. There is a "Happy Birthday Katya," but in Russian, and a dog holding a cake.

"Thank you," I say, in Russian, flipping through the pages. "This is so beautiful. You are so talented."

She shakes her head. "No, I'm not. I just didn't know what else to get you."

"This is my favorite thing that I have," I tell her. A knot of emotion wells in my chest. I love her so much. "Kristina, have you thought about becoming an artist when you grow up?" I ask her, looking at an owl that has amazing detail. "These are incredible."

Kristina shakes her head. "No, no. I need to focus on a job that makes money, I think. This is just for fun."

I remove my eyes from a drawing she did of a parrot who is crying.

"Don't say that," I say, taking her hand. "You can do anything you want. I promise."

"This is just because I'm bored," she says, pointing to her notebook. "I can't do it for a job. I have to be realistic about my future."

I go back to her notebook, flipping to a page with a hamster eating a piece of cheese, a clock behind him like he needs to eat quickly.

"How did you come up with this?" I ask her.

She pauses, looking up.

"I just draw how I think," Kristina says. "I guess maybe, how I feel."

She pauses, looking down at the eye she's drawn.

"I want to make video games," she says, like it's a secret. "But video games with lots of monsters. Girls aren't supposed to like monsters, I know."

I feel mad, but not at her. I feel mad that she thinks something is off limits for her. "You are allowed to like whatever you want," I say, resolutely. I look into her eyes so she knows I'm serious. "And, you will have whatever career you want."

"OK," she says. Her face is drawn, serious, like she is listening intently. I can't tell if she doesn't want to argue, or if she really believes me.

I look at her and remember myself when I was close to her age. I remember how I failed the standardized test in the fourth grade. I remember how I stupid I thought I was.

I pull her in for a hug. I feel her shoulders drop, like she's relaxing. Warmth blooms in my chest. I hold her tight. She's so small, only seven.

I will make sure she can do anything in this world.

Kindergarten

Fall, Mid-2000s, Eleven Years Old, Sixth Grade

WE LOST THE court case. Well, it wasn't lost. It was just that we can't move to California. I both wanted to move and didn't. I like the idea of starting a new life, but I didn't want to leave Dream behind. I don't want to make new friends. It was hard to make this one.

Today is Masha's first day of kindergarten. I started sixth grade last week.

Masha turned five this summer. Mom and Adam are taking her to a doctor after school today to get a brace for her thumb so she will stop sucking it. Adam says if the kids at school see her sucking her thumb, they will make fun of her. I don't know about this, but it's enough to scare Masha not to suck her thumb at school today. My school starts later than Masha's, so I can go to the school to help her settle in. Adam keeps leaning over her, posing for photos. None of the other parents take as many photos as Mom and Adam are. I wonder what everyone else is thinking.

"I need to go potty," Masha says to me, after posing for a photo where Adam is pointing to Masha's name on her name plate. Masha looks scared. She just got fully potty trained last week. Adam's Mom said she was the one who potty trained Masha, but I think Masha potty trained herself. All Adam's Mom did was take away her diapers.

I hold out my hand to Masha and tell Mom I will take her to the restroom. Mom nods at me, but she's not really paying attention because she's taking pictures of Adam at Masha's desk. Mom and Adam are trying to prove they deserve a marriage visa so we can get our green cards, and to do that we have to have a bunch of photos of Adam and Mom being good parents and in love so the immigration people don't think their marriage is fake.

I walk Masha to the bathroom and hear her go into a stall.

"The toilets are just right," Masha says.

I open the stall next to hers. The toilets are very small.

"Perfect for your stinky butt!" I say, trying to lighten the mood. Masha doesn't respond.

"Don't be nervous," I say, when she gets out. She tries to leave the restroom without washing her hands but I point at the sink. "Wash," I say. "Or the kids will make fun of you."

She rolls her eyes and turns on the sink.

"Are you scared?" Masha asks me. I feel like someone has pushed me, the question surprises me so much.

"Scared?" I ask. "Why?"

"I don't know," Masha says. "I feel like you're scared."

"I'm not scared of anything," I lie. Masha can read me very well.

"I think you are," she says. She is drying her hands in the blower. I never use those because they are too loud, and I don't like extra noise.

"Can you tell me the truth if I ask you something? But don't tell anyone I asked you." I ask, since we're alone. I ignore Masha's accusation of me being scared.

Masha nods. Her face is very serious. Maybe to a stranger, Masha's freckles and buck teeth would make her look even younger than five. But her expression makes me think she is eleven, like me.

"Does Da—does your dad ever ask about me?" My hands start shaking. I'm not supposed to ask about him, I know I'm not, but I want to know so bad.

Masha looks up, like she's thinking. "No," she answers, simply. "Dad never says anything about you."

My face falls. I can't help it. "I talk about you though," Masha says. "I tell him about how we played with those fake spiders, and how we went on a boat in Austin."

I smile at her so she knows I'm OK, even though what she said has broken my heart.

"That's great," I say, opening the bathroom door. "You're going to have an amazing day today," I say, trying to change the subject.

Masha takes my hand and squeezes it because I think she knows my feelings are hurt.

One day I will take Masha, and we will leave everyone behind.

It turns out I am not dumb. My grades were so good the first six weeks and I kept getting hundreds on all my tests, so my teachers had a conference with Mom and Adam and decided to put me in Gifted and Talented. They said they are surprised I am doing so well since my end of year standardized testing scores were very low. I wanted to tell the teachers that I passed them this year, unlike last year, but I don't in case they won't let me be in smart classes anymore.

We're at Outback Steakhouse, celebrating. "I'm going to the little boy's room," Adam says, getting up from our booth. We just ordered our food. I wanted to go to Outback Steakhouse because they have good mashed potatoes. I don't like steak but if I cover up the meat in the potatoes I almost can't taste it.

"You need to tell Adam that your grades are because of him," Mom whispers to me when Adam gets up. "He thinks you don't appreciate him."

"Did he say that?" I ask, surprised. I thought we were here because everyone is proud of me. Not because I'm doing anything wrong.

"I can tell," Mom hisses. She steps on my foot under the table. "You haven't told him thank you."

"But I've been the one reading the books and doing my homework! It's not because of him," I argue. I feel like something has been stolen from me, with her words.

"Without him, you wouldn't be in these special classes. He helps you a lot. If you don't say thank you, he will leave us," Mom presses.

My face warms up like it's been slapped. I nod and look down, trying not to cry.

Adam comes back and as soon as he sits down I say "thank you" to him, but I can't look at his face.

"For what?" He asks.

"Because of you I got good grades," I say. I think about when Babushka was here and how I got good grades then too. I wonder why sometimes I get good grades and sometimes I fail.

I feel a warm hand on my cold one. I look up and see Adam, his eyes shiny. "Of course," he says. "I would do anything for you. Your Mom and I started a college fund for you. When you graduate high school, you'll get twenty-five thousand dollars to go wherever you want for college. Hopefully you'll want to stay close to us."

I think about how many hundreds from Adam's wallet that is.

A lot.

I never thought about college before. I always thought I would be a stripper because Mom says they make the most money. She said she couldn't be one because Chris would take Masha away from her, but she would if she could.

"Thank you," is all I can manage, but I meet his eyes when I say it so he knows I mean it. I want Chris as a dad more, but Adam is good too.

It's November. This weekend we are going to Dallas with Lenora and Sophia. Masha is with Chris again. I don't miss Chris as much as I used to, but I still think about him. I would rather be with Masha and Chris than Sophia. I would rather be with the devil than Sophia. I will never forget how mean she was to Masha because she was jealous that her Mom spent time with Masha. But I still feel like I owe her because her Mom helped us keep my sister.

I was alone last night because Mom and Adam wanted to go to Dallas first, without me. So they can have time together without the kids. Lenora picked me up from school with Sophia in tow, and the three of us are driving the four hours to Dallas.

"OK, girls, are you hungry?" Lenora asks from the front seat. Sophia has been reading the new *Warrior Cats* next to me while I've been reading the third *Cirque Du Freak*.

"Yes, Mom," she says, like she's annoyed.

"What do you want to eat?" Lenora asks.

"Hot dogs from James Coney Island," Sophia says without consulting me, even though the question was for us.

"Do you want hot dogs too, Katya?" Lenora looks at me in the rearview mirror.

I can feel Sophia's eyes staring holes into my side.

"Sure," I say, because I like to be uncomplicated.

"James Coney Island it is," Lenora says.

I go back to my book. After what feels like ten minutes, the car starts to slow down and make a weird noise, like the engine is getting hit with a metal spoon.

"Mom, what's going on?" Sophia asks.

"This fucking—this fucking car," Lenora says, pulling to the side of the road.

"Weren't you supposed to get it checked last week?" Sophia asks. Sophia is really good at being unhelpful.

Lenora doesn't say anything. After she pulls over, she gets out of the car and walks around it, like she's looking for something. I watch her, waiting for her to pop the hood of the car or bend down to hit a tire, like I've seen Mom do when our car was acting weird.

Lenora does none of those things. She gets back in the front seat, sighs, and says, "We're sitting ducks, girls, sitting ducks!"

"What are we going to do?" Sophia asks. Her voice crawls to a whine.

Lenora sighs louder. "I'm going to call AAA. Then I am going to call your parents, Katya. I don't know."

I know to stay silent in times like these because no one likes when kids ask a bunch of questions, but I want to know what she thinks is wrong with the car.

"Fuck!" Sophia says, slamming her book down. "I'm still hungry!"

"Shut up, Sophia!" Lenora yells, turning around. Her hand is to her ear, holding her phone. I guess she has already dialed AAA.

Sophia starts to cry. If she were Dream, I would put my arm around her, but because she's Sophia I will pretend to read my book.

When Lenora gets through with all her phone calls, she says, "We have to wait for an hour, girls. I have some mints and water. That will have to do."

I have never seen Lenora like this. She's acting like we are absolutely helpless.

"What is wrong with the car?" Sophia asks.

"I don't know, Sophia!" Lenora screams. Sophia is spoiled because she doesn't know when to keep her mouth shut. She doesn't have a fear of being yelled at so she hasn't been yelled at enough, obviously.

We sit in silence. The sky is turning dark. It feels like it's been more than an hour but I haven't been able to get a good look at the time because I don't want to move too much. I know Adam gave Lenora sixty dollars to take me to Dallas with them. He said that should cover gas and also my food, but I wonder if it covers the repair of the car? I was here when the car broke down. I don't know if that means I'll also need to pay. I have four hundred dollars saved from when I stole from Chris, but no one knows I have that money. I don't want to tell anyone in case of an emergency. If Lenora asks me, I will say I have no money.

Finally the AAA guy comes and checks out the car. Lenora says she will handle it, and to sit in the car and be quiet. It is seven and already very dark outside, and three women on the side of the road means we will probably get murdered.

I watch Lenora talk to the AAA guy from my window. She comes back five minutes after he arrives and tells us that she has a coolant leak, and he will fill her up, but she needs a patch when she gets to Dallas. It shouldn't be expensive. The repair man only takes ten minutes to fill up the coolant and then he leaves. Lenora lets out a breath and says, "Thank God," and she starts driving again. I hope the sixty dollars Adam gave Lenora helps cover the patch.

I wonder how much money I have cost Lenora over the years. I wonder how much I owe her for food and electric and gas. It scares me to think about. I don't want to owe anyone anything.

Visiting

Winter, Mid-2000s, Twelve Years Old, Sixth Grade

My real father is coming again. He's here today, but I haven't seen him yet. Mom says she is letting him visit so he can see how big our new house with Adam is. After he came last time, Mom said she wouldn't let him come again because she doesn't need him anymore. Mom and I are in her closet while she picks her sexiest outfit. Adam says it's OK for her to look sexy so my real father can see how great she is doing in America.

I am sitting on Mom's floor, playing with my braid. Babushka is supposed to come this summer and that is all I care about. I don't want to see my father just to show him how great Mom is doing.

"When he is here, you need to ask him to take you shopping," Mom says. She's looking at herself in her full length mirror, patting down her mini skirt.

"Shopping?" I ask, confused.

Mom nods. "He hasn't sent any child support after all these years. He hasn't helped me with you. He owes you. You need to tell him to take you shopping for school clothes."

"School has already started," I say.

"Well, it's for next year then. Also, I am going to write down my sizes on a piece of paper. You need to buy me clothes too. Tell him it's for you. He won't know the difference."

I look around at Mom's closet, which is as big as mine and Masha's bedroom was in our old apartment. It's full of clothes.

"Will anything else fit in here?" I ask her.

"It doesn't matter!" She snaps, turning around to look at me. "He owes me and you. Go to the good stores. Coach. Abercrombie and Fitch. Guess. When he asks what you want to do, tell him you need clothes for school."

I don't want to do this. I don't even want to see this man at all, but I will do whatever Mom says. I don't want her to be mad at me. Since Adam bought us this big, new, house, Mom has been a lot nicer to me. I don't want to ruin it.

"OK," I nod, crunching my legs to my chest. "I'll ask."

"Also, Katyusha," Mom bends down to my level. She has put her nicest voice on. "Make sure you talk about how great Adam is, OK? He has done so much for us. You need to start calling him Dad like you called Chris. I don't know why you haven't started."

Chris will always be my dad. I can't just switch Adam to "Dad," when that was what I called Chris for such a long time.

I nod my head anyway.

I am in Coach, a very fancy store in the mall. My father is here with me. Mom, Adam, and my father's new wife are outside of the store on a bench, talking.

I have picked random stuff from all over the store and have handed it to him because I know he'll buy it for me. We did the same thing in Abercrombie and the same in Guess. I don't like doing this. It feels the same as when I was stealing money from Chris.

"Do you want anything else?" My father asks me. He has been nice, except for when he brought me a toy Porsche car as a gift. Mom says it was thoughtless of him because I am a girl and don't like cars.

"It's my company," he said. "It's the car I helped them design."

I liked the car but Mom is right. I don't actually like cars. It was thoughtless of him to bring it for me. He doesn't care about what I like. I try to remember this as I nod at him, telling the sales ladies at the Coach store that I want a Coach duffle bag. Leather.

My real father doesn't flinch. They ring him up, and he owes them six thousand dollars. He pays in cash, like it's nothing. He already paid several thousand dollars to the other stores we went too. I know he's not rich because I heard my father and his new wife arguing in Russian about how he took out all their money to come here and visit me. My father doesn't know that I know Russian because Mom said I couldn't tell him.

My father takes my bags. "I'll carry these," he says. I nod. I haven't said much to him. He tries to talk to me about learning English, how he has practiced every day. He even bought a fancy translator where I can put in the English word, and it gives it to him in Russian. It looks like a calculator but instead of numbers the buttons have letters.

"Are you hungry?" he asks me. He always asks me if I'm hungry.

I look at Mom and Adam, who are now talking to just each other, ignoring my father's wife. I don't like to answer without Mom's approval.

"What did you say, Ivan?" Mom asks. "Your accent is too strong." She gets up from the bench and walks over to us. She doesn't even look inside the bags, like she doesn't care.

"I asked her if she was hungry," my father says.

Mom looks at me, but I can see in her eyes that she is angry. I don't know what I did wrong.

"Hold on," she says. "She needs to go to the bathroom."

Mom points at me. When we are inside the bathroom, Mom turns to me. Her face is bright red.

"Why haven't you gotten me any clothes?" She spits.

I move my head to the side. "What?"

"You are so ungrateful! You forgot about me. You haven't gotten anything in my size."

I look down. She's right. I don't know how she knows, since she doesn't look in the bags. She must be watching me in the stores. I want to cry. I feel stupid. I spent this whole day shopping without getting clothes for Mom.

"I got you some purses from the Coach store," I say. "I just think my father would know if I'm not buying clothes my size."

"He's an idiot. All men are." She stands up, straightening her bangs in the mirror. "Tell him we will go to one more store and then get food. Don't miss this opportunity!"

I nod. She walks over to a stall and I hear her pee. I don't want to go to the bathroom. I just want today to be over.

When we make it outside, Mom puts on a big, fat, fake, smile. "Are you hungry, Katyusha?" She asks me, innocently, like we didn't just have a conversation in the bathroom about shopping.

I shake my head. "Not yet," I say. "I want to go to one more store."

I feel greedy saying this, like I'm a bad kid.

"Where do you want to go?" My father asks.

I look around. My eyes snag on Bebe. I know Mom likes this store.

"Bebe," I say. "It's one of my favorites." My father's eyes scan around us until he finds Bebe too. The clothes on the display window look like clothes for clubs. Lots of short skirts and see-through shirts.

He frowns but says, "OK," and he follows behind me. I scan the racks at the front of the store, since those are where the most expensive clothes are, and find a mini skirt I think Mom would like. It looks like it's leather. I also find a few going-out tops.

My father says, "Will these clothes fit you?" when I give them to him so he can pay.

I swallow. "Yes, they will. I know my sizes."

He nods. The total is high, again, but he pays it without questioning me anymore. I want him to know this is not my idea.

"Are you hungry yet?" he asks, when he's done at the register. I look at Mom, who is smiling. That is good. That means I did well.

"Yes," I say, finally. My job is finally over.

After my father leaves, my mom takes everything he got me to her room. She lets me keep some things, a few pairs of jeans and some shoes. She also lets me keep one small Coach purse, but she says everything else is hers as repayment for years of no child support. I know I shouldn't cry, but I do anyway.

"But I got you clothes!" I say. "Can I keep the stuff I got for myself?"

"No," Mom says, automatically. "You will be too spoiled."

I try to swallow my tears away, but this just makes me cry more. At least I'm not sobbing. They are silent tears. I don't know if Mom even notices that I'm crying since she's putting the things I got her into a separate pile.

Later, Mom and Adam leave me home alone as they go to the mall to return the things I got. I feel betrayed. I hit my chest, trying to push this feeling out. I need to trust Mom. Mom knows what she is doing. I shouldn't be spoiled. She let me keep some things.

I hear Mom and Adam come home but I don't greet them. I am lying in my bed, staring at the ceiling. I feel bad, like I did something wrong, but if I was just doing what Mom says, was it bad?

"Do you want to see my watch?" Mom asks, bursting into my room. I turn to see her in the doorway.

I nod and put a smile on so she doesn't get mad at me for feeling guilty. I look at the watch on her wrist. It's beautiful and has a diamond on it. "It's white gold. From Coach."

"Did you return the stuff I got from Coach?" I ask her. I can't help it. Mom always wanted to shop at Coach but never could. She wouldn't shop there unless someone else was paying for it. She wouldn't even ask Adam to buy her anything from there because his money is her money now.

Mom grabs her wrist back. "It's an investment in your future. Better than these purses. I returned them all and bought me a watch because jewelry is always better."

I nod. I know not to be upset. I push all the words I want to say down. I push down that my dad bought me those things because they were for me, and he came to see me, not Mom's huge new house. I push, push, push down so I don't explode.

"Cool," I say.

She smiles.

Sometime after the watch, when she is gone, I go into her closet. She has a lot of new clothes from the stores I went to with my father.

I guess she didn't just buy jewelry with the clothes he got for me. She bought stuff for herself too.

Goodbyes

Summer 2021, Late Twenties

WE'RE SUPPOSED TO be playing Uno, my sister's favorite game, but she's sitting in my lap and we're crying instead. My father has his arm around us. My stepmom, brother, and husband are still playing Uno.

"When will I see you again?" My sister asks me.

"Next summer, I promise," I say. "I promise." I kiss her head. "I'm going to Russia."

"I love you a lot," she says.

"I love you too," I answer. "So, so much."

We hold on to each other. Our father is here too, but he's quiet. He hasn't said anything to our wailing, but he's here.

"I want to see you every day," my sister says. "Not just in the summer."

I nod. The idea of going back to my life without them is excruciating. How am I supposed to go home and live my life while they are on the other side of the world? How can I deal with not seeing them for holidays and birthdays? How can I accept pictures and video calls as my only connection with my family?

"You will be alone when you get home," My sister comments. She knows I no longer speak to my mother.

"I have my other little sister," I say. "But I won't have you."

"You don't have a grandma and grandpa and cousins," she says. "You have all of us in Russia. Why don't you come with us now?"

I think about my life in America. I think about how lonely it is, how I grew up not having family other than my mom and sister with my grandmother occasionally visiting. It's isolating and hard. Russia is more appealing, certainly, but what about the freedoms I have in America that I wouldn't have there? Could I give them up? I squeeze my sister tight.

Tomorrow we leave Greece, and I don't know what I'm going to do without her.

Zelyonka

Spring, Mid-2000s, Twelve Years Old, Sixth Grade

IT STARTS WITH a crop of pimples. Mom tells me that the pimples on my forehead will eventually grow to infiltrate my brain and kill me. She calls the pimples "*cheeries*," rolling the "r."

"Come here," she commands, eyeing my forehead. It's the morning, right before school.

"Is it another one?" I ask, feeling the top of my head. There is a large bump directly in Mom's line of vision. "A *cheerie*?"

I don't want to die, but it also hurts when Mom starts popping these bumps.

Mom nods gravely, bringing my head to her face. She has claw-like nails that dig into my skin as she presses her fingers together at my hairline. "It's a bad one," she whispers.

I squeeze my eyes shut, bracing for the pain. It hurts so bad I have to move her hand away. I start counting. Since we moved, the lice have gone away, but I miss them sometimes. Counting can be stressful. Like now, when "*cheerie*" is seven letters and leaves me with three spaces. I feel a little better because seven is a good luck number according to Babushka, but still.

Mom responds to me moving my head with, "Do you want it to get to your brain? Shhh! I'm almost there!" Mom presses and presses, but nothing is happening.

Finally, grabbing my head as tight as she can, she pops the *cheerie*. She moves her fingers from my head and when she does, I notice the blood all over them.

I maneuver myself to the closest bathroom, which is in her room. I look in the mirror and see what appears to be a gash on my forehead. It looks like she didn't just pop a pimple, but also dug a hole into my forehead in the process.

"Uhhh. . . ." She says. She also looks shocked at my face. "It was bad one. Lucky I got it before it got you."

I grab several sheets of toilet paper and start wiping at the cut, hoping to staunch the bleeding.

"I do it," Mom says, when I'm not getting anywhere. She pulls the tissues out of my hand, moves my face to be level with hers, and starts dabbing what I know is the Russian medicine *zelyonka* on the bloodied toilet paper, bringing the medicine to my head. She's almost out of it since Babushka brought her last batch, so this must be bad.

"Ow!" I say, closing my eyes against the sharp sting. "Ow, ow, ow," I bite my lip and grab her arm.

"There. It's fine now," she says, moving me off.

I turn around to face the mirror and my mouth falls open in horror. Now, not only is my forehead bloody but it is green. *Zelyonka* is also a green dye, but now I'm green and want to die.

"What you want me to do? Let it kill you?"

"No," I mumble, turning on the sink.

Maybe I should have let it kill me. It's better than walking into school like this. Especially because I'm still known as the new kid since I started sixth grade late.

I stick my head under the faucet, moving the handle so that it is all the way hot. I scrub at my forehead with soap, getting it in my hair, in my eyes, everywhere.

I don't know how long it takes, but I finally stop and look again. Nothing has changed, except now everything is wet.

"Mom," I say, tears welling up in my eyes. "I have to stay home today."

She looks at me, then at my bleeding forehead, and narrows her eyes. "You will be fine. You need to go to school."

"*Mom! You did this!*"

"I was helping you!"

I continue to stare at myself in the mirror in horror.

"I went to school with *zelyonka*. Everyone goes to school with *zelyonka*. You will be fine."

"Come on, you'll be late for your bus," Mom continues, lightly pushing me towards the door.

"Mom. I'm green," I respond, planting my feet. "You had it in Russia, where it's common!"

"It's medicine! There is nothing wrong with medicine. Everyone will think you are cool," she says, picking up the backpack that I had dropped outside the door. She motions with her head for me to leave the room. "It's cool Russian medicine."

Cool. Russian. Medicine.

"I'm green!" I shout. "And bleeding. *And wet! I look like Kermit got shot in the head!"*

"You don't look like dead frog. You look like Christmas tree!" Mom exclaims, but I notice she is refusing to look at my forehead. "Christmas is always beautiful," she tacks on.

"Please let me stay home," I beg, following her out. "Please."

She looks around, like she is considering it. "No. You have to go to school today."

Mom squishes up her face, contemplation swirling across her features.

It's pointless to argue with her.

"I have an idea," Mom says, pulling out her compact. She takes the soft sponge and dabs at my head.

"There." This time she bites her lip, like she is trying to hold her laugh in. I check myself out in the mirror again. Where the left side of my face was white, the right side has a giant green spot with a tanned, clayish circle in the middle, and a red, bleeding pimple in the center of that. My face resembles a hurricane on a weather map.

"You have to catch your bus!" Mom says, hurriedly. "You'll be late!"

I close my eyes and make my way outside, trying to wipe the tears away.

"Love you!" Mom shouts, and shuts the door.

When the bus comes, I lower my head and hold my hand to my forehead, leaning against the seat in front of me. It isn't until the very last stop, the stop my friend Megan is on, that I tentatively move my head off the seat, leaving my hand where it is.

"What's wrong?" She asks as soon as she sees me. "Did you hit your head or something? Why are you covering it up?"

I close my eyes and move my hand.

"What the—why did you—*Katya. Why did you color your head with marker?"*

"It's not marker! It's a Russian medicine! If I don't put it on my head I'll get brain tumors."

She raises both of her eyebrows. *"What?"* she asks.

I explain to her my situation, and she stares, open mouthed, at me.

"It doesn't come off?"

I shake my head no.

She laughs a high pitched, all-encompassing laugh. "Brain cancer! You think pimples are brain cancer?"

I never thought to question mom about this, but the way Megan put it is right. Pimples can't be brain cancer. My mom is lying to me.

The realization hits me hard. My mom is lying to me to get her way.

How often does she do this?

The rest of the school day is horrible, with everyone making fun of me. What hurts the most, though, is the realization that my mom would hurt me to get me to do what she wants.

Home Again

Spring, Mid-2000s, Twelve Years Old, Sixth Grade

BABUSHKA COMES BACK on a cool spring day. It will be summer soon, and then after that I will be a seventh grader.

Mom lets me miss school so me, her, and Masha can pick her up from the airport. I have not seen Babushka since I was eight. I am now twelve. I have thought about her every day since we last saw each other.

As soon as I see her coming out of the international arrivals door, my shoulders drop. I feel a warmth bloom through my chest, like a flower opening its petals to the sun. She goes through the line, not seeing us, but moving her head like she's looking.

"Mama!" Mom shouts. Babushka turns her head. She puts a hand over her mouth, like she's shocked.

I wave frantically at Babushka, to make sure she sees me. With the hand that is not at her mouth, she waves. She lifts both hands now, waving together.

"Mama, beestra!" Mom shouts. Babushka looks ahead of her, sees the line has moved, and moves with it.

Mom and I automatically start moving towards Babushka. When we are only a few people away from her, I look up at my mom and see the tears melting from her eyes. Her face softens, like butter that's been left out. She looks like she has a weight lift off her chest too. She looks like my nice Mom.

Babushka finally reaches the end of the line and she runs into our arms. She kisses me and Mom a million times, then leans over to Masha to kiss her too. I can tell Masha doesn't remember her. Masha gets shy and hides behind me.

"I . . . am. . . . your. . . . grand . . . mother." Babushka says to Masha in broken English. Masha nods her head and returns Babushka's hug.

"She doesn't remember me, does she?" Babushka asks Mom.

"She will," Mom says, holding Babushkas arm.

I grab Babushka's hand. She looks at me.

"Finally," she says, in Russian.

Babushka can only stay for three months, but she says she will come back every year now. She won't overstay her visa again. I am almost out of school, finally, so I can spend all day with Babushka at home like we used to do in the summers.

I am on the bus on my way home from school. When it pulls up in front of my house, I hop off and run to the front door. Babushka has been making me *katleti* every day, and I don't eat lunch so I am hungry enough to eat everything she makes without tossing out any food. When I open the front door, I hear shouting.

Mom is shouting at Babushka. I put my backpack down and rush into the kitchen.

"I didn't know!" Babushka says in Russian.

"How can you say you didn't know! There was a sign that said no swimming!" Mom says.

"I can't read English," Babushka counters.

"It wasn't in English! It was a picture!"

Babushka huffs. I go over to her, and she kisses my forehead. Babushka's hair is wet and she smells like grass.

Babushka starts getting me food. She has made me soup today, instead of *katleteka*, but that's OK because I love her soup too.

"Mama, you will get us into trouble," Mom says, softer this time. "This is America, and the rules are different."

"It is stupid you cannot swim in the water!" Babushka says, handing me my bowl. I sit down at the counter, close to where Babushka is standing. She puts her hands on her hips. "How do you have a whole lake, and it's not for swimming!"

"It's for decoration, Mama," Mom says. "It's not a lake. It's a fountain."

"It's big enough to be a lake," Babushka argues.

Babushka did say she was going to swim in the fountain at the front of our neighborhood. I guess she did it while I was in school. I told her not to because the water is dirty. It's dark green because no one cleans it.

I try not to make a face.

"It's not, Mama. This is a nice place. It's exclusive," Mom says.

"Pah!" Babushka answers, slapping her thighs. "Who cares? It is too hot here. I can't drive. I can only walk. And I see a lake, and you tell me I can't swim or fish? Ridiculous!"

"Babushka, you tried to fish too?" I ask her.

She starts patting my hair and saying, "Shh, don't ask any questions, Katushinka."

"She tried to fish," Mom said to me. "With a bucket. She brought it because she thought the fish would be good for dinner, but there are no fish in this lake. It is only frogs there."

"See! You said it is a lake too!" Babushka says, catching Mom.

Mom sighs, heavily. "I will take you somewhere to swim."

"You are in school all day," Babushka complains. "You have chosen a house that isolates you from everyone. There are no resources here. At least where you used to live we could walk to get food, to the library, to the pool. Here there is nothing."

Babushka crosses her arms as I chew on some chicken. I know Mom wants Babushka to be impressed with her big house, but Babushka is never impressed with money or wealth. She thinks it corrupts people. She tells Mom this all the time, which has caused a lot of fighting for them.

Adam walks into the kitchen from his home office and gives Mom a kiss on the head. He walks over to me and kisses me too. "How was school, kiddo?" He asks.

"Almost over," I say.

This makes him laugh, which makes me smile.

"What did you say?" Babushka says in Russian. She always wants to know what I say if it's funny, which I like. The only problem is that Adam doesn't like it when we speak Russian because he can't understand what we say. He says either me or Mom need to be speaking English to translate to him always.

I am quiet, waiting for Mom to translate. Mom doesn't say anything. She's cutting fruit, probably for Masha for when the bus drops her off.

"I just said I'm ready not to be in school anymore," I say to Babushka in Russian. I can't tell which one of us is supposed to be speaking Russian or English, so I talk, and I hope I don't get into trouble.

Adam walks over to Mom and takes an apple slice off the cutting board. "Did you talk to your Mom about the fountain?" He asks.

Mom nods her head. "Yes. She is having a hard time understanding why she can't swim in it."

"Tell her in America, we respect the rules," Adam says. He has a sharper edge to his tone of voice. I know I'll get into trouble if I try to say something about it, so I don't.

"I'm not going to tell her that," Mom snaps. "She will tell me that Russia has rules too, but that they make sense. I am tired of arguing with her and with you!" Mom slams the knife down and walks out of the kitchen. Since Babushka has arrived, I've noticed that Mom has been more stressed when Adam comes into the room. It's like her battery for stress gets drained and she explodes.

"Yuliya, wait," Adam follows her. Babushka looks at me and nods, and I know that means we will talk about it in her room upstairs, where I normally brief her about what Mom and Adam are fighting about.

It's mainly about her. Babushka and Adam do not like each other. I think they are both in Mom's ear about each other, and Mom doesn't want to choose between her Mom or her husband.

I have started to like Adam less because of how he treats Babushka. He always asks me if she is talking about him and most of the time she isn't. I can see why Mom is tired too, but mostly of Adam. All Babushka says about Adam is that he is annoying for being paranoid all the time.

I am practicing roller blading up and down the street with Babushka since the weather finally feels OK, but today I fall, and Babushka is very concerned because now I have a hole in my jeans and a scrape on my knee.

"We'll pee on it," Babushka says in the bathroom, after thoroughly examining my scrape. "The urine will clean it."

I am sitting on the bathroom floor, Babushka bent in front of me, her beet-dyed hair grazing my cut.

"I'm not going to *pee* on my leg, Babushka," I respond, shaking my head. "That's gross."

"It's the same as *zelyonka* except it comes from the body," she says, motioning to herself

"Why can't we just use *zelyonka* then?" I whine. Babushka brought half a kilo of *zelyonka* with her.

"You need to learn how to take care of yourself without it." She stands up, her knees popping with strain. "You won't always have modern medicine."

I didn't know *zelyonka* was that modern, but I don't tell her that.

I scan her moon-shaped face, looking for a pocket where I can fit in an alternative solution, like literally anything else.

"If you don't pee on your cut, I will, and my pee smells because I'm old."

I scrunch my face.

"*How*, even?"

"Come on," she pushes, tapping the toilet seat. "You're going to take this toilet paper and you're going to hold it under yourself as you pee on it."

"Babushka—"

"*Katya.* I don't want to argue with you. I told you, I'll do it if you don't."

I sigh, wincing as I get up.

"I really don't want to—*Please* Babushka, can't I just use soap and water?"

"You understand, Katulia, it won't disinfect it. Not really."

"OK," I sigh, all resistance gone as I poise myself over the toilet.

"Don't forget the paper," she urges, handing me several folded pieces of toilet tissue.

Babushka says I never complained this much when she cleaned my scrapes with pee as a child, but I don't remember her ever peeing on me. Maybe I blocked it out.

After I am done, she takes the soiled toilet paper from me and gently places it on my cut, holding it on the shredded skin. "Babushka! It stings!" I say, pushing her hand away. She holds on tighter.

"That's good! It means all the bacteria are dying!"

I press the heels of my hands to my eyes.

After a few minutes, she finally lets up. "There we go," Babushka says, patting the urine-soaked cut. "It will heal more quickly now."

It didn't heal more quickly. Actually, it started to itch, which my Babushka decided was because we didn't put *enough* pee on it.

Gold Digger

Fall, Mid-2000s, Twelve Years Old, Seventh Grade

"YOUR MOM IS a gold digger," Megan says to me. It's Friday, and we are riding home on the bus. "My mom told me." It's the first week of seventh grade.

Megan has been my friend since sixth grade started. We saw each other a lot this summer since she lives a few streets down and there is nothing else to do in my neighborhood. Babushka doesn't like her. Right now, I agree with Babushka.

I am not sure if I should agree with Megan or be mad at her. I don't want her to stop being my friend because we sit together on the bus, but I also don't want her to think my mom only loves my stepdad because he's rich.

"No she's not," I laugh. I don't want to be laughing, I want to be mad, but I am trying to lighten the mood.

"How much older is your stepdad than her?" Megan asks. "Like fifty? My mom says only women who want money marry men that old." I don't tell Megan that it's not only money that my mom likes about Adam. We are also in the process of getting our green cards.

"I think maybe twenty," I say. That's less than half of what Megan guessed.

"She doesn't have a job, he's rich, and she's Russian. Mom says she was probably a prostitute in Russia, and she came here for money."

James and Mike sit in the seats across from us. Megan is not talking directly to me, even though she is addressing me. She is talking to them. I think she is upset because James said he wanted to go out with me, and she likes him. I told her she could have him. I don't like James as a boyfriend.

"My mom came here because Russia is a dangerous place. She didn't come here to marry anyone for money. She wanted us to have a better life," I say sternly. Megan brought this subject up randomly. No one was talking about my mom or my family. We were talking about the new PSP that James brought to school.

"She talks like this," Megan says, donning a bad Russian accent. "And she wears miniskirts and ten-inch high heels. Of course she only cares about money."

I move my head forward because I feel the tears bubble behind my eyes.. I decide Megan is not my friend anymore. She is dumb.

Megan tries to talk to me, prodding me for the rest of the ride, but I give her one word answers until it's my turn to get off.

When I open the front door and walk inside the kitchen, there is a bowl of *borscht* waiting for me. Babushka isn't here.

"Baba?" I call to the echoey house.

"Ah-ooo," Babushka answers from upstairs. "I'll be down in a minute," she says. "Just zipping up my suitcase."

My heart sinks. Babushka is leaving tomorrow. I keep pushing it out of my head hard enough so that I forget. But now I can't avoid it.

I start eating my soup. It's August and boiling outside, but for some reason this is the best time to eat soup. Babushka says the heat from the soup makes my body cool itself down. I am chewing a beet when she comes in.

"Katyusha, how was school?" She asks. She is very smiley. I know she is happy to be leaving. She doesn't like it here, in our new house.

"Bad," I answer, honestly. "You were right about Megan. I don't like her either."

Babushka nods her head, like she understands. Babushka doesn't understand English but somehow she knew Megan was bad.

"What happened?"

I shrug. "She was making fun of Mom."

Babushka narrows her eyes. "I can tell that she doesn't like people who aren't like her. The way she talks to me—I don't know what she is saying, but she expects me to know. She isn't kind to visitors." Babushka says to be friends with poor kids and Black kids and immigrant kids. They aren't spoiled and annoying.

I don't say anything. I suddenly don't care about Megan. I care only that Babushka is leaving. Every time she comes I feel better, and every time she leaves it feels like someone has taken away my heart. I feel the tears I had behind my eyes on the bus threaten to fall. I look up, hoping they don't.

"What is the matter, Katyusha?" Babushka asks. "What did this Megan say?"

The tears fall fast. I can't hide them from Babushka. I shake my head. "It's nothing."

Babushka comes over to me and wraps me in a tight hug. "I know. I will miss you so much. I want you to come with me."

"Why can't I?"

Even though our life is good here, better than the last time Babushka left, I still want to go with her. I don't want to be without her. I would leave everything except Masha and go with Babushka. Me and Masha could go to Russia together.

Babushka shakes her head. "Your mama says you have to wait until you have your green card. Then you can come with me."

I imagine my plane landing in Russia. I wonder what it would feel like to be there. To be surrounded by family.

"Did you know it was going to be my last time in Russia when I left?" I ask Babushka. I am still leaning against her pillowy chest. I want to stay here forever.

Babushka pauses. I feel her grip me tighter. "No," she whispers. "I wouldn't have let you go." I look up and see that she has tears in her eyes.

"Why did Mom take me, Babushka?" I ask her, looking away. I can't handle Babushka crying.

"She wanted you two to be safe. I understand. Now Russia is safe. Now it's OK."

"Do you think she wanted to come to America for money?" I ask, thinking about what Megan said today.

"No," Babushka answers. "Who would want to leave their whole life for money? She wanted you to be OK. She was tired of looking over her shoulder. She wanted to feel safe walking in the streets."

I press closer to my Babushka and think about how there is nothing in the world that would make me leave her.

Adam will not let me have my new best friend Ayana over. I've tried asking him a million times, but every time he says no. He says it's because she lives in a trailer park, and he doesn't want me hanging around people like her. Ayana is my best friend in the world, so I'm going to have her over when he and Mom leave to go to Tennessee this weekend. Mom doesn't agree with Adam, but he pays for everything so we have to do what he says.

After me and Megan broke up, Megan and her friends started calling me Russian trash. Every time I would see Megan she would hold her nose and say, "What's that smell? It's Russian trash," and start coughing. I went home and begged Mom to let me be home-schooled. Mom got annoyed and said if she didn't let me get bullied then how was I supposed to learn to stand up to anyone?

I still haven't stood up to Megan for calling me Russian Trash. But Ayana has.

Ayana found me crying in P.E. and asked me what happened. I told her about how Megan called my mom a gold digger and started to call me Russian Trash when I defended Mom. Ayana marched over to Megan and called her white trash, and now me and Ayana are best friends.

Mom and Adam leave every other Thursday and come back on Sunday, before Adam drops Masha off. They do this every weekend that Masha is gone. They go to lots of different places, but Mom hasn't been to Nashville yet, so Adam is taking her there this weekend. Ayana is going to spend two whole nights with me.

I am waiting next to the front door for Ayana.

I see headlights pull up to the house and immediately go to open the front door, waving at her. She rushes to me.

"Hi," Ayana says. "Wow, your house is huge." I didn't tell Ayana that she's not allowed to come over because she lives in a trailer. I just told her that my parents were going to be gone.

I shrug. "My stepdad picked it out. He's rich," I add. "But that's not why Mom married him."

Ayana comes inside. I have warmed up fish sticks for us. They are left over from when Babushka was here. She loves fish sticks and ice cream sandwiches. I also convinced Mom to let me rent two movies. I picked out two movies in a different language because me and Ayana like weird stuff like that.

Ayana and I eat fish sticks and crawl into Mom and Adam's bed to watch *Amelie*. When the movie is over, Ayana and I put on Mom's facemasks. In the bathroom, I see cuts all over Ayana's wrists.

"Ayana, do you slit your wrists?" I ask.

Her eyes get big, like she's in trouble. She looks down.

"Sometimes," she mumbles.

"Why?" I ask.

"I—I don't know," she says. "It just makes me feel better when I'm angry."

"Do your parents know?" I say, looking at the mean marks across her arms.

"Yeah. It has actually made them stop being so mean to me. They yell a lot less and let me do more stuff."

I pick up Ayana's wrist and study it. "Does it hurt?" I ask.

"It depends on how deep I cut. I use a razor, and sometimes that hurts. But it hurts less if I use a paperclip."

"Can you do it to me?" I ask her, looking into her face.

"What?" She asks, pulling her wrist back quickly, like I've upset her.

"I didn't tell you this," I say, sitting on the edge of Mom's counter where her bathroom sink is. "But Adam won't let you come over because you live in a trailer park. I didn't think he was mean, but he is sometimes. If Mom and Adam come home and I have slit wrists, maybe he'll be nicer."

Ayana looks at me for a long time. I can't tell what she's thinking. Her lips are in a thin line, but they don't look angry. "I can show you where to cut so you don't hit any important veins," she says. "You don't want to kill yourself."

I nod, presenting my wrists to her.

"Do you have something sharp?" She asks, looking around Mom's bathroom.

I open and close drawers quickly, looking for something that can slice my skin but not cause real damage. I find a broken pair of Adam's glasses and break the glass some more, so that it's at a point. I hold the shard up to Ayana.

She nods. "This is good."

I show my wrists, and she gently cuts them for me. It doesn't hurt that bad. I don't know why Ayana's parents are so concerned.

When Mom and Adam get home on Sunday, after Ayana leaves, I keep asking Mom to hand me things, hoping she'll notice my wrists. She doesn't. The scabs look bad and they are pretty obvious, but Mom doesn't say anything. Finally, when it's bed time and Mom has said goodnight to Masha, she comes in to my room. I am already under the covers. She comes over to me and sits on my bed.

"What is wrong with your arms?" Mom asks, her eyes looking where I have wanted them to look all day.

"I'm upset because Adam says Ayana can't come over because she lives in a trailer park. She's my best friend and the only person in school who is nice to me and doesn't call me Russian trash. Please let Ayana come over, and I'll stop hurting myself."

Mom sucks in her cheeks. I think she's mad, not sad, because she can't look at me. She is supposed to be sad. My chest squeezes. I think I did something wrong without meaning to. This is not the reaction I was hoping for.

"I'll talk to Adam," she says, and gets off my bed. "We'll see."

It's a week after I showed my mom my slit wrists, and they have mostly healed, but Mom has not spoken to me much. After Babushka left, she got angry at me again. I love Mom most when Babushka is here because she is nice and relaxed, but when Babushka isn't here I feel like we aren't on the same side.

I'm doing my math homework in my room, when I hear Adam come up the stairs. His footsteps are heavy and clunky so I know it's him.

He opens my door without knocking, which I don't like, but he says it's his house and he can do what he wants.

"I heard you were being mean to your Mom," he says. The words walk from his mouth like they are holding a dagger. "Because I said you couldn't have your trailer trash friend over."

I swallow. I have never seen Adam like this before. He has a bright fire in his brown eyes.

"I—" I say, but in the span of a blink Adam is across the room. He has grabbed my arm, his face inches away from me. "Don't fuck with my rules. Don't threaten your Mom, you manipulative brat." His hamburger breath is so vivid in my face that I can smell the toppings he must have asked for. Onions. Mustard. Tomato. I wince.

"I—" Adam slaps me, hard, with the palm of his hand. He hits me so hard I fall over.

"Don't back talk me!" He screams. I didn't say anything. I was just going to say sorry.

Adam picks up my wrists, the one with the cuts, and says, "Stop being an ungrateful brat. I will ship you off to Russia so fast you won't even have time to pack your things."

Tears sting my eyes. He grabs my hair and pulls my head back. "Say yes, damn it!" He screams. I can't smell any alcohol on his breath. I don't think he does drugs. He is completely sober.

"Yes," I mumble.

He lets go of my head and walks out of the room. I look at the treacherous scars on my wrists.

This wasn't supposed to happen.

Later, Mom comes up to my room. I can tell because her footsteps are quiet. It's the middle of the night. I'm lying on my bed, staring at the ceiling fan. I don't look at her.

She comes up to me. I think maybe she will kiss my forehead but she says, "Don't tell anyone what happened. You have a big mouth. We could lose Masha if anyone finds out he hit you. Don't be ungrateful."

Layla

Spring, Mid-2000s, Fourteen Years Old, Eighth Grade

In social studies we are learning about voting and the government. I like voting, but I also like the idea of being a leader. At lunch, I decide to ask our table to sign a decree to kick out a girl I don't like, Layla, from the lunch table. She is annoying and I am mad, so I wrote a list of why she should be kicked out. Mostly it's because she talks too much. I gave her the list of what makes her annoying plus our signatures, and she started to cry. I told her life is hard.

I have also started to write because Ms. Abrams says I am talented with words. I am glad Ms. Abrams told me this because now I have someone to tell about what's going on in my life. Sure, a notebook is inanimate but at least it won't call me trash.

I'm too embarrassed to talk to real people about how I feel about my parents except Ayana, so I am glad I have paper.

Mom and Adam surprised me at school one day because they said they wanted to see who I was talking to and see who was putting bad ideas in my head. They followed me to every class and sat in the back. My face burned from embarrassment.

Adam says they had to do it because of me trying to slit my wrists and getting low grades in math. Adam says it's because I'm probably hanging out with the wrong crowd at school. He told me I look like the girls he used to fuck in high school, which made me feel weird since I'm not in high school, and I don't want him to think about sex when he's looking at me.

I think Adam is paranoid. He always thinks we're talking about him. He also thinks I have had sex with boys, which I haven't. How? I'm not allowed outside of the house unless it's to Adam's approved list of people. He has turned Mom against me too. She says I'm not allowed to go anywhere with her since I'm too annoying and needy.

I have thought about killing myself, but I don't want to leave Masha and I know Babushka would be mad, so most days I lie in my room. I can't wait to be older. When I graduate from high school, I will leave this place and never come back.

Passports

Mid-2000s, Fourteen Years Old, Summer Before Freshman Year

MOM AND I are on the way to pick up our Russian passports. They have been expired for a while, but if we want our green cards, they can't be expired. Every single document we submit has to be perfect and up to date. After we get our passports, Mom says we will leave America and come back inside, which will mean border control will stamp our passports and validate our American visa.

The last Harry Potter book is open on my legs. It just came out last week but I'm taking my time finishing it. Every time I think about reading the last page, panic that feels like fire licks at my throat and chokes me. I know when I finish Harry Potter, my childhood will be over. When I read, I forget I'm in the real world. I go to a better place. I pretend I am Harry and that I have a lot of friends and am loved.

Mom is in the passenger seat of the car, nervous, her hands shaking. I can tell she wants a cigarette. She keeps scratching at her wrists. I think she's nervous at the idea of leaving America and coming back inside. The thoughts in her head are ones she says out loud at home a lot. "What if they turn us away? What if we can't get back in?"

We park in front of a brown building and walk inside. Mom and Adam hold hands, and I walk behind them. We get inside the elevator and Mom grabs my hand, squeezing hard. I am surprised by her doing this. She doesn't ever touch me.

We get upstairs and Adam says, "Shit, I forgot my wallet in the car."

Mom's eyes get big. She looks like she is going to lose it.

"I can get it," I say, because I want my Harry Potter book too. We're right in front of Mom's lawyer's door. Mom's lawyer renewed our passports because Mom didn't want to give our address to the Russian embassy when we applied to renew them.

Adam eyes me, like I'm stupid for asking. "You? Get my wallet? So you can steal money from it?" He smiles like he just made a funny joke.

Sometimes Adam shames me for when I stole money from Chris. It hurts every time he brings it up. I want to forget about when I lived with Chris, but he doesn't let me.

I look at Mom but she's looking at the ground like she didn't notice what he said. Or maybe she did and it didn't matter to her.

"Can someone get the fucking wallet?" Mom spits. She looks at Adam expectantly. He grimaces and heads towards the elevator.

"Wait for me in the waiting room," he says.

"Where the fuck else would we wait?" Mom asks, in a low voice, but only I hear it. She grabs my arm, and we sit in her lawyer's waiting room until Adam comes back with his brown leather billfold. Mom goes to the front desk and says something to the receptionist, who gestures to the seat I'm already in.

I wish I asked Adam to grab my Harry Potter book, even though what he said was mean. The waiting room is full of people, and there's nothing for me to do but stare.

"We're the only white ones here," I hear Mom mumble to Adam when he comes back.

I wonder if everyone else here is undocumented, just like us, or they are visiting Mom's lawyer for other immigration reasons.

"You're the only ones who deserve to be here," Adam whispers back. He has a smirk on his face. Adam hates people who aren't white. Mom says it's because a girl from Guatemala broke his heart in high school, and he never got over it.

Mom and Adam have different political views. She says she's a Democrat and he's a Republican, but if the Republican governor in office helps us get our citizenship, she will turn into a Republican. She promised him because he said it's the only way he would help her get her citizenship. Mom says health care should be free, like it is in Russia. She also says there should be more taxes on rich people and more access to things like government-funded child care. Adam doesn't agree with Mom. He says what she believes isn't capitalist and that people should get benefits based on how hard they work. He thinks too many people take advantage of "the system." By "system," I think he means "the government."

I frown at the idea of Mom voting for someone just because they helped us. Aren't you supposed to vote for the best person for everyone?

"Adam, can you get me a water?" Mom asks. I think she says this so she doesn't have to respond to what he said about us deserving to be here.

Adam grunts as he gets up and goes to the vending machine outside of the office.

Mom looks at me hurriedly. She starts biting her thumb nail.

"I talk to Adam," Mom says. "You need to start behaving better."

I frown. "What?"

"He is going to try to adopt you," Mom waves her hand in the air like she's waving a fly away. "Anyway. We need to contact your dad, and you need to tell him you want him to sign over his rights. OK?"

"To Adam?" I ask, looking at the door.

"Yes. You need to start calling him 'Dad,' he's getting angry.

I move to bite my own thumb but Mom slaps it away. "Stop, you'll ruin your nails."

"I don't want him to be my dad," I say simply. "I would rather not have one."

Mom rolls her eyes. "Don't be stupid. He will be your dad if I say he is."

The door to the office opens and Adam comes back inside, handing Mom a water bottle. If this was three years ago, he might have gotten something for me, but he knows he doesn't need to impress me anymore so he doesn't.

Mom nudges me. I know this means I need to smile at him.

"Do what I say," she hisses. "I know best."

PART 7

Bella Swan

Fall, Ninth Grade, Fourteen Years Old

IT'S THE FIRST day of high school, and I have Adam drop me off at six-thirty in the morning even though school does not start until seven-thirty. I didn't go to orientation because Mom says it's a waste of time. I am going early today so I can find my classes and not be late, because I don't want to be called out. I don't want any attention on me. The goal is to get through these next four years without any incidents.

"You're lucky I love your Mom enough to drop you off so early," Adam grumbles, as he pulls up to the front of the school. It's still pitch black outside, but there are lights on that make the school look warm. Almost inviting.

"Thanks," I say. I breathe through my nose because I know that is supposed to help with anxiety. I have a plan for high school, on how to act, who to talk to, how to be. The plan is to endure.

"Have a good first day. High school is where everything really counts," Adam says, as I gather my backpack from the floor of the car. Backpack. *Eight letters.* I'm missing two fingers, but if I add a space and period, it could count. Maybe today will be a good day.

I nod and hop out, closing the door behind me. I hear Adam pull the car away before I make it to the front door. It opens, thankfully.

After these next four years, I can leave my house and never come back. I can take Masha with me. We will escape. But I have to push through. Four years isn't an unsurmountable period of time. Four years ago I was in the fourth grade, going into fifth grade. I can do it.

I walk to the front office, where a woman is sitting behind a big white counter.

"Hi, I'm a freshman, can I have my schedule?" I ask. It feels weird to say "freshman." I just learned the different levels last week: freshman, then sophomore, then junior and senior. I wonder who invented the labels for the different grades. Maybe I'll look it up on a computer later.

The lady at the front desk asks for my details, and I give them to her. She hands me a printed copy of my schedule.

"Did you go to orientation?" she asks, "Or do you need a tour?"

This school is huge. The last graduating class was fifteen hundred seniors. The idea of being a senior makes my stomach drop. What will happen these next four years for me? I wish I knew the future.

"No, thank you," I say, and take the paper from her. I will figure my own way around. I start with my first period, which is math. Not the best way to start my day.

I have decided to pretend to be Bella Swan, from *Twilight*. Or at least act like her. If I'm quiet and focus on my grades, maybe no one will notice me. Maybe I won't need friends. I set a cap of twenty words a day for myself. I'll be known as the quiet girl, not as Russian trash. Bella Swan had everything good happen to her because she wasn't like the other girls. She wasn't annoying or loud, she was quiet and well-mannered. She is perfect, and I want to be exactly like her. I have to be. I don't feel like I have a choice. If I show my real personality, I'll get made fun of again. I'll be punished. I have to push myself down. My books will be my friends. I'll be perfect for Mom and Adam. I'll get into the best college. And then I can leave forever and be myself again.

I walk to the rest of the classes, the only sound the soft taps coming from my shoes. I like when the school is this quiet. I doubt Adam will drop me off at this time every morning, but maybe sometimes he will if I tell him I have to do something for school.

Too soon, other students start filling the halls. I come back to my first-period class and sit outside, my back against the wall. Adam bought me a phone a few weeks ago. It's called a Pebl because it looks like a rock. To me, it should be called "egg" because it's in the shape of an egg. I flip it open and start to text Ayana.

I remember I decided that I don't want friends in high school. I don't want distractions. I close my phone and slide it back in my pocket. I look out the window, where the sun is coming up.

"Hey, what are you doing here?" a man says, unlocking the front door of my first-period class. I guess he's the teacher.

"Just waiting for school to start, I guess," I answer. That's already eight words. Do teachers count? Teachers aren't people. Maybe my limit of twenty words should just be for people my age. I have to talk to teachers, or they won't give me good grades.

The teacher who unlocked the door holds it open. "Come on in," he says. "You can help me set up."

I get up, holding my folders in my arms. The classroom looks the same as our classrooms did in middle school. Motivational posters. Red chairs. Desks attached to the chairs. A chalk board. A smart board.

"Sit anywhere. Perks of coming early," he comments. I hear him pop a lid open. It comes off with a snap. I look at him as he takes a sip of what looks like Snapple. He sighs.

"What's your name?'

"Katya," I say.

"Cat-ya?" He asks.

"Kat," I answer. I hate teaching people how to say my name because I don't even say it right. "You can just call me Kat."

He nods. "OK Kat, can you put one of these papers on every desk?" He nods to a stack of crisp, white worksheets. "This will keep everyone busy, hopefully. It's a test to determine if this is the right level of math."

Ice cubes clog my stomach. I wonder if there will be multiplication tables on it. I still don't know my multiplication tables. I glance at the tests as I hand them out. It looks like mostly some division and the order of operations. I remember that from last year.

My breathing evens out a little.

"Can I start the test early?" I ask, when I'm done passing the papers out.

He cocks his head when he looks at me, like he misheard.

"I don't have anything else to do," I explain.

He shrugs. "Be my guest. Maybe you'll do so well you'll test out of my class, and I have one less of you to worry about."

I sit down and within five minutes I know that's not the case. These questions are difficult. I've never been good at math. Even though I'm in Gifted and Talented classes, I am in regular math. It makes me feel dumb.

It takes me the entire period to finish the test. I'm glad I started early.

The bell rings, and I tell my math teacher bye. He makes a motion with his hand like he's dismissing me, and I go to my Pre-AP geography class. I am mostly looking forward to Newspaper and this class. I'm the first one in the class again, even before the teacher, but her door is unlocked. I sit down in the furthest chair from the door.

So far I haven't seen anyone I know from middle school, and I haven't had to say anything to any students. Maybe twenty words is doable.

The class starts filling up slowly. When the bell is about to ring, Layla from middle school walks in. She's talking to the teacher. She's the first person I recognize. She has long, brown hair that reaches her butt. It's in a loose braid. She is also very tall, which makes her look like an Amazonian warrior. I look away, hoping she doesn't see me. I feel bad for how I treated her when I kicked her off our lunch table.

She comes to sit down next to me.

"Hi," she says.

Did she forget I bullied her last year?

I nod and give her a small smile. Maybe I've changed a lot more than I thought. Maybe I don't even look like myself.

When the teacher, Ms. Lynn finishes up her introduction, she gives us a worksheet. We have to fill in all the countries of the world. It's our homework. She puts on rock music. We're allowed to talk, she says, as long as we leave her alone.

"How was your summer?" Layla asks. There's one other person at the table with us. She doesn't say anything either.

"It was fine," I say. *Three words.* I have seventeen left. I should ask her how her summer was, maybe, but I don't know how the rest of today will go, and I need to save my words.

"I went to Paris. And London. And Syria," she says, even though I didn't ask. "Paris was good. I think I want to live there one day. Maybe study French Literature or something."

She's coloring the countries of the world but not labeling them. I thought we were supposed to label them. Am I doing it wrong? The teacher said not to bother her. I don't want to ask Layla.

"Aren't we supposed to just label them? Did Ms. Lynn say we had to color them?" I force out, because I don't want to be doing one of my first assignments in high school wrong.

Layla shrugs. "I don't know, I think you're right, but I like to make things pretty first."

It doesn't necessarily answer my question, but I will keep labeling the countries. I am struggling with African countries right now.

"Did you read anything good this summer?" She continues.

Should I be rude and just ignore her? Why is she talking to me anyway?

"I finished Harry Potter," I say, because I don't want to be known as the rude quiet girl. Just the quiet girl.

"Me too. Wasn't it good?" She asks. "When Fred died I—" The bell rings. I hop up and head to the door. I don't want to give her any more of my words. I keep the image of Bella Swan in my mind. Good things will happen to me if I'm quiet. I will get through high school if I put my head down. I don't have another choice.

Gas Light

Fall, Ninth Grade, Fourteen Years Old

I'VE BEEN GOOD. I've made straight As. I haven't fought with Mom and Adam. I haven't had any friends over either. I've been focusing on school. But today, everything I've been pushing down has boiled to the surface. I can't hold it in anymore. I hate Adam.

I came home from school and found Mom crying in her closet. I asked her why, and she said because of Babushka. She said Babushka was a bad Mom to her. She said Babushka hit her when she was a child.

I reminded Mom that she hit me too. And so has Adam. I told her it happens. I was trying to be comforting, but she started to cry harder.

Adam came in at just that moment, when I was pleading with Mom not to be mad at Babushka, and said he never laid a hand on me.

Mom didn't respond.

And now the three of us are here, in her closet. She keeps crying.

Her knees are to her chest. Adam is towering above us.

"You did hit me!" I roar at Adam. He's looking down at me, like I'm a speck of dust. He almost looks like he's smiling but that might be the light. "You hit me hard. When Mom told you I was slitting my wrists! It was last year."

Adam shakes his head. "You're a liar. Just like your grandmother. You're just trying to hurt your Mom." He walks past me to where Mom is pressed against the wall. He bends down to her. "This is why she shouldn't come, Yuliya. Look at how Katya is acting already."

I want to scream. I want to pull my hair. I want to kick Adam so hard he bursts. I want to tell him he is a pimple that needs to be popped.

Mom nods, looking up at Adam, like she doesn't even see me. "You're right," she says to him. "I'm going to tell her to leave me alone. I'm going to tell her not to call anymore. She's manipulative. So is my brother."

"No! Mom! Don't!" I scream. "Please!"

I can't live with Babushka not coming back this year. She's my light. She's the only thing that keeps me going. She is all I have. I haven't seen Babushka in a year. She's the only good thought in my head, other than Masha.

"Don't listen to him!" I shout.

"Get out!" Adam says, pointing to Mom's closet door. "You're making your Mom more upset. This is already a bad situation. You're making it worse."

Doesn't Mom see that Adam is manipulating her? Why is she turning against Babushka? I don't understand what he said to her to make her want to stop talking to Babushka.

"Mom," I beg. "Please. Babushka loves you. Uncle loves you. Please. I don't know what is going on, but he's lying to you. He did hit me. You know he did."

Mom shakes her head and wipes her eyes. "Stop," she says to me. "You're too young to understand what real abuse is. Adam is right. My mother is not a good person. She only cares about my brother."

I feel like my mother is slipping through my hands. I want to scoop up what's left of her, but I'm losing her. I whisper, "Please, Mom."

"Get out," she says to me.

I feel a nudge against my back and realize Adam is pushing me with his foot. I don't want him to touch me. I force myself to stand up and walk towards her closet door, leaving her behind.

"You're doing the right thing," I can hear Adam say behind me. "Look how Katya defends her. She's a bad influence on her too."

When I get upstairs to my room, I look at my thyroid pills on the counter in mine and Masha's shared bathroom. I have been taking them since I was 13. I know too much of anything can kill you and right now, I want to die. I unscrew the lid of my pills. I can't survive without my grandma. I can't make it four years. It's torture.

I take all of them. I hope these will kill me.

Suddenly, the bathroom door opens and Masha comes in. "What's wrong Katya?" She asks.

My stomach plummets.

How can I forget about Masha? How can I forget how much I love her?

"I'm sick," I say. It's not a lie. "I need to throw up."

"Should I get Mom?" Masha asks.

"No, don't get Mom. Mom is sick too. Can you play in your room? And I'll come out in a little bit and we can watch *The Simpsons*."

Masha smiles and nods. I stick my finger down my throat and heave. I don't know if my thyroid pills can kill me, but I need to live for Masha.

Adam told Mom she needed to see a therapist because she was crazy. Mom saw him, didn't like him, and gave him to me. Mom and Adam both agree that I need to see him and say I don't have a choice. They tell me they think the family will be happier once I get my mental issues resolved. They have started blaming a lot of stuff on me, so they are happier now that they have a scapegoat. I learned that word in English class, and I use it all the time now because I feel like it's very relevant to my life.

I am sitting in the office of a man who looks like Santa Claus. He is probably older than Babushka. Mom says he questioned her too much and made her think about things she didn't like, but insurance pays for him, and she wants him to fix me. She says it's too late for her. Talking to a therapist goes against my twenty-word goal, which I have finally started to meet. It is November and at first I talked a lot in school, but now I can meet my goal because people know I'm not approachable or nice, and I usually won't help.

"Have you heard of *The Velveteen Rabbit*?" The man asks me.

I shake my head. Mom also said I can't tell him anything bad about her or Adam or we could get Masha taken away. If I didn't have Mom's words in my head, I would tell him that Mom didn't read to me, Babushka did, but this probably makes Mom sound neglectful.

"I have it here. Let me read it to you."

I frown at this therapist. Does he not know I can read?

The therapist grabs a book with a rabbit on the cover. He crosses his legs and reads me the book, showing me the pictures. I feel sleepy. I don't like the therapist, not really, but I like being read to.

"Do you know the moral of the story?" The therapist asks when he finishes the book.

I think. "You are only worthwhile if someone you love loves you back," I say.

He frowns at me, and I panic that I've said the wrong thing.

"Well, that is an interpretation, certainly. I think about this book a lot when it comes to perfectionism. Do you remember how the rabbit got dirty and raggedy, but the boy still loved him? In fact, I would argue the boy loved his toy rabbit even more. Not because the rabbit was beautiful, but because the rabbit was always there."

It's my turn to frown. I don't know what this book has to do with me. Maybe the therapist just wanted to read the book because I wasn't talking a lot.

"You don't need to be perfect to be loved, Katya."

When it's time to leave his office, I feel confused, but like I want to come back next Thursday.

"The therapist says you are depressed," Mom says. I have been going to the therapist for a few weeks now. I didn't realize they were talking.

"He didn't tell me that," I say. If I was depressed, wouldn't he tell me?

"It's because you are sitting in your room and reading too much without any exercise. Me and Adam decided that if you want a new book, you have to work out for forty hours. We will have a sign in sheet in the exercise room where you need to log your workouts. If we find out you are lying about your time, we won't buy you any books for the rest of the year. Got it?" Mom asks, her voice stern.

"OK," I say. "Did the therapist say I wasn't exercising enough?" We haven't even talked about exercise.

"I'm your mother. I know that's why."

"Babushka used to walk with me every day. For hours," I say. I take every chance I can to bring Babushka up and how good she is. All Mom wants to do is talk about what a bad Mom she was. I still don't understand why.

"Well, you're never going to see Babushka again, so you need to learn to exercise yourself."

Her words are like a punch to my gut. I wonder, for a moment, if I'm really here or if this is a nightmare.

"Why are you being like this?" I whisper.

"She's a bad influence on you. Adam's right. She fought with me all the time. And him. She was never thankful. She thinks America is horrible. We don't need her in our life."

I don't think these are Mom's words. They sound like Adam's. He did this with her friends too. She sees Lenora, but about once a year now. She doesn't have any more Russian friends because Adam told her they were hitting on him and were in love with him. I feel sick. I feel like Adam wants to isolate us.

"She was just Babushka," I manage. "She just said what she thought."

"She was a horrible Mom," Mom says. "You're lucky I love you so much."

I don't feel very loved.

Ms. Lynn

Fall, Ninth Grade, Fourteen Years Old

I AM IN MY second period class, taking a test on India. I want to move there someday. I want to join the Peace Corps. Layla and I have started writing fanfiction about joining the Peace Corps, but only to each other. It's not really fan fiction, it's more like our own fiction.

Somehow, Layla has become my best friend. We never talk about how I kicked her out of our lunch table. We never talk about middle school. One day she asked me for my email, and I gave her Mom's. She started emailing me, and I write her back. That way I don't have to use my twenty words on her. She uses a million words on me, every day, but she's happy with my nods. Somehow, she seems to know. She has asked for my phone number what feels like a thousand times but I always reject her. I am not ready to talk out loud yet. Maybe this summer.

After I turn my test in, I look at Layla's desk to see if she's done. She's only halfway through. I sigh, pulling out my homework for my next class.

"Katya, hey, come here!" Ms. Lynn says from her desk. Her brown hair is in a high ponytail that looks like it would hurt, but is very fashionable. Ms. Lynn always dresses like she's going to lunch with her friends, kind of like Mom, but showing less of her boobs. She's a few years younger than Mom. I wonder if they would be friends.

"I need to ask you something," Ms. Lynn says.

I get up, hoping that she's not accusing me of cheating. I studied a lot for this test. I felt like I knew all the answers, which is unusual. There are usually one or two questions I overthink.

"Hey, do you want to join Olympiad?" Ms. Lynn says, when I reach her desk. I cock my head.

She nods, like she knows I don't know. "It's like . . . I don't know. It looks really good on your college application. It's a club for nerds. I'm the sponsor, and I think you'd love it."

"I . . . don't know," I say. "I'm not a very good nerd."

My cheeks get hot. I feel embarrassed. I may not be in the dumb classes like I was when I was a kid, but I am only in two Pre-AP classes this year. All the other Pre-AP kids are a lot smarter than me.

"You are the best nerd," she says, taking my hand. She is looking at me earnestly, and I don't know why. "Look. You need more friends like you. That's this club. Every year the Olympiad organization picks a subject, and it's our job to study everything there is to know about the subject. This year it's evolution. Then we take a series of seven tests. Whoever scores the highest gets to go to the next round. We compete against all the schools in the district. You have nothing to lose."

I look down at Ms. Lynn's hand on mine. She's squeezing it, like she's trying to comfort me. I don't think she knows the truth about me. "Ms. Lynn, I'm not very smart. I'll make you guys lose."

Ms. Lynn rolls her eyes. "Are you kidding? You're brilliant. Who's telling you you're not smart?"

I don't want to tell her how I failed the standardized test in the fourth grade. Or how I didn't go to the last part of third grade. Or how I still don't know my multiplication tables.

"Trust me, Ms. Lynn. I won't be any good at this. I'm too dumb. I don't want to go and be the only idiot there."

Ms. Lynn moves my chin up so that I have to look at her.

"Don't you ever say that about yourself again, do you hear me?" She asks. "You're not dumb. Anyone who has ever said you were dumb didn't know what questions to ask you. You're one of my smartest kids, you just don't believe in yourself."

She lets go of my chin and sits back down. "One meeting," she says. "Then you can decide. OK? You're smarter than everyone in there. I promise."

I groan. "Ms. Lynn, please."

She groans. "Katya, please."

I think about it. Ms. Lynn says it looks good for college, and I need to go to college. Especially with a scholarship.

"Fine," I sigh.

"You won't regret it!" Ms. Lynn claps.

Christmas Surprise

Ninth Grade, Fourteen Years Old

EVERY YEAR FOR Christmas since the last time my biological father visited me three years ago, Mom gets me clothes from Abercrombie. I know that after she returned what she got me and got herself what she wanted, she has used the rest of the credit to buy me Christmas presents. I also know I'm not allowed to ask for anything not from Abercrombie for Christmas.

I have finished opening my last wrapped present, which is a brown sweater with a giant hot pink moose in the corner. I don't tell Mom I hate Abercrombie. What I really wanted was a gift card to Borders, or to talk to Babushka on the phone.

"We have one last surprise," Mom says, looking at Adam. Adam nods at her, like he's approving something.

"We're going to London!" Mom shouts. Masha jumps up next to me and starts wiggling her butt in a little dance. Masha's always happy. We could be going to the middle of nowhere, and Masha would think it was the best place. I think it's because she sees how I get yelled at when I express any emotion that's not happiness.

"How?" I ask Mom, shocked. I know we have our green cards now, but I didn't know we could leave the country yet.

"We can! Isn't it exciting?!!"

I don't know what to say. I thought the first place we would go once we could leave the country was Russia.

I smile at Mom. Ever since our argument in the closet, I have mostly avoided Adam. He has turned Mom against our family. He has taken all of Mom's friends away. Mom looks at me, and then looks at Adam, and I know she wants me to say something to him.

"That's great," I say in his general direction. He is the reason we got our green cards, so it's true that we can leave the country because of him.

Mom prattles on about the details of us going to London. As she's talking, I start cleaning up the wrapping paper to throw in the trash. When the living room is clean, I take my clothes and go upstairs to my room, closing the door. I want to cry. I should be happy, but I want my grandmother.

Mom comes in a few minutes later. "What's wrong with you?" She asks. "Why aren't you happier? You love this Harry Potter and British books. I thought you would be jumping up and down."

"I—" I know not to talk about Babushka, but the words are having a hard time meeting my lips. "I am happy," I mumble. "Really happy."

"Good," she says. "Don't be so ungrateful. It's obvious."

Before we go to London, I decide to call Layla and tell her. It's our first phone call. Masha, Mom, and Adam went to Masha's friend's house. Mom is friends with one of the moms down the street whose kid Masha plays with all the time. Adam approves of this friend, which is why Mom's allowed to go to her house.

At first, when Layla and I talk on the phone, it's weird. I keep having to stop myself from counting my words. It's not school, I keep reminding myself. I am on break. There is no homework for me to be doing.

"Do you want to watch a movie?" Layla asks.

"How?" I question. Meeting her isn't an option. I don't want Adam to know about any friends.

"I'm going to email you a website. Just click on the link, and we can watch the movie together on the phone."

Mom's laptop is already in my room. I told her I needed it for a school project, but really I was reading fanfiction. I turn the computer on and click the link Layla has sent me. It opens to a website that has strange, pixelated, blinking ads.

"Is this safe?" I ask Layla. "Will it give my mom's computer a virus?"

"I use this website all the time," Layla says.

"What movie are we watching?" I ask, through the speaker. Me and Layla have already been on the phone for over an hour. We got comfortable halfway in, and now I'm even OK with the silences between us as we do other things.

"It's called *The Quiet*," Layla says. "My friend told me about it. She said it was really good."

"If my mom comes home, I'm going to hang up, and I might not say 'bye,'" I say to her. I don't give her a reason why, and she doesn't ask.

"If that happens just write me an email."

Layla and I watch half the movie. At first we are making jokes about it, but when the main character, who is a girl in high school, starts sleeping with her dad, my lungs fill with chunks of ice. I remember when I lived with Chris in fourth and fifth grade, how I dressed in tight clothes because I knew Chris liked them. How I kept telling him I wasn't Mommy when he felt me up in bed. I remember trying to be a wife.

"That happened to me," I whisper to Layla. She is in the middle of calling the dad ugly when she goes quiet. She hasn't been quiet this whole time. She's never quiet.

"What do you mean?" I hear her say. Her voice isn't shaky, like mine. It feels like a pillar to me. Strong and steady. I am the storm.

"That. The dad and the blond girl," I blurt. "I had that with my sister's dad."

I feel a wave of tears crash over me. My throat closes up. Is it possible to drown without water?

Layla is talking, saying something, but I can't comprehend what.

"Don't tell anyone what I just told you," I snap at her. "Don't say anything. Just forget it."

"Katya, it's OK. I won't tell anyone," she says, but she sounds scared.

"I'm fine. Everything's OK," I say, even though I am dizzy while I'm saying it.

"I have to go." I hang up on Layla, my hand shaking.

I finish the rest of the movie by myself, holding my knees and crying.

I am making it up. Adam is right about me. I make everything up. I can't have been molested. Other kids get molested. Not me. This was my life. This was normal.

It's not normal.

I turn off the laptop and clear the history, putting the computer where Mom told me to, in Adam's office. I feel sick and full, like watching that movie made me pregnant. I remember telling Mom about how I slept in Chris's bed. I remember how Adam said it would make her look bad. No one ever used the words, though. No one ever said "molested." Did it really happen if I'm the only one who acknowledges it? Did it really happen if no one cares?

I won't bring it up again. I can't.

Mom says she chose London, out of all the places we could have gone for our first technical trip outside the US, because of my obsession with Harry Potter. She says this trip is for me. I don't know if I believe her reasoning, but I'm happy to be here.

We walk around the city until our feet hurt, and I marvel at everything. I don't even care about the blisters on my feet.

The toothpaste is different. They don't advertise teeth whitening anywhere. They spell favor with a "u." The portions are smaller. Everyone has an accent, like Mom. They don't sound like Mom, but they sound different.

I love it.

The first hotel we stay in is very broken down. It's a hotel brand that Mom and Adam stay in a lot in the US, but Mom says it's the worst quality one she has ever been in because the building is over two hundred years old.

That's normal here. All the buildings feel ancient.

After a few days walking the city, Mom has Adam rent a car so we can go all over the UK.

"This is our new hotel," she says, when we get inside the tiny car. There is a huge piece of luggage in between me and Masha.

The car barely fits us and our four bags. I don't know how Mom wants us to sleep in here or why, but I know not to question her.

We drive to Stonehenge, to Bath, and all the way up to Edinburgh. It's been five days and we haven't stayed in a hotel or had a shower. We're on our way to Wales now, and although I love the UK, I really hate being dirty and using the bathroom on the side of the road. We keep begging Mom to stay in a hotel, and she says we don't need to, that we can handle no showers, but everyone is in a bad mood from smelling bad. Now that Mom and Adam are married, Mom is obsessed with saving money because everything that is his is hers too.

"Mom, I've got to pee," Masha says. She says it in a sleepy voice.

Mom sighs. It's pitch-black outside. The car smells like old oranges left in the sun for too long. I want to roll down the window but it's cold because it's January.

"Adam, pull over," Mom says. She points to the field we're driving next to.

"It's too dark. She won't know where she's peeing," he says.

"I don't want her to get infection! Pull over!" Mom says, getting angry. I can tell Mom wants a shower too because she sprays her perfume every thirty minutes.

Adam pulls over. Mom gets out and opens Masha's door. I guess that means Mom wants to go too because normally I'm the one that goes with Masha. Masha gives me a look like she doesn't want to be doing this with Mom.

"You don't want to go?" Mom asks me. "We're not stopping again for the rest of the night. You should go."

"No thanks," I say. I try not to sound irritable.

"Fine," Mom says. She and Masha disappear into the dark field.

I close my eyes. After a few minutes a scream wakes me up. I jolt forward.

"Is everything OK?" Adam shouts, rolling his window down to shout outside.

No one answers. My heart starts racing. I shouldn't have let Masha go with Mom. I unbuckle my seatbelt but before I can pull it all the way off Masha races into the car. Her pajama bottoms are all the way down, her bare butt red and in my face.

"Get it off, Katya! Get it off!"

"Masha! What's wrong!" I yell, trying to focus my eyes on what she is showing me with her butt.

"I sat in something!" She screams. "It burns!"

"Shit," I mumble. I look around frantically and find my sweater, trying to wipe Masha's dry butt with it. She screams harder. "It burns!"

Mom pops open the passenger side of the car, getting inside.

"She sat in poison ivy!" Mom says.

"Are you sure that's what it is?" Adam asks. "I don't know if they have that here. It could be serious."

"I don't know, I didn't see," Mom says, frantically.

"Should we go to the ER?" Adam asks.

Masha is bawling. I grab water from the front seat and pour it on her butt.

"That's better," she says, through tears.

This seems to also soothe Mom. "And pay a million dollars? No. We just have to get a hotel for tonight," Mom says. "She needs a bath."

After I pour out all of the water we have on Masha's butt, and wipe it with my sweater, she sits on my lap and cries. "Can we please go to a hotel now?" Masha asks.

"Yes, we will go," Mom says. "You win."

Therapy

Winter, Ninth Grade, Fifteen Years Old

I HAVE BEEN IN therapy for several months. I normally like it because the therapist listens to me. Except for today. Today I messed up. I am in my room, staring at the ceiling, wondering what I should do.

I told the therapist about watching *The Quiet* with Layla and how I think I was molested. Today, for some reason, I felt safe.

I was wrong. I was stupid.

After I told the therapist the room got dizzy. I started breathing hard, like I was going to pass out. My life with Chris came pouring out of me. I don't even remember how or why, or what prompted it.

When I was done, I realized that he could report Chris. And Mom. That's when I felt like I was going to pass out.

"Please don't tell anyone," I said to him. "I am scared Masha will get taken away. Please."

"Katya, calm down," he said to me, in a firm voice. It sounded like he was yelling. I don't remember what happened after that, just that I was getting in the car with Mom. I told Mom what I told the therapist. She told me I made a mistake. We could lose Masha. Masha and I could go into foster care. I could never see anyone again. Mom will be called neglectful.

I ran upstairs to my room when we got home. I haven't been able to move out of bed, or do my homework. Tomorrow I have a test in English.

What if Masha and I get put into foster care? What if we never see Mom again? What if we lose our green cards?

I can't think. I can't breathe.

Eventually, I let myself close my eyes, but I can't help feeling like I am going to lose everything.

Liam

Spring, Ninth Grade, Fifteen Years Old

LAYLA AND I eat at the library every day for lunch. We don't really eat, mostly we do homework, but there's no homework to be done today, so I told Layla that it was OK for her to invite the new kid, Liam, since she thinks he has no friends.

The new kid is not that new, he's been here since January, and it's April, but I've decided to stop counting my words so much.

"How's therapy?" Layla asks, when we find a place to sit in the back. She flips her long braid over her shoulder. She says she likes her hair really long, but I feel like it would be too much to take care of. Layla and I are sitting against the windows, and Liam is cross-legged in front of a bookshelf, so we can all see each other's faces. Liam has shaggy black hair and big brown eyes. He's tall and lanky, and he has big bags under his eyes, which I think make him look mysterious.

Layla asks me this every day after a session. Normally I answer her honestly, but today we have a rando in our midst.

"It's fine," I say, looking down.

"Didn't you go yesterday?" She prods. "What did you talk about?"

I shrug, thinking how to answer without giving too much information about myself. "Deaf people."

It's been several months and neither I nor the therapist has brought up what I told him about Chris. It's like I never said it. I was going to quit therapy completely, but then I thought he for sure would report something, so I kept going as though nothing happened and now we have a good rhythm. We mostly talk about how stressed I am about school and also a lot about philosophy. I don't think he reported anything.

I'm lucky.

"Deaf people?" Layla reiterates. "What about deaf people?"

"What they dream about," I say. "Or how they dream since they can't hear."

"That's a really interesting thing to think about," Liam says. His eyes are on mine, and I feel my cheeks heat up so I look away.

Layla looks at Liam, and I can tell she's surprised he said something. Liam is normally silent in class. I was half expecting him to be quiet all of lunch. Initially I didn't like Liam because he got better grades than me, but then I started to beat him again so now I'm neutral about him.

"Yeah. I mean . . . Or blind people. What do their dreams look like?" I add.

"Vivid in a different way," Liam says. I don't know why but I suddenly feel self-conscious. I didn't brush my hair after dance class, I just threw it up in a bun, so I probably look bald. I put my hair down. I'm always prettier with my hair down.

"What's your favorite book?" Layla asks Liam when I don't keep the conversation going.

"I like *The Once and Future King*," he says, after thinking for a while. "What about y'all's?" He asks, but he's looking at me.

"Never heard of it," Layla says. "*Harry Potter*, obviously."

"Katya? What's your favorite book?" Liam reiterates.

I want to say *Twilight*, but I don't want to admit that I am that into love. I also don't want to say *Harry Potter* because I want to be mysterious, but I don't know what else to say.

"*Peter Pan*," I say, because I think it makes me sound smart since it's a classic and British.

Liam nods, thoughtfully. "What do you like about *Peter Pan*?" He asks me.

"It's whimsical," I answer, because this sounds intelligent. "And imaginative." This was a dumb answer. It's not like *Harry Potter* isn't imaginative. Or whimsical.

I look to Layla, hoping she will bring the attention back to herself.

"*Peter Pan* is weird," Layla says, resolutely. "Who likes kidnapping little kids? Why not rich adults?"

This catches Liam's attention. He and Layla start arguing about *Peter Pan*. Liam does not think *Peter Pan* is weird. I am relieved that I don't have to talk anymore. I watch Liam talk, and realize I think he's cute. I don't like thinking anyone is cute. I don't have time for that. I push the thought down, hoping it will go away.

Babushka Calling

Spring, Ninth Grade, Fifteen Years Old

THE PHONE IS ringing. I look on the caller ID and see Babushka's number. Without a second thought, I pick up.

"Privet?" I say.

"Katyusha!" Breathes the voice on the other end. My heart tears in two. My Babushka. It's been a long time since I've heard her voice.

"I'm here," I say, in Russian. I want to tell her to come, please, come. I want to tell her that Adam has convinced Mom she is bad, that our whole family is bad.

"Katyusha!" Babushka says, again. "Oh, my Katyusha."

"Katya?" I hear, behind me. It's Mom. "Who are you on the phone with?"

"I—"

"Is that your Mom? Katyusha, why hasn't she called me? Are you OK?" Babushka asks, frantically. "What is going on?"

Mom comes closer. I am frozen.

"Who is that?" Mom asks again.

Mom snatches the phone from me and looks at the caller ID. She hangs up immediately. It feels like someone has stabbed me and twisted the blade.

"I told you not to talk to her! I told you not to pick up when she calls!" Mom shouts.

"Please, Mom—"

"No!" Mom says. "No, you don't understand. She never loved me. She never loved you. She was using us. Using me. Adam is right."

"How?" I scream. "How was she using you? How does she not love you? She came to watch me and Masha every chance she could. She stayed with us. She brought you money."

Mom gets tears in her eyes. "She could have lived here, Katya! She could have stayed here with us permanently! I was struggling! She chose to leave! She chose Russia!"

"She can't even go to the doctor here—" I start, but with a hand Mom cuts me off.

"Don't pick up the phone again. Don't talk to her again," Mom says. "You will regret it if you do."

Olympiad

Spring, Ninth Grade, Fifteen Years Old

My heart is beating a million miles a minute. I don't want to go to this stupid meeting. Ms. Lynn was wrong about me. I am dumb. Everyone is going to know it.

I want to be home, writing fanfiction. Or doing homework. Or pulling teeth. Anything but be here. I take a gulp of air and push open Ms. Lynn's door because I promised her I'd go to one meeting. But after this one she'll see what I mean about me being dumb.

Ms. Lynn's room has been taken over by several boys. There's only one other girl. I recognize them as the smart kids. The AP kids. I know a lot of them are in pre-calculus, even as freshman. I'm the only one in pre-algebra.

"Katya!" Ms. Lynn yells. "I knew you'd come. I told them we weren't starting without you."

I give Ms. Lynn a small smile and go to the very back of the class. The boys and one girl all watch me take my seat. I want to cry.

"OK, who coined the theory of evolution?" Ms. Lynn asks the group, once I take my seat.

My heart sinks. I have no idea. I'm not going to know any of these questions. They are all so far ahead of me. I shouldn't be here.

I want to leave but Ms. Lynn is now blocking the door, like she knows my thoughts.

"Darwin, easy," a kid I recognize as the student with the highest GPA in our class, says. I swallow.

"Good," Ms. Lynn says. "Next question. What *primary* animal did Darwin use to help prove his theory?"

"A tortoise!" Someone I don't recognize yells.

"Wrong!" Ms. Lynn says, but she says it in a funny way, like she was making fun of the kid's enthusiasm.

"That one is easy. It's monkeys. Duh," the girl says.

"Nope! Not monkeys either. Man you guys are a bunch of dummies today," she laughs.

"Finches?" Someone says.

"Yes! Finches—correct!" Ms. Lynn shouts. She pelts someone with candy.

The class goes on like this, answering Ms. Lynn's questions. I stay silent. It's like I'm not there, which is what I want. When Ms. Lynn asks her final question and some kid answers correctly, she gets a blowhorn and starts honking it. Everyone covers their ears.

I can't help myself. I smile.

"Remember. District test is next week," she says, when we're gathering our things. "Make sure you have a ride there and back. Katya, where do you live?"

I turn to her, surprised. She must be crazy. She knows I can't take a test on evolution. I didn't answer any questions.

I don't even know why she asked me to come here.

I swallow. "Uh, I live like ten minutes away," I say. I feel my brow break in a sweat.

"Hey, I know her. She's in regular math and science. She'll bring down our average," one of the kids I don't know says. I wonder where he knows me from. "You can't let her test with us."

"Shut the hell up," Ms. Lynn snaps at him, almost immediately. "I get to decide who tests. Not you."

My face is on fire. I can't look up or I'll start crying, so I gather my things more slowly. The only thing worse than one of these smart kids calling me dumb is all of these smart kids seeing me cry.

"You're not supposed to say 'hell,'" the kid who called me out says to Ms. Lynn.

"I can say whatever I want when you're being a jerk," Ms. Lynn responds.

"Whatever," he says. The other kids laugh.

"Don't forget to wear your shirts!" Ms. Lynn adds, as everyone heads to the door. They all walk out in a group, talking animatedly about who is going to ride with who next week.

I finally feel safe enough to get up too. My things are already packed, and I rush towards the door.

"Wait!" Ms. Lynn says, before I'm even halfway there. "Don't leave. I have something for you."

I turn around but I keep my eyes on the ground.

"Look. Study these," she says, coming up to me. She hands me a huge binder. "Don't tell anyone you have them. Promise?"

I look up at her, confused. "What?"

"They're just a study guide for the tests next week. I don't want the kids thinking I'm giving you special treatment, so don't tell them I made this for you."

"You are giving me special treatment," I say. "Why?" I narrow my eyes. "And I'm not taking the test next week," I add.

She pauses. "Because you deserve to be treated like the special person you are. You are smart. Not enough people have told you that; otherwise, you wouldn't have fought me so hard about joining. You would feel like you deserved to be here, because you do. These tests? These classes? It's all part of a messed up system that you need to figure out if you want to get ahead. Being an AP kid isn't about how you test, it's about learning how to play the game. And you will. Now study this, and show up next week for the test. And don't tell anyone I'm giving you these, OK?"

I don't know what makes me agree. Maybe it's because she looks like she really believes I'm smart, but I nod and take the binder from her.

I stare at my medals in disbelief. Ms. Lynn said I have to wear them to school today. It feels wrong. But she made me promise, so I start to drape each medal around my throat like they are diamond necklaces.

There are five of them, total, for the seven tests I took. I placed in every single test in every subject except math, and then I won overall in the district.

I put the district medal on last, staring at myself in the mirror.

I won because Ms. Lynn helped me cheat, and I didn't even realize we were cheating. The study guide she gave me was just a copy of the tests we took, all the correct answers circled. After I won, my mouth open in shock, she pulled me to the side and asked for the study guide back, making me promise not to tell anyone about using it.

I promised her.

"I feel bad," I told her. "I'm a fraud."

"No, you're not. These kids grew up with so many resources you didn't have. So what if you get some help too?"

I looked down at the medals in my hands. So many of them.

"You're going to win this game," she whispered to me, before we walked back to the rest of our group together.

"Guess it was a good thing Katya came with us, huh, AJ?" Ms. Lynn said to the boy who told her I would bring down their scores.

It felt good to see his face drop and for him to look at me with jealousy in his eyes.

I feel different this morning as I go downstairs, better, for some reason, even if we did lie.

Mom made breakfast for me. She's never done that. She made me fruits and yogurt.

"For my winner!" She says, kissing me on the forehead. "I always knew you were smart. Always."

I smile at her and eat my yogurt until it's time to go. In the car she tells me stories of when she knew I was a genius as a child. The time I fixed the. TV. The other time I stole a kid's toy in the sandbox. She said this made me an entrepreneur, which was an early sign.

It's the last week of summer. At the beginning of the year, I would have loved this. But now, when I think about not going to school for several months, my heart sinks. I don't want this year to be over, not yet. I don't want to say bye to Ms. Lynn or Layla. Or Liam.

I get to school, my medals clanging against my chest. I feel proud to wear them even if I didn't earn them. Ms. Lynn is beaming when I walk into her class. The morning announcements are in second period, and she screams when she hears the principal announce my wins.

"That's my girl!" She shouts. I blush and look down.

At the end of class, she grabs me into a tight hug. "You can do anything. Always," she says.

Today is the best day ever. The kids who treat me like I'm dumb look at me in shock, like I have a superpower. I like feeling smart. Ms. Lynn is right. I feel like I have a seat at the table.

The nagging truth of the lie sits in the back of my mind, calling me a fraud, but Ms. Lynn's words echo over it. I deserve help too.

"Hey, congrats," Liam smiles at me, when I get to English.

I have been putting mascara on in the mornings ever since I decided he was cute. It never stays on though. Today I don't even feel bad about my appearance. It's like the medals take away all my insecurity.

"Thanks," I say, putting my books down.

He sits across from me.

"What are you doing this summer?" I ask, in an uncharacteristic start to conversation. Normally he starts it.

He looks away, suddenly.

"I'm moving. To Oregon."

I feel my face fall.

"Oh," I say. I want to put my hand to my heart, but I don't. I don't want to show him that I'm sad he's leaving. I barely know him. It's dumb to be sad.

"My dad got a new job," he explains.

I nod. I don't want to spend any more time getting to know him. I don't want to use my words on him. I stopped counting my words, but maybe I should start again.

"I wish I could stay," he says.

I mess with my papers, pretending I don't hear him.

Layla comes in. "How big is her head?" She asks, sitting down next to me. "Huge, right?"

I nudge her, grateful for the distraction. I won't be sad about this random kid I don't know and will never see again.

People leave. It's a part of life. I should be grateful freshman year is over. Three years left. Then I can leave, finally.

Smart Kid

Fall, Tenth Grade, Fifteen Years Old

"I THINK BELLA SWAN is an idiot," I say in English class to my friend Jen. We're supposed to be working on our essays but we're talking instead. We're a few months into sophomore year. Thanks to winning the Olympiad competition last year, I am known as the smart kid. I am in all the same classes as the kids in the Olympiad were in, except math, but I upgraded to honors math, which is not a class I thought I was qualified for. I have an A in it now.

"Why do you think that?" Jen asks. I have a lot of friends this year. I don't know how, but Olympiad made people take me seriously and like me more. I have stopped counting my letters, and I still make good grades.

"She is in a horrible relationship with Edward. He controls everything she does. She's not allowed to do anything without his permission. It's weird. It's like Stephanie Meyer is telling the reader that it's wrong for women to think."

Jen nods, like she's considering what I'm saying. "Yeah, that makes sense." Last year I would have never argued this, I would have never even thought of debating, but now I argue all the time. I like myself more this year.

The bell for lunch rings, and Jen and I walk to the cafeteria, except she goes to eat and I go to the library because it's the only time Layla and I can see each other since we don't have any classes together this year.

"Hey," I say to Layla, setting my books down.

"Hey," she answers, glumly.

"What's wrong?" I ask. I pull out a granola bar and quietly unwrap it so the librarian doesn't see. We're not supposed to eat in here. She knows we do, but she says we just can't do it in front of her.

"Driver's ed," Layla says. "It's kicking my ass. My dad won't fucking drive with me without yelling. Today is the test, and I am afraid of failing."

My stomach sinks. Everyone is taking driver's ed this year. I tried to sign up for driver's ed with just my Russian passport and green card but they won't let me sign up for it unless I have a social security card because I'm under eighteen.

I don't know when we'll get our citizenships. Mom says soon, but it's always been soon. I should be thankful that I'm legal, I know, but it's hard to watch everyone get their permits and licenses when I know I won't have one.

"At least you're in driver's ed," I say to Layla, because I have nothing better to say. I am jealous.

"You'll get there soon," she says. It's not very comforting. I hope I get a social security number before applying for college or else I don't know if I'll get financial aid.

"Hey, guess who added me on Facebook?" She says, changing the subject.

"Who?" I ask.

"Liam."

My head shoots up. "Like from last year? Liam who moved to Oregon?"

She nods. "He asked about you. You should really get Facebook."

I shake my head. "I don't have any room in my life for distractions."

She nudges me. "So, he's a distraction?"

I roll my eyes. "Whatever."

"He said he missed us," Layla adds.

My heart picks up the pace. I've thought about Liam a lot since he moved.

"Well, he's the only one," I lie.

She punches my arm playfully. I pull out my homework. "Shouldn't you study for your driver's test?" I ask.

When school lets out, instead of doing my homework, I make a Facebook page.

I'm at home, researching my biological father on Mom's laptop. When she's not studying for college I'm allowed to use it. Mom is almost done with her master's program, so she's almost done studying in general, which means I can have her computer a lot more. This is good because my phone is no longer safe, so I can use email instead. Adam has started to read my text messages. I'm not allowed to have my phone upstairs with me. There is no reason for this, just something he told Mom was necessary. Mom doesn't think this is an issue that is worth arguing, although she does argue other things with him that don't seem as important, like what she's allowed to wear when she goes to class.

I pull up a picture I found of my dad online. It's a business page. His business. He owns it. I study his face and try to see myself in him.

"Katya?" Mom says, walking into my room.

"What?" I ask, annoyed that she didn't knock, even though she's never knocked.

"What are you doing?" She says. I can hear the frown in her tone. She has probably spotted the photo I'm staring at, but I don't care.

"I'm researching my dad," I say.

She comes in my room and closes the door.

"Why?" She asks. Her voice gets cold.

"Because he's my dad? I want to know more about him? Am I not allowed to be curious?"

Mom comes over to me and sits next to me. She leans into me. She never sits with me at night, and I like that she's here, even if she's being annoying.

"You know, his sister called me a few years ago. I didn't want to tell you but she said that he was trying to kill her."

"What?" I ask, in shock. I turn towards her. "What do you mean? How? Why didn't you tell me?"

She shrugs. "I didn't want to upset you. She died a little later." The accusation hangs thick in the air.

"But why would he do that?" I ask.

She shrugs, again. "I don't know. He's evil. I got us away from him for a reason."

"I thought we left because of the mafia."

"That too. And him. I was trying to protect you from him. He's not a good guy. He didn't even want you."

"Why would he kill his sister, and how would she know? Why did she call you?"

"Me and her were friends," Mom says sadly. "She called me sometimes and asked about you. I told her. You know."

"You gave her your phone number?"

"She was my friend," Mom says sharply. "Of course I did."

"But if her brother was dangerous—"

"You asking me too many questions," Mom snaps. "And give me my computer back. You said you was studying."

I close the tabs and hand the computer over. Mom takes it and leaves the room without saying anything.

My body feels frozen at the idea of my dad killing his own sister. I want to call Layla and tell her, but I don't want to pass Adam's office to get my phone from downstairs. I pull my notebook out and write.

Who am I? Who am I made of?

Citizenship

Spring, Tenth Grade, Sixteen Years Old

We got approved for our citizenships a few months ago. I didn't let myself believe it at first, especially because Adam couldn't adopt me, but today Mom is going to the swearing in ceremony without me since I have to be in school. She will promise both of us to this country since I'm under eighteen.

The last interview we had, where I was asked if I had a criminal record, I signed a document that said I didn't. I gave my thumb prints. Mom showed my report cards.

I'm in my homeroom, brainstorming for fundraising for our class, but I can't focus. I count down the minutes. Am I American yet?

I haven't counted my words or my letters for a while, but occasionally I'll run my hand through my hair when I'm nervous, looking for ghost lice.

Will we be safe now that Mom has pledged our loyalty? Will we be protected, like Mom has always dreamed? Will the courts listen to our words and not focus on Mom's accent? Will we be treated like we deserve to be here?

The bus takes me home after school. My heart beats a million miles a minute because I'm scared something went wrong. I sent Mom a text asking if she took the oath but she never responded.

"We're Americans!" Mom says, when I walk through the front door. She approaches me and hugs me, giving me a kiss on the forehead. "Finally. Thirteen years ago we came to this country, and now we truly belong here." Mom still has her makeup on from this morning, and I can tell she cried a lot today because of the smears of black under her eyes. The air around Mom isn't so heavy. She's walking a little taller, like she feels supported.

Mom leads me to the kitchen where there is BBQ food in take-out containers. Mom, of course, doesn't eat any. I guess being an American hasn't changed her that much yet.

"We belong to the best place in the world. We have freedom, here, Katya," she says, loading me a plate. Grilled chicken. Vegetables. No ribs or BBQ sauce. Freedom doesn't apply to food, I guess.

I take the plate from her and we sit down together at the dining table. Adam comes in too. Masha's school lets out a few hours after mine so she won't be home for a while.

"You know, your mom didn't have to get you a citizenship," Adam says, biting into a rack of ribs and looking at me. My body automatically tenses when his eyes are on me. I feel like he's searching for my weak spot. "The reason it took so long is because she wanted to make sure you were documented too. She could have just waited for you to be eighteen and have you apply for yourself. You should be thankful to her." Adam takes a large chunk of flesh off a bone. There is BBQ sauce on his lips as he smacks loudly.

"Thank you, Mom," I say, because I know this is a happy day for her. I want to go upstairs. I don't want to be down here. This day feels bad with Adam here, watching us.

"I couldn't have done it without you, sweetie," Mom says to Adam. She kisses his BBQ covered lips. "Thank you for applying for us. Thank you for all that you've done. I found the best man in the world." She is beaming at him.

I feel nauseous looking at her earnest, thankful face. I don't want to be part of their America. I don't want to be part of a place where women have to be abused to get a citizenship, or a place where people who don't have documents aren't believed in court.

I am in the car with my friend Maritzia. It's summertime. Mom left me cash, and we're going to Walmart since it's the place with the best A/C, and Houston has consistently been over a hundred degrees every day since the beginning of June.

Mom and Adam are in Italy, and it is nice not to have them home. I can do what I want, and not feel like I'm being monitored. I can have my phone in my room. I can stay up on Mom's computer all night. I can go over to other people's houses and invite them to mine. I mostly invite other people over since I still can't drive.

Mom, Adam, Masha, and I are going to Ukraine in a few weeks, where my Dedushka lives. Mom says she feels safe to go to Ukraine since we have our American passports. Mom has recently started talking to Dedushka again, after not talking to him for a long time after he and Babushka divorced when I was eight. Dedushka has married someone new. I am afraid of how Adam will influence this relationship too, but Mom only talks about how much Dedushka says he loves Adam.

"Hey, we're here," Maritzia says. I look up from my phone, where I have been texting a boy I like. Maritzia's hair is always in a messy bun. She's as tall as me, but much skinnier. She also wears a lot of eye liner, so most of the time she looks like she can compete in *America's Next Top Model*.

"Thank God," I say and open the door to her car. The sweltering humidity suffocates my throat. We hurry inside to where the ice cold Walmart air is a balm to our boiling skin. Maritzia and I go to the fishing section and find a quiet aisle to sprawl in.

"When are you getting your car? I'm tired of driving your lazy ass around," Maritzia says, smiling.

I groan. "I just got my permit. Also, I just found out you have to wait six months after you get your permit to drive without a real adult in the car with you."

"Loooser," Maritzia says, making an "L" with her thumb and forefinger and holding it up to her forehead.

I roll my eyes.

Maritzia and I have known each other since middle school, but we recently got close because we were in the same Home Economics class and sat together. Also, Layla is in Syria the whole summer and normally I spend my days on the phone with her but Syria has bad internet.

"Do you want to get drunk?" Maritzia asks, after a bout of silence. I like Maritzia because we can be quiet together.

I look up from my phone. The boy I like replied, and I'm trying to decipher, "nothin much, you?" Does that mean he likes me too?

"How?" I ask.

"How? Are you dumb? With alcohol," she says, laughing.

"No, I mean, how are we going to get alcohol?"

"My parents have some tequila. We can get junk food here and get drunk off tequila at your house."

I consider this. I haven't been drunk before. Not really. I've had alcohol, sure, but not in a *bad* way. I'm not a rule breaker, but I am American and not undocumented. It's not life or death if someone catches us. Not anymore. Plus, I like Maritzia. I want to bond more. I want to do dumb high school stuff.

"Sure," I say, standing up. I give her my hand so she can pull herself off the ground. We buy a bunch of chips and ranch dip and Fruit Roll-Ups, and she drives us to her house where she puts a bottle of tequila under her shirt and kisses her Mom "hi." Then we go back to my house.

Maritzia pours us each a shot and then tells me to bite into a lime after I've downed the liquid. I do as she says and immediately feel nauseous after my first shot.

"Is that normal, to feel sick immediately?" I ask.

She frowns at me. "It's cause you're white. Aren't you from Russia? Isn't Russia part of Asia or something? Can y'all have alcohol without it fucking you up?"

I think about how Mom drinks, how flushed her face always gets.

"I don't know. I think that's just a stereotype," I mumble. I sit down and put my head in my hands to stop it from spinning.

I hear Maritzia put her glass down.

"Did you take another shot?" I groan.

Something cold taps my arm, and I see that she's brought me ice water. I drink it gratefully. "You might be allergic to tequila, bro," she says, smirking. "If this is you after just one shot. I've already had three, and I'm fine."

Maritzia comes to sit down next to me. I lean on her shoulder.

"You can't drive after this, OK?" I say. "You have to stay here."

I realize we didn't discuss whether she'd sleep over.

"Duh, I'm not stupid," she responds. "I was always planning on staying the night. You're closer to my job anyway." Maritzia works at a fast food restaurant with her cousin.

I nod. "Let's get up. Maybe get food," I groan.

She helps me up, and I go to the fridge. Nothing looks good. Everything makes me feel dizzy but I should probably get something to soak up the alcohol, so I take out a container of ice cream. I put it down on the table with two spoons.

"I'm not sure ice cream is the best thing if you're nauseous. . . ." Maritzia says, taking a spoon and shoving a bite in her mouth.

I shrug. "Nothing else feels like it will go down."

Maritzia picks up my permit, which is always on the kitchen table, under my house keys.

"This is a permit, huh?" She says. I can hear the slur in her voice. "They changed the design." I know I'm not drunk, I just feel nauseous. But Maritzia might be.

"Yeah?" I say, but I make it sound like a question. "Do you not know what a permit looks like?"

Maritzia shakes her head. "Never got one. Still don't have my license."

"What?!" I shout. "You've been driving us around!"

"Shhh," she says, putting a finger to her lips. "You're so loud."

"How have you been driving us without a license? Don't you need one for insurance?"

"Nope. Just can't get caught," she says, taking another spoonful of mint ice cream.

"Why don't you have a license?" I ask her, cocking my head.

She's quiet. She doesn't look drunk. She looks like she's thinking about something serious. Suddenly it hits me. I wonder if Maritzia is undocumented.

"I just got my citizenship," I offer, because she looks like she feels like she said too much. "We didn't have papers for our whole time here. That's why I'm getting my permit later than everyone else."

Maritzia's shoulders go down, slightly. She nods.

"Yeah, we don't have papers. And I have to pick my little brothers up from school and go to work. They're in sports. That's why my parents let me drive. I know English the best so I won't be as in as much trouble as them if I get pulled over. At least that's what we're hoping. I don't know, though."

Mom drove without a license for a long time. I remember how scared she was every time we got in the car.

"It took us a long time for me to get my green card. Nine years," I say, another offering. I hope Maritzia feels safe enough to open up. I know how lonely it feels not to be able to talk to anyone about feeling like an outsider.

"We've been here since I was one, and we haven't had papers that whole time. We've gone to so many lawyers but somehow our documents always get lost in the application process, or the lawyers are busy, or I don't know," she says. She puts her spoon down. "They reject us when they've met their quota, but they always meet their quota."

"Don't pick me up anymore," I say. "I don't want you to risk it. It's not worth it."

She nods. "I know. I should only drive when I have to. That's what my mom says too. But I want to leave the house for myself too! I do everything for them."

Maritzia looks like she has something else to say but she sighs and gets up, taking the ice cream to the freezer.

She's a year older than me so she'll be a senior this year. I wonder how she'll apply to college. I wonder if my mom can help her, since she applied to college as an undocumented person. I wonder if I should ask.

Maritzia is rinsing our spoons. I remember too, when we got our citizenships, Mom agreed with Adam. He said we're the type of people who deserve to be here. What makes Maritzia not deserve to get her documents, then? What is the difference between us?

Kerch

Summer Before Junior Year, Sixteen Years Old

I NEVER WANT TO go back to America. How did Mom want to leave here? Ukraine is my favorite place in the whole world. Dedushka's house is on the coast, looking over the ocean. He has a rich garden, full of the best tomatoes and apricots I've ever tasted. Mom says we lived here when I was a baby, before we came to America. I grew up missing this place, but not fitting the puzzle pieces together until visiting now. I didn't realize how empty I was until being home. My soul has found its body here.

There's no plumbing, the electricity goes out all the time, there's no internet, and the TV barely works, but I don't want to be anywhere else in the world.

Masha's and my room smells like pepper and peaches. Every night I sit by the window and write about my future life. I will live here one day and write novels about mermaids who travel the world. I plan how I will travel everywhere, how I'll never get married, how Masha and I will make a life together. I write about surprising Babushka in Russia. I write about all the things I will do once I am an adult and have escaped from my mom and Adam.

We have been in Kerch for three weeks. Today is the start of our last week here. I am plotting how to stay. I beg Mom not to come back to America. She tells me I am ungrateful. Adam says Mom should have left me to rot without a citizenship since I don't know how lucky I am.

Dedushka comes outside while I'm writing and gives me a cup of hot tea, even though there is sweat on both of our brows.

"How's the most beautiful granddaughter in the world?" he asks. He's a little blind, so I don't think he can see that I'm crying.

"I don't want to leave here, Dedushka," I say to him in Russian. My mother tongue has completely come back to me. "I want to stay with you."

"I know, Katyusha. We didn't want you to go. Your grandmother and I. We aren't together anymore, but that was something we did agree on. Your mom should have left you with us."

I want to lean into him and cry but I don't. We sit together in silence, sharing a cup of cherry tea.

"I'll be right back, Dedushka," I say, and leave my journal on the table. I have to use the bathroom and it's a whole ordeal since there's no plumbing. We have to use a bucket to flush.

When I come back, Adam has taken my spot next to Dedushka. He has my journal open on his lap. Dedushka doesn't speak English, but he looks alarmed.

"Katya, you left your journal here, and I went to go get us cookies and I come back and he is reading it like it is his. I told him to put it down but he acts like he doesn't understand what I am saying," Dedushka says, pointing at him.

Adam's legs are crossed, and he's flipping through my journal like he's reading a book. My insides twist and grunt.

"Hey," I say to Adam. "That's mine."

Adam looks up, like he knew I was there. He slams my book down on the table. "Ungrateful bitch," he says, and walks back to the house.

"What did he say?" Dedushka asks, shaking his head. "Why is he reading a young girl's journal? So strange."

"He's mad," I say. "He probably read about how I don't like him."

"Ah," Dedushka says, nodding. "You're not wrong."

I sit next to Dedushka again, and we eat our cookies quietly.

Mom comes out of the house a few minutes later, Adam on her tail.

"She's writes whatever bullshit she wants," Mom says, turning around to Adam. "Stop yelling at me. I can't control her."

Adam doesn't look at me as he follows Mom to the kitchen, which is on the other side of the courtyard, away from where we sleep. The kitchen is underground because there's no refrigerator, and it's the only way to keep food cool.

I can't make out what they're saying, but they're shouting, loud. Loud enough for the neighbors to stop and peer over Dedushka's fence.

"God, what are they yelling about?" Dedushka asks. "They are causing a scene. We live in a quiet neighborhood. They are disturbing everyone."

"They are fighting about my journal," I say.

"Still? Did you put the secret to life in there? You are so young. Who cares?" Dedushka gets up and goes to where Mom and Adam are still yelling in the kitchen. He pokes his head through the door.

"You are disturbing the neighborhood," Dedushka yells. "Stop fighting like children. Adults do not fight like this! Grow up!"

Adam storms out, pushing Dedushka out of the way so that he has to hold on to the door to keep from falling over. Dedushka looks at Adam like he has gone crazy.

"Fuck you!" Adam yells, pointing to me. His eyes are shiny with hate. "I've done everything for you. The stuff you say about me in your journal is sick! You should be kissing my ass!"

Adam runs across the courtyard and tries to open the gate. He can't figure it out so he starts climbing over the fence. Dedushka comes by me and watches him.

"If he wants to leave, he just has to ask," Dedushka says, frowning. "He's going to break my fence trying to climb over it."

Mom stands next to Dedushka. "Just leave him," she says, waving her hand. "Maybe he'll get kidnapped."

Mom, Dedushka, and I sit and have another cup of tea from the samovar as we watch Adam struggle to get over the fence. Finally, he is successful. His face is red and sweaty, like he just ran a marathon. A gaggle of neighbors has circled around, watching the spectacle.

"Fuck all of you!" Adam says, walking away from the property. He's crying, I can tell, because his face is bent.

"This man is in his fifties, and he is throwing the same kind of tantrums that two-year-olds throw," Dedushka observes. Adam gets to the end of the street and turns around, probably to see if anyone is coming for him.

No one makes any moves to go to him.

"He is like a child, Yuliya," Dedushka says.

"I know," Mom says, finishing her tea. "But he's all we have right now."

She sighs, straightens up her shorts, and goes to open the gate.

My heart sinks. Why does Mom think Adam is all we have when we have all this?

Honesty

Winter 2022, Late Twenties

My father is irritating me. After coming home from Greece, something clicked. I realize I am not afraid of losing him, like I was afraid of losing my mom. I don't think he'll leave me. I don't feel the need to please him. I am honest with him in a way I've never been honest with anyone before, which has resulted in me also being impulsive with my feelings. I tell him when I don't like something. I tell him when I find him annoying. He feels safe, in a way that older men have never felt safe before.

We're on a call, talking about Masha, about how I don't like that she relies on Chris to pay for college. "I met Chris," my father tells me. It's January. We're on the phone. We talk on the phone every day, especially after Greece. "When I was in Houston. He was picking up Masha for her visitation. He didn't seem that bad." I have to remember that my father still doesn't know a lot about how I grew up.

"He's not a good guy," I tell my dad.

"Are you just saying that because your Mom told you bad things about him?" My father asks me. "You have to remember what your Mom said about me as well. They were lies."

I feel red hot anger rising in my throat. "No," I say. I can hear the spike in my voice. "I have my own experiences with her dad. They aren't good. I don't like when you defend him."

"What were your experiences?" my father asks me. His face is curious but defensive on the screen, and I don't want to deal with him anymore.

"He. . . ." It's on the tip of my tongue. "I have to go," I say. "Sorry." I hang up.

I know that if I tell my father what Chris did to me, and he tells me it was my fault, I won't be able to talk to him again. It would hurt too much. I don't want to risk it. I feel tears burn my eyes.

Liam walks into the kitchen, a mug in his hand.

"What's the matter?" He asks me, putting his hand on the small of my back. "You look like you're going to cry."

Liam leads me to the table where we eat and sits me down. "Katya, what's wrong?"

I hesitate. I don't like talking about it. But if I hear my father defend Chris one more time, I don't know how I can continue having a relationship with him. "I almost told my dad—I almost told him what Chris did to me."

Liam rubs my back.

"What stopped you?" he asks, so quietly I can barely hear him.

"I can't—if he doesn't believe me—I don't think I would keep talking to him," I say.

Liam nods.

"I just—I can't have another adult not believe me," I say, looking up, hoping the tears stop. I hate crying. "I can't have *him* not believe me. That would just, it would ruin everything."

"What are you remembering?" Liam asks me. "Is it your mom or the district attorney?"

I pause, releasing the breath I was holding.

"The district attorney," I say quietly. Liam scoots his chair closer to me, so that he can better wrap me in his arms. "I'm so sorry," he says. "That was a horrible time."

I start to remember details of the thing that I've buried for years.

When I was a sophomore in college, Chris tried to take full custody of my sister again. Imagining her living with him as a teenager by herself ignited a fire in me. As a nineteen-year-old, I went to the police and reported to them what he had done to me as a child. A few months later the district attorney dismissed my claims because the only evidence was my word. I remember crying into Liam's shoulder when I found out. He and Layla had missed their classes so they could come with me to court that day.

"How are they supposed to get evidence ten years later?" Layla had asked my mom's lawyer. "How is a fourth grader who was told something terrible would happen to her family if she spoke up supposed to know she needed a rape kit?"

My mom's lawyer had shrugged. "This happens a lot," he said.

Going to the police about what had happened to me was the hardest thing I ever had to do. The worst thing that ever happened to me was not being believed afterwards.

"I think—I think if you don't tell your dad about Chris, about everything, it will make it hard to have a relationship with him," Liam says.

"I don't trust him," I respond, wiping my eyes.

"You should give him a chance," Liam encourages. "What if he does believe you?"

I haven't even let myself think that my father believing me was a possibility. My heart starts to flood with an unfamiliar softness. I push the thought away. I can't let myself think of that.

"I don't think you'll be able to have the relationship with your father that you want unless you tell him everything," Liam says.

"I can't risk our relationship," I say.

"You already are by not being honest," Liam answers.

Drunk

Fall, Eleventh Grade, Sixteen Years Old

Coming back from Ukraine is painful in a searing way. I want to stay there forever. I have never felt more like myself than swimming in the water of the Black Sea and drinking my Dedushka's cherry tea from his samovar that is over a hundred years old. I belong there, and I will make it back one day.

"Mom, I need to talk to you about something important," I tell my mother. We are shopping for clothes at Gap. It's November of my junior year. I never get time alone with my mom, but Adam is on a business trip, and this is my chance to tell her something that's been sitting heavy on my mind since we got back from Kerch this summer.

Mom sighs. "This is why I don't like spending time with you," she says. "You always trap me when we're alone."

Her words are biting.

"I think Adam is turning you into an alcoholic," I tell my mom, ignoring her words to me. "Every time he's with you, he makes you drink a bottle of wine. He just keeps filling your cup, and you keep drinking it," I press.

I look at her while she is looking at the racks of clothes. We're shopping for Masha, in the back, where the sale section is.

Mom rolls her eyes. "You don't know anything about alcoholics, Katya. He is not turning me into an alcoholic."

"Yes he is!" I say. I feel this passionately, with my whole body. "He pours and pours you more glasses, even when your eyes are rolling in the back of your head. I think I figured him out, Mom. I think he is doing it because you graduated with your degree, and we have our citizenships. He needs you to be dependent on him. It's all mind games with him," I say, pointing to my head.

Something twitches in Mom's jaw. She's annoyed. She's not going to listen. I know in my heart that what I am saying is true. Adam takes videos of Mom drunk. He smiles at me as he pours her more, like he knows I know what he's doing. He plays psychological games with her, and she thinks he's better than Chris because he doesn't cheat on her.

"Mom, please, listen to me. You have to stop drinking. He's doing this to you on purpose. He takes videos of you with his camera. He wants to have evidence against you. He needs you to need him. That's been his trick this whole time."

"I am not going to take you anywhere with me anymore if you just accuse me of being an alcoholic!" Mom shouts, turning to me. Her eyes are glaring and bright.

I step back. She really doesn't believe me.

"An alcoholic can't control themselves. They drink every kind of drink in the house. I don't drink the gin we have, Katya. I don't drink the bourbon. I am not a fucking alcoholic. You are the psycho."

Maybe I sound crazy. Maybe Mom knows what she's doing. Maybe I really don't know what I'm talking about. She's right. Don't alcoholics drink every ounce of everything in the house? Mom only drinks wine.

She just drinks so much of it.

Mail-Order Bride

Spring, Eleventh Grade, Seventeen Years Old

I'M SUPPOSED TO be cleaning the garage, there are still tons of boxes that need to be moved to the curb, but I can't bring myself to do anything but call my friend, Jen. I'm not sure if I'm calling Jen because I want to make fun of the fact that I found my mom's mail-order bride magazine or that I'm calling her to cry.

I remember going home to my mom after career day in first grade and asking her what she did for a job. She told me she was a model. She showed me the same magazine I have in my hands now. I didn't know how to read, so I assumed she was holding the Russian equivalent of *Vogue.* My mom had always told me she modeled and waitressed in Russia. She had a degree, but she could make more money with her appearance than her brains.

"I think my mom is a mail-order bride," I blurt to Jen, who has just picked up the phone. I'm looking at my mom's ad, because that's what this picture of her is. An ad. She was selling herself.

"I wonder why she would tell you she was a model," Jen asks, after I explain how I found the magazine.

I shrug, my back against a wall in my bedroom. "It's so weird. I remember her going to her closet and pulling out this magazine from behind her shoes. She was, like, proud of it."

"What does her ad look like?" Jen asks.

"It's small," I say. She's posed suggestively over a barstool, her boobs peeking through her shirt. "Kind of same as how she dresses now. She's bent over."

"I'll have to come over and see it," Jen responds.

"I remember being so impressed and telling everyone my mom modeled for Coke," I tell her. "She had this whole shoebox full of glamour shots and I just . . . I. thought they were for clothes."

"Your mom does tend to embellish things," Jen muses. Jen has been over a lot. She knows my mom well.

"I remember Mom, like, egging the story on. She talked about how famous she was, she described the photoshoots, how she dyed her hair red for the "Coke" brand."

"What did your mom's ad say?" Jen asks.

"That she is looking for a family and eternal love."

This makes Jen laugh. I laugh too because we know Mom would never say these things now.

"Did she know any English before she came over?" Jen asks.

"No," I scoff. "She must have had someone write it for her."

"What do the other ads say? Like, the other women?"

I flip to a different page and start reading the descriptions out loud to her.

"Natasha loves to cook and wants nothing more than to be a pleasant wife to her husband."

"Interesting," Jen comments, after the first one. I continue.

"Vera is looking for a deep commitment and relationship for life."

"Ksyenia loves children and keeping a clean house. . . ."

"There are *so many* women in this catalog," I continue. "All around twenty years old, some with kids, some without, some that had red hair, brown hair, blonde hair. I feel like I'm flipping through one of those Sky Mall magazines, except instead of reading descriptions for luxury items for sale, it is full of outlandishly beautiful Eastern European women. Is *this* how we got out of Russia? Did Joe *buy* Mom?"

"Who is Joe again?" Jen asks, and I forget that there are details of my life that I haven't told her because I haven't thought of them in so long. But I remember Joe. I remember him so clearly.

"He's the guy who helped us cross the border," I tell Jen. Suddenly I feel embarrassment.

It hits me—again.

My mom is a *mail-order fucking bride.*

I think about all the weird details of my life. Details I knew weren't normal for other kids, but were normal for me. My stepdad is so much older than her. We have a huge house. I remember how she had a salary requirement when she was searching for a husband.

I scoff.

I think about Jen's mom, who is a lawyer. Maritzia's mom cleans houses, Layla's mom raised Layla and her siblings.

All my friends have issues with their parents, but they have mothers they can *respect.*

A chilling feeling emerges in my gut.

I have to be better than my mom. If I'm not better than her, I will end up like her.

Dependent on a man.

I can't have that life.

"I have to go," I tell Jen. "I'll call you later." My throat feels hot. I feel tears spring to my eyes as I stand up. I am going to put the magazine back. I never want to see it again.

I head downstairs from my room and toward the garage. My hand is on the doorknob when I hear Mom's bedroom door open.

"Katyusha," she says. I look around me and realize I don't have anywhere to hide the magazine. "Are you done cleaning the garage?"

She comes closer to me and her eyes brighten when she notices what is in my hands.

"Where did you find this?" Mom asks, a crease in her forehead, her tone sharp.

I thought I was sad, but when she asks me this, I realize I am so angry I could explode.

"In the garage, when I was cleaning."

"I don't appreciate you going through my stuff," she says, back.

"You told me you were a model for Coke," I say, "I didn't know you were actually a *mail-order bride*."

"A *what*?" she asks, like she is confused.

I point to the magazine. "Mail-order bride. That's what we call women who *sell* themselves." Mom is usually the mean one. Now it's my turn.

Mom sighs, closing her eyes. I can't read what she is thinking. I can hardly ever read what she was thinking.

Finally, she says, "Everyone I know was doing it."

I don't respond.

She adds, gently, "It's how we got out."

Mom is wearing a mini skirt and a tight, hot pink, spaghetti-strapped shirt. When I was little, I remember asking her to wear pants and regular-sleeved shirts like my friend Dream's mom. I always wanted my mom to be the same, and this just proves how different she is. I hate it.

Mom comes closer to me, her face red. I don't know if she is angry or if she is ashamed.

"You could have had a more respectable occupation," I say. I stand up taller; I feel better than her. More powerful.

"A *what*?"

"A job. You could have had a regular *job*. Come here on a worker visa or something."

I am more American than she is. I'm not as *low* as she is. I speak in words she doesn't understand.

"I—You don't understand how it was back then. Besides, I didn't marry anyone until later."

"Who was Joe?" I ask.

Our story is clicking into place for me, and I hate it.

"He helped us cross the border. It was different with him."

"Did you promise him sex to do it?" I spit the words, aiming them at her.

She looks away. "It's none of your business," she responds.

I bite down on my teeth. I want to call her a prostitute. I want to keep pummeling her. I want my words to *hurt*.

"Why did you tell me you were a model?" I seethed. "Why didn't you tell me the truth?"

"What else did I have?" She shouts, her eyes watery. For a Moment I think she is going to slap me. "You came back from school and talked about how everyone had a job for this fucking job fair. What did you want me to say? I show you the magazine. I—I had nothing else."

I feel deflated. I want a normal mom. A mom who respects herself. An American mom, who wouldn't be caught dead in a catalog, waiting to be bought.

I want her to be more than a mail-order bride. I want her to stand up for herself, to stand up for me, to not have had to sacrifice everything, including her own daughter.

I want her to be strong. I want to be proud of her. I want her to use her fucking voice instead of this chopped accent that she has, this accent that people label as whorish because she is Eastern European.

I slam the magazine down, leaving it for her.

"You sold me too!" I yell, walking away.

Shrimp Tacos

Spring, Eleventh Grade, Seventeen Years Old

I'm with Jen and her family. It's Friday. We're having dinner at her parent's favorite Mexican café. I love that about Jen's parents. They have traditions. They are stable. Jen's mom, Andrea, stabs her fork into her taco salad. She has just finished telling us about work. She's worked for the same company for twenty years. She has a law degree. She's the breadwinner, Jen's father making much less money than she does.

"So Katya, where do you want to go to college?" Andrea asks me. Her hair is a sandy blonde and in a ballerina bun. I wonder if she's ever done dance. She isn't wearing a lot of makeup, maybe just mascara. She has wrinkles, and I like that she doesn't try to cover them with makeup.

"Anywhere that will give me a scholarship," I respond, almost immediately, lifting a shrimp taco to my mouth. I take a bite, watching Andrea's face. She frowns, like she doesn't understand something I've said. Andrea has seen how big my house is when she's picked Jen up. She knows that my stepdad has a lot of money.

"Do you need a lot of aid?" Andrea asks.

"Yes," I say. "I don't want to rely on my stepdad for anything."

Andrea nods, like she understands now. Maybe Jen has updated her on how much I hate my stepdad and the whole mail-order-bride-mom situation, I don't know.

"Are you going to stay in Texas?" Jen's dad asks me. I don't know his name, so I just call him Mr. Sky, Jen's last name. He is bald and very skinny. He doesn't look or talk like someone I would say is particularly warm, but he feels like he would be protective.

I shake my head no. "I'm going to go to the furthest place that offers me the most money," I say.

My phone vibrates in my pocket. I take it out and flip it open.

What are you having for dinner?

It's Mom. I told her I was going out with Jen and her family tonight.

I close my phone. Before I left for Jen's, my mom told me to order the most expensive thing on the menu. I hate when she does that, especially in the context of her being bought.

"Scholarships are so hard to get," Jen's mom comments. "Especially out of state."

I take another bite of taco, not wanting to go into why I'm desperate to leave and never come back. I am going to start a new, shiny life, so far away from my mom and our history together that people won't even know I wasn't born in America. I don't have an accent. My name gives me away, but I can just ask people to call me "Kat."

"Won't you miss your mom?" Andrea asks, smiling at Jen. Jen rolls her eyes at her mom. Her hair is in a matching ballerina bun like her mom's, though I don't think Jen notices that. Jem has some of the prettiest eyes I've ever seen. They're brown and feel like you're looking into a forest.

I think about how involved Andrea has been in Jen's college applications. I wish I could ask my mom to edit my essays or to just read them in general, to tell me if they're any good. She says I am the best writer but doesn't read my writing.

I wish my mom was as old as Jen's mom so people wouldn't assume I was a teenage pregnancy. I love that Jen's mom doesn't wear shirts that emphasize her boobs. I love that she's been married for over two decades.

I want Jen's life.

"Yes," I say to Andrea. "I will. But I need to leave her so I can know how to be on my own."

Andrea raises her eyebrows. "That's so mature of you," she says.

I smile at her, not knowing how to respond. I don't feel mature. I just want to run away.

Jen changes the subject.

I focus on the shrimp in my tacos. I didn't want shrimp tacos. I wanted cheese enchiladas. I only got the tacos because my mom taught me to always order seafood, if it's available. I didn't order the most expensive thing, but it was close. A habit.

If Mom were having dinner with us, she would talk about how healthy shrimp tacos are, and she would talk about how rare fresh seafood was for her when she was growing up.

At seventeen, I have had seafood more times than I can count. I have grown up with food my mom didn't even know existed when she was my age. I have choices now that she will never have, because she brought me here.

I finish my plate and look at Jen and Andrea. They are talking about Jen's list of colleges she wants to visit. My mom doesn't even know what colleges I'm applying to.

Shrimp tacos I text my mom, in response to her question.

She doesn't know that I'm trying to leave her.

Good Mom texts back. ***Healthy. Be careful and text when you get back to her house***

It hits me that very soon, my mom won't know what I eat at all. She won't know if I'm eating healthy or where I'm sleeping or what I'm doing.

It hits me that I will miss my mom when I leave to go to college.

It's Mother's Day.

A week ago I took Masha to a wildflower field so we could take photos. I printed out our photos at Walmart and bought frames to put them in. We also got Mom a salad from a restaurant she loves with money from the fast-food chain I'm working at. I'm saving for a car and for college. I'm trying to save as much money as I possibly can so I can leave.

Masha and I artfully display the photos we took for Mom on the counter. There is a picture of Masha and me sitting next to each other, Masha leaning on me, her blonde hair draped over my shoulder. Her big blue eyes are like blueberry halves, her freckles like little specks of sand. We look so similar, it's hard to believe we don't share both parents. In the photo, my hair is as long as hers, so you almost can't tell which hair belongs to which sister. We have the same eyes. I'm not as freckly as she is, but, next to her, it is startling how much I still look like a child, even though I'm almost eighteen. I haven't felt like a child in a long time.

We also decorate the living room with drawings Masha made that say "#1 Mom" and "Best Mom with an Accent." I hear her and Adam fighting behind their door so I tell Masha to go upstairs and change into a dress. Masha in dresses is a rare sight, and it always makes Mom happy.

"You can change as soon as she gets a picture with you," I promise Masha.

I want Mom to realize she only needs us. She doesn't need a man.

The door to their bedroom opens and Mom steps out. She's been crying, I can tell. Masha comes down just in time.

"Happy Mother's Day!" We both shout.

This makes Mom smile. Adam trails after her, his face clouded in shadow. Lately they have been fighting about Mom getting a job. She wants one because she is bored at home but he doesn't want her to work. He says she'll cheat on him or leave him, and it's not worth it when he already makes money.

"Wow, guys," Mom smiles. She looks at the photos on the kitchen. "Did you guys take these yourselves?" She asks us.

"Katya took them," Masha says. "But I helped put them in the frames!"

There are six pictures of us total, each in different size frames. I used my first paycheck to purchase them. It felt good to pay for something with money I worked a real job for. Adam can't say I'm stealing now. No one can.

"Look at your drawings," Mom says to Masha. "You're so funny!" She laughs. Watching Mom with Masha, I realize that Masha is the kid Mom wanted most. I was the kid that Mom got stuck with. I'm OK with that. She'll be a better Mom once she's not married anymore.

"I wasn't done with our conversation," Adam says, in a low voice. His eyes are trained on Mom like they are lasers following her every move. He crowds her. I want to push him off.

"It's Mother's Day, and I want to see my kids," Mom says, turning around to face him. She has Masha's hand in hers. "They care about me, and they did this for me. It's not always just about you."

"They only did what I told them to," Adam says. He shoots me a look and smirks. "This was my idea. They didn't do this on their own."

My mouth opens in shock at his lie.

"He's lying!" I roar. "He didn't do anything! This was me and Masha's idea!"

Adam shakes his head. "Ungrateful bitch," he says to me, like it's a joke. "You know how ungrateful she is. And what a liar she is," he says to Mom.

Rage is building in my chest. I want to explode. I bite down on my teeth and remember to breathe through my nose like the therapist taught me.

Mom looks defeated. She looks like she's tired of fighting. Maybe she is.

"Come back to our room and finish the conversation," Adam commands, his voice a low growl.

Mom nods her head and follows him. "I'll be right back, guys," Mom says to us.

I feel desperate. I need to get Mom out too. I need to get us all out, but I don't know how when Adam has his claws in every crevice of Mom's life.

Deported

Fall, Twelfth Grade, Seventeen Years Old

It's September. Maritzia is on the phone with me, crying. I'm in my room, on the floor, my mom's laptop open in front of me. I was supposed to be writing an essay for college, but I can't focus. Her dad ran a stop sign, just barely, and they took him to the border and he's there, waiting to see if he'll be sent back to Honduras.

"It was his first time, Katya! His first time doing anything wrong!" Maritzia says. "I should have been driving. It should have been me."

"You were in school," I mumble. "You couldn't have driven him to work. It was just—it was an accident."

She sobs, hard, not breathing. I don't know how to help. I don't know what to do.

"I'll ask my mom what to do. When we didn't have our documents I remember Mom got into a wreck. She gave a lady whiplash. It was bad. But we didn't get kicked out."

We're quiet. I can hear Maritzia sniffing on the line.

"My dad was supporting us. I'm going to have to drop out. I have to get another job," she says, sighing. "Something that pays more."

How do you even get a job without papers? How did my mom do it? It dawns on me. She's white. That's how she got a desk job, that's how we crossed the border.

My cheeks redden, and I feel embarrassed that I even brought up that Mom gave someone whiplash.

"Don't drop out," I say. Maritzia started at the community college nearby. She applied under DACA, deferred action for childhood arrivals. She called me after her first day of school, so excited because she could be here with a student visa. She could be here legally, finally.

I think about Maritzia's family. Her dad mows lawns every day and does odd jobs. He never has a day off. Her mom cleans houses. They do jobs my mom, who had the same status as them for a shorter period of time, did not have to do. My mom, without documents, worked a desk job. Our time in America wasn't easy by any means, but we have our citizenships now. Maritzia's dad is at the border waiting to be deported.

"We have to pay for another lawyer too," she says. "It's just not fair."

"It's not fair," I agree. "It'll get better, Maritzia. I promise. It has to."

It has to, because it's America, and America is supposed to be the best place in the world.

Mom is on the floor of her closet when I knock on the door. She has stacks of receipts in front of her, like she's trying to organize them.

Her closet is like another room. There are shelves on the wall that I know is meant for shoes and purses, but Mom fills them with wrinkled papers. Mom has gotten into the habit of not throwing anything away, because "You never know what will be important for citizenship." It's been obvious how men have traumatized her, but what about the citizenship process? What scars does she have from being constantly afraid we're going to be kicked out?

"Mom, I have a question" I say, when she asks what I need. "My friend . . . she needs help."

"What kind of help? Which friend? Never give out money," she adds.

"She's undocumented. Well . . . her whole family is. From Honduras. Her dad ran a stop sign, and they took him to the border. I remember when we got in a car wreck and that lady got whiplash. We weren't documented then. How did we not get sent to the border?"

Mom looks up at me, like she's surprised. I've learned not to bring up citizenship questions, ever, because Mom gets angry. She usually says she doesn't want to talk about it, or that I wouldn't understand because it's complicated. But Maritzia needs help.

"You remember that?" Mom asks me, her eyebrows going up. Her voice is soft, almost like Masha's voice.

"Yes," I say. It was before Masha. I will never forget the car spinning, the fear I had when my mom came back to our car and told me that the lady whose car she hit was going to call the cops. At that point I had already stuck the Barbie shoe up my nose and knew the police scared my mom, but I didn't understand why. Mom started to cry. I remember she scrambled, pulling her red Russian passport out of the glove compartment.

Mom looked at me for a long time without saying anything. I wonder what else she thinks I don't remember.

"They didn't ask for my documents," Mom says, finally. "They just ask if lady is OK. I say sorry a lot and say I will pay for her medical bills," she shrugs.

I chew my lip, thinking this information over.

"What can my friend's dad do?"

Mom sighs, putting the receipts down.

"Well, if he doesn't have police record, maybe they let him stay, I don't know. It's hard. Does he have dark skin?" Mom looks down at her arm.

I nod.

"If we was darker I think we get kicked out a long time ago," Mom says.

College

Spring, Twelfth Grade, Eighteen Years Old

I HAVE GOTTEN SEVERAL scholarships to places all across the country. They are obscure schools, but I don't care. Money is money. I've accepted a full-ride scholarship to Eastern Michigan University.

I'm sitting at our kitchen counter, waiting to tell Mom. She said she's bringing home dinner tonight. She's taking another class at her university since Adam still won't let her get a job, and she has nothing to do at home.

The knob to the back door twists, and Mom walks in. "Hey," she says. Her face is drawn. She looks exhausted.

"Hey," I say to her. She's carrying a bag with take-out containers. I get up so I can take the bag from her and start laying the containers on the table. I examine Mom's face, from the table, trying to see if she's had anything to drink. Her cheeks are a little flushed. Maybe she's had a glass of wine, but nothing severe enough to impede our conversation.

"I—I made a decision about college," I start, when she finally sits down. Might as well get it all out. I don't know how Mom will react. I don't know if she'll be proud or angry or petty or happy. It depends on how she's feeling about me, I guess.

"Oh yeah?" She asks, her eyebrows up. She picks up a fork and pops open a container filled with salad. "Where did you decide?"

"Michigan," I cough, watching her.

She stabs a bite of salad and puts it in her mouth. My heart is galloping. I don't know why, we've been in worse situations, and this isn't a bad situation. It's happy. I just feel like I'm doing something wrong by leaving her.

"It's cold there," she says, chewing. "Unbelievably cold. You will freeze." She swallows her salad and goes to the fridge to pull out a bottle of wine.

My heart sinks. She pours herself a glass, pauses, and gets out another glass, pouring another one.

She puts the second glass in front of me. "Here," she says. "Might as well practice getting warm."

I frown, taking the glass from her. "I—yeah. Well, they offered me the most money and I don't want to be in debt–"

"I have an account for you that Adam made. It has twenty-five thousand for college. So you can use that too," she says, simply.

"I don't want to use any money from him," I spit. I can't even look at Adam without my body burning from anger.

"Don't be stupid," she says. "It's half mine too. I work for it by being married. It's hard. Don't let it go to waste."

I swallow. I hate the idea of taking anything from Adam.

"OK," I say, because Mom is not having a crazy reaction like I was afraid of.

Mom looks old. She's not energetic anymore. She looks like someone took a vacuum to her life. It cracks me open.

"Will you visit?" I ask, smiling.

"Pah! Michigan? No. You'll come back home," she says, confidently.

I can't tell if she means to visit or if she thinks I'll drop out. I don't ask.

Confession

Winter 2022, Late Twenties

You haven't called me for a while my dad types to me. I haven't called him since I hung up on him when he started to defend Chris. It's been a few weeks.

Why? he asks.

He has asked this several times this week. I keep telling him I'm busy. I'm writing a novel about a young girl whose mother is an alcoholic and comes back into her life after her dad tells her she died.

I'm focusing on my book I type back to him.

You can focus and still talk to me he responds.

The same impulse I had when we had talked every day for months is creeping its way into my fingers. "I am afraid of your reaction if I tell you something important," I want to type. Or, "I was molested and I'm afraid you won't believe me." I don't type these things. I look at the word document I'm editing instead, minimizing my WhatsApp window.

I hear the familiar ding of WhatsApp and open the window again. ***Kristina wants to talk to you too*** my dad has written.

My younger sister, Kristina, doesn't have a phone yet so the only way I can talk to her is through my dad. My eyes slide to the photo I have of us on my desk. We're on a beach in Greece, smiling. My heart aches whenever I look at the photo because I know she will be so much bigger the next time I see her, whenever that will be.

I have to tell you something I type. I press enter without thinking about it.

What's wrong? his response comes immediately.

I clear out all the noise from my head. I'm going to tell him. I'm just going to be direct. If he doesn't believe me, so be it. I've been doubted before. I can deal with it again.

The reason I don't like Chris, the reason that I don't like that Masha relies on him to pay for her college, is because he molested me when I was a child

I hit enter and snap my laptop shut. My heart is flapping in my chest. I want Liam here, I don't want to be alone, but I don't have it in me to go to his office. My legs feel shaky like they do when I'm hungry, even though I know I'm not hungry. I move from my desk chair to the ground. My head is spinning. This isn't a big deal, I know it's not a big deal, I just told my dad something that happened to me, and his reaction doesn't matter. I am an adult. I am in my late twenties. I have handled a lot in my life. I can handle this.

After what feels like an hour, I stand back up and open my laptop screen. WhatsApp pops up immediately.

There are several messages from my dad.

This is sick. What happened? I want to know.

Is this when your mother left you with him?

I have found several lawyers in America. He needs to be in jail, at the least.

Have you spoken to any lawyers about this?

I found several lawyers in Washington and Texas and wrote them this letter:

The next few messages include the email he sent to the lawyers he found. In it he says that he is in Russia but his daughter was taken away from him when she was three, and he was at the whim of my mom for most of my life if he wanted to see me. He describes how I had several stepfathers and one of them sexually assaulted me when I was a child. He asks the lawyers what his options are.

I blink at my screen.

Katya? he types, thirty minutes after he pasted his email. ***Are you there?***

I look at my world clock. It is four in the morning in Russia.

My fingers start shaking.

I didn't think you would believe me, I type to him.

Why would I not believe you? What motive would you have in lying to me? he types back. ***If you tell me something, I will always believe you.***

I swallow but my throat is dry. I feel a lump form in the base of my neck. My fingers shake on my keyboard as I start answering his questions.

I haven't been talking to you because I didn't think you would believe me, I start. ***No adult has believed me.***

I will always believe you, he types back.

Summer

Summer After High School Graduation, Eighteen Years Old

I AM OUTSIDE OF my favorite bookstore with Jen.

It's a few days after graduation, which I did not attend. Mom and Adam said that's when tickets to Spain were the best price. They've been in Spain for a few weeks now.

Jen and I went to a music festival instead of graduation. We never talked about it, but I think Jen skipped her graduation because I had no one here for mine.

Jen has stayed with me for most of the summer. She has helped me take care of my mom's cats, and also made sure I wasn't alone.

"Are you excited to see Liam?" Jen asks me. Her hair is in a messy bun. Mine is in a fishtail braid she did for me this morning. I'm wearing a chiffon dress dotted with sunflowers, and she's wearing jean shorts we thrifted together a few weeks ago.

We're in the grass, the blades scratching our thighs as we picnic in front of Borders, the bookstore. It's almost time to meet up with Liam, and my heart can't control the drum it's playing in my chest.

"I haven't seen him in three years. What if he's not real?" I respond. "Just like, I don't know. A forty-year-old dude trying to get with a teenager?"

She laughs. "He's not. You've been talking to him for years now. He found you. His picture is the same, right?"

I bite my lip.

"You're nervous," Jen says, cocking her head. "You? You're actually nervous. I don't think I've ever seen you nervous."

I look away from her. Towards the sun. I want it to blind me. Nervous girl is not the vibe I'm trying to give off.

"I'm not," I lie.

"You are!" She hits me, laughing. "Don't be nervous. You're a catch. You're hot and smart. You're the whole package."

I sigh, not believing her.

"You know, for as long as I've known you, I didn't think you wanted a relationship," Jen says as I throw our food away. I had crushes throughout high school, and one boyfriend, but I was mostly detached. "Men are the worst," was my mantra.

We walk across the street to the Borders. The cool air hits us like a wave when we open the doors and I automatically head upstairs to the YA section.

"I don't know what I want," I say. Liam is going to college here, in Texas. I'm not, so it doesn't matter. I just want to see him one last time before I probably won't ever see him again. College is supposed to mold you into a different person. I am ready to be molded. I am ready to change.

Hey, where are you?

The text is from Liam. I shove my phone to the bottom of my purse. I change my mind. I don't want to meet him. I want to leave.

"Actually, I think those blueberries I ate for lunch were bad. Let's go home. This was a bad idea."

Jen cocks her head, studying me. "What? No. You're meeting him. We're staying."

I walk to the edge of the stairs and start my descent. "No, no, no," I say. "This is a bad idea. I'm dumb, I'm—"

I run into someone. "Sorry!" I say, and look up.

My heart skips a beat.

It's Liam.

Three years later.

After he moved away.

He's here now.

"Katya?" He breathes. "Hey. You didn't answer-"

My body stiffens. I feel like an icicle. "I—" I don't have the words. He looks the same, but better. More grown up.

I turn around and walk back up the stairs.

"Katya?" Jen says, behind me. "Where are you going?"

"Katya?" Liam echoes.

I want to pass out. I want to faint. I run to the children's section, to where there are board books, hoping they don't follow after me.

I want to cry. Why do I want to cry? The idea of being around a man terrifies me.

I sit down in one of the aisles with board books and pull out a random one, opening it to hide my face. I was fast, and I outran them. Hopefully this cover will hide me.

My eyes narrow in on the pictures in the board book.

I've pulled out an alphabet book with rabbits on the cover.

It reminds me of *The Velveteen Rabbit*, the book my therapist read to me our first session together. I put the book I'm holding down and scan the shelf for *The Velveteen Rabbit*.

I find it quickly.

I flip through the cardboard pages, focusing on the illustrations. I read the story of the rabbit. The same story my therapist read to me four years ago.

You don't have to be perfect to be loved, he had said. I didn't understand then. Do I now? What even is love?

I think about Lenora and Chanel and how Mom wouldn't have even partial custody of Masha without them. I remember that night on the phone with Layla, and how I opened up to her like I've never opened up to anyone before when we watched *The Quiet*. She's in Syria for the summer, and I wish she were here too.

I wish I could talk to Ms. Lynn right now, but she's not here. She passed away this year from cancer. I wish I could ask her why she was so desperate for people not to call me stupid that she made me smart even when I didn't feel like it. I want to tell her how her encouragement helped me excel in school after we cheated, and how I ended up placing in Olympiad for the third consecutive year without her help.

I think of Maritzia, how her dad is still at the border. How she dropped out of college.

I hear Jen and am reminded of how she missed graduation to be with me. How she's meeting Liam with me right now. Liam, who messaged me every day even when I didn't want to talk and how good it felt to have someone care about me.

I get up, the book in my arms.

Liam and Jen are in the international section. "She wasn't in the YA section, this is her next favorite," Jen says. "She likes looking at the Russian books—"

"Hey," I say, breathless. I stand up straight.

"Where the hell did you go?" Jen asks, turning around. "He could be the Craigslist killer for all I know," she says, pointing to Liam.

Liam and I laugh, and Jen cracks a smile.

"Do y'all want to get a coffee?" I ask, so I don't have to say out loud that I ran away.

"Yeah," Jen says. I am so glad she is here. She gives me courage.

"How was the drive?" I ask Liam. The first thing I've said to him in person in three years.

"Air conditioner in the car broke," he answers. "But nothing was going to stop me from getting down here to see you."

"Katya, I'm scared," Masha says, when I pick up her call in the middle of the night. I'm packing for Michigan. I leave in a month and a half, but I'm already mostly packed. I'm ready to never look back.

I'm only ever at home when Mom and Adam aren't, but tonight is Masha's first night back from Chris's house, and I wanted to be here.

"Mom is driving, and she's really drunk." Masha also knows all the signs and signals for Mom being drunk. "I don't want to die."

"Where are you?" I ask her, urgently.

"I don't know," she says.

"Shut up!" I hear in the background.

I hear a squeaky noise, and a muffled cry. It's Masha, trying to hold her tears in. I know that sound. Mom is angry. She's never a nice drunk. I wish I knew where Mom was. I have never felt more helpless.

"Can you tell me what's around you?" I ask Masha.

"Trees," she whispers. "She's swerving on the road."

"Shit," I say. "Only trees? Any buildings?"

"No buildings," Masha bites out.

"Where were you guys? Can you tell me if you were in downtown?"

"We were dropping Adam off at the airport. Then we stopped somewhere to meet Mom's friend and Mom got a lot of Margaritas. We went on the highway but we're not on there anymore. She got off."

What the fuck kind of friends lets you drive a car with a child after several margaritas?

"What are you saying?" I hear Mom's slippery words in the background. "Are you on the phone with your bitch sister? Did you call her to tell on me?"

"I'm not on the phone," Masha says. My heart sinks. I don't want Masha to have to know how to lie. I don't want her to know how to survive.

If she was on the highway and got off, maybe she's close.

"Stay with me on the phone," I say to Masha.

"OK," Masha squeaks out. I know she's trying to be brave.

"You are so strong," I tell her. "It's going to be OK. Are you wearing your seatbelt?"

"Yes," Masha whispers.

"Good, that's good," I say.

"I can hear her voice," Mom says. "Your bitch traitor sister's voice. I work my life to get her citizenship and she leaves me for fucking Michigan? Fuck her."

Masha lets out what sounds like a hiccup, but I know she's holding in a sob.

I bite my tongue so hard I can taste blood.

"Mom, please, can we pull over?" Masha asks, after a few minutes. "Please?" She starts crying.

"Oh, why, so your sister can come rescue you from me? Fuck her. You don't need her. You have me. I'm your Mom. Not her. She hasn't done shit for you. She's leaving you!"

Masha lets out another sob.

I go outside to the driveway. I don't care if I have to walk to find Masha.

When I'm further down the road I see headlights approach like the driver is driving too slow. It's Mom. I let out a breath and quickly start walking back.

It takes me three minutes to get back to the house, but Mom isn't even close to pulling in yet. She's driving so slow I wonder if she has fallen asleep.

She hasn't, because the car is moving forward little by little. I wait as she pulls into the driveway because I don't want her to see me.

"We're home," Masha whispers on the other end of the phone.

"I know," I say. "Go to your room, OK? I'll be there."

"You're here?"

"Yeah," I say.

I hear the back door open and Masha's footsteps hurry inside and up the stairs. She slams into my arms. Her face is red and she's shaking.

"Where's Mom?" I ask her.

"She's in the garage in the car. It's running."

"Fuck," I mutter, and rush downstairs to turn the car off.

Mom is slumped over the steering wheel, her mouth open.

I turn the key in the ignition, the engine turning off. I let out a breath. Thank God they are safe. Thank God they are here OK.

I take the keys inside and leave Mom in the car. She can sleep it off in there.

Upstairs, I cuddle with Masha in bed.

I look at her, sleeping safely in my arms, and make a decision I hate myself for making.

I can't leave her.

Leaving

Summer After High School Graduation, Eighteen Years Old

I CAN'T LEAVE MY sister, but I will leave my mother.

I gave up my scholarship to the college in Michigan and have decided to go to the University of Houston. It's an hour away from the house. It was a devastating decision, but I couldn't bring myself to leave Masha. Not with Mom. Not with her dad. Not without me.

I am packing up my car. Today is the first day I'm allowed to move into the dorms, and I do it with fervor. It's August. I am ready.

I use trash bags to gather all my things. It reminds me of moving out of our apartment and into a storage unit when I was a kid.

I take the stuff that I know I won't need in a dorm but will be useful in an apartment. Queen size sheets even though my bed at the dorm is a twin. Curtains, even though there are blinds on our windows already. A microwave even though we have a kitchen. I am saving these things until it's time for me to move into my own place, because I will never, ever, live under the same roof as my mother or any of her husbands ever again.

The car is so packed that it looks weighed down, but I don't care. It only takes me an hour until I'm at my college. An hour away from Masha isn't bad. I can be here if Mom drives with her drunk. I can be here when she needs me, and when she doesn't anymore, I can leave Texas for good.

I sigh. Nothing else will fit into this car. I look around the garage, as though it's hiding something.

My eyes snag on Mom's box, in the corner. I remember when I found the mail-order bride magazine while I was cleaning a year and a half ago. I'm surprised to see the box still there. I thought Mom would have moved it after I found it.

I go to the box, curious, and open it up.

There's the magazine, on top. Mom put it back.

I flip it open to the dog earned page.

Mom, seductively posing for the camera.

I think about the woman who chose to put herself in a magazine. Only five years older than I am now.

I think about how it was this advertisement that got us here. This advertisement, that led us to become American citizens. Our road to get here has been twisted and painful. It has been too much, and so many times I didn't know if I was going to survive. I didn't know if *she* was going to survive. I remember how angry I was when I found this magazine, and I understand why now.

I have the words.

Mom was not only sexualized, *I* was also sexualized. In buying young, beautiful, helpless women, these men looking through this magazine for a young bride were looking for innocence they could exploit.

Children are also young and helpless. It's a power dynamic. It's a pattern.

When I was molested, I was not only learning how to survive as a person, but I was learning to survive in this country that didn't want me. I didn't have the words to explain what happened to me. I knew it was bad, but I didn't know why. No one around me cared. There were signs, but the adults chose to ignore them.

I did too.

I remember the moment I acknowledged the sexual abuse with Layla.

"That happened to me," I had whispered to her.

I had the words. "Molested." "Sexual assault." "Sexually abused."

Chris had treated me exactly how he treated my mom. I cooked for him, cleaned for him. I cringe. I remember picking out clothes that I thought he would like, the same clothes my mom wore. Skin tight. I emulated what I saw—what he wanted. I wasn't even out of elementary school.

This catalog I found—it was glaring evidence that Mom had sold not only herself, but me too. The words written in the catalog, the words that she didn't even write because she didn't know English at the time, were indicative of her signing us away without knowing the terms.

I am angry at her for putting me in those situations, for finding these terrible men that left me with ugly, deep scars. I am angry at these men, these monsters, who are most attracted to innocence because it makes them feel more powerful.

I am angry at all the adults in my life who knew bad things were happening to me and didn't do anything.

I am mad at everyone who has not used their voice to speak up against people who are doing bad things, especially if they have the privilege of an American citizenship behind their words.

Finding this magazine at seventeen made me feel powerless all over again.

Not anymore.

Now, I will use my voice. Now I am the powerful one.

I look at the magazine and make a vow to one day tell our story.

I will exercise my freedom of speech. I will fight tyranny. I will take every opportunity available to me. My mom did not grow up with these rights. My mom fought for this. She lost so many pieces of herself fighting for these freedoms, and I will make sure she didn't lose them for nothing.

"Katya? When are you leaving?" I hear Mom shout from the kitchen. She thinks I'm upstairs. She doesn't know I'm in the garage, about to leave.

I don't answer her.

"Katya?" I hear her head upstairs.

I think about leaving without saying goodbye. I stroke Mom's face in the magazine. That poor girl, what was she thinking?

I will never get back what I lost. I will never get back my childhood.

"Katya?"

I can leave here if I want to. I can cut her off. I don't have to say goodbye. I can disappear forever.

I don't know yet what to do, but I know that it's my choice.

I have my American citizenship, and I know it's value.

Home

Summer 2024, Early Thirties

We are waiting at passport control in Istanbul. It's July and very hot. We have been to several countries at this point, so I'm used to sliding through border control with my blue passport. My heart still skips a beat when the border control officer of any country asks me what nationality I am, but I always say that I'm American.

I wonder how passport control will be like for my Babushka. If she will be able to slide through as easy as I can with her red Russian passport.

Upon rekindling my relationship with my father, I was also able to get in touch with my Babushka.

Liam and I are next in line. A man waves us forward.

"You are American?" He asks, after I hand him our passports.

We both nod.

He places a stamp on the last page and gives our passports back, waving us through. Every time we cross a border, I can't help but think about how me and Mom crossed over to America. How border control looked at our faces, as though they were as good as the blue passport my mom fought years for, and let us through with no other questions.

I think about the people who have died in the back of hot trucks to get across the Mexico border into the United States.

I think of Maritzia's dad, who, fourteen years after he was arrested, now lives in Mexico City. He's from Honduras, but he wants to be as close as he can to the border, in case he can figure out how to come back.

My blue passport is the most valuable thing I have. I will never not appreciate how lucky it is that I have one.

Liam and I find a bench close to our baggage carousel and sit down. I don't know how long the wait for my grandmother will be. She was supposed to land soon after us. Ten minutes ago, to be exact, but there has been no updates.

I found out a few years ago that the reason my mom didn't take me back to Russia after we got our American citizenships was because she was afraid of what legal action my dad would take against her, since she took me without his permission. I wish I could go back, but with Russia's invasion of Ukraine, I don't trust that I wouldn't be made an example of, like other Russian American's who have visited Russia and been taken into custody for frivolous reasons. I don't want my American citizenship to be used against me.

The flight to America is now too long for my eighty-five-year-old Babushka, so we are meeting in Turkey, one of the only places that allows Russians in without a visa.

Babushka visited America one last time when I was in college, eight years after her last visit to the US, when I was in middle school. I was recovering from an injury I got while waitressing, and don't remember much of that time. Babushka and I didn't talk at all when I was in high school because of Mom's estrangement from her. Mom and Babushka rekindled their relationship after my mom's divorce from Adam my freshman year of university.

A few years after I graduated from college, I became estranged from my mother. While they were married, Adam attached himself to Mom like a toxic mold, fitting himself in every crevice of her life and leeching away everything that made her strong. When they divorced, he walked away with her sobriety, her vitality, her motivation. I didn't recognize her. I was not strong enough to watch what remained of her fade away, so I left. I had done everything I could to save her, and it had cost me my health. I realized I was going to go down the same path if I didn't choose myself.

When I first started talking to my babushka again, I was so nervous. I was embarrassed to call my grandmother on my own, without my mom being present, because my mom had convinced me that my Russian was terrible and that I needed her there when I spoke to Babushka, otherwise she wouldn't be able to understand me. I found out after talking to my Russian sister for hours, that I've never forgotten my Russian. I hope I never will.

My hands start shaking. I'm worried something happened to her plane. Since the start of the war, airplanes have been unreliable and dangerous.

"Do you see her?" I ask Liam. "She was supposed to land an hour ago."

We collected our baggage. I have messaged her several times, but haven't gotten a response.

"Not yet," Liam says, also scanning the massive room. There are so many people here, all of them speaking different languages.

What if something happened to her plane? What if border control doesn't let her in? Liam squeezes my hand in a gesture I recognize as letting me know he is here, with me.

"There she is!" Liam shouts. He lets go of my hand and stands up, pointing to the top of the stairs. I look in the direction of his finger.

There she is. She is hanging onto the arm of a young woman, maybe eighteen years old. I don't recognize her.

"Babushka!" I shout. Tears spring to my eyes. I feel my shoulders relax. She's here.

I run up the stairs to her.

"Oh!" She says. "Katya!" She turns to the woman whose arm she is hanging on to.

"This is my granddaughter," she says. "The one I was telling you about."

I hug her, hard. My Babushka. The safest person to me, still, even after all these years. The memories I have with my grandmother are where I hide when I feel scared, her voice is the sound I hear in my head when I want to be soothed. The happiest memories in my childhood all have her face in them.

I take in her peppery smell. I am twice as tall as her now.

We walk down the stairs. She's unsteady on her feet, her balance not the same as it used to be.

"I met Mira on my flight. We sat next to each other. She and her brother are also visiting family here. She helped me through this whole process," Babushka says, waving at the Turkish border patrol.

"Thank you," I say to Mira.

"She wouldn't stop talking about you," Mira says to me, in Russian. "She is really proud of you. She says you have written a book about how hard life in America is!"

I laugh that my grandmother is describing my book like this to other people.

"Yes," I say, simply.

"Thank you for all your help," I tell Mira again.

Mira nods and hugs Babushka before leaving.

"My girl," Babushka says, turning to me. "Finally."

Acknowledgments

THANK YOU TO my agent, Natalie Lakosil. I can't imagine being on this journey with anyone else. You are the big sister in publishing every writer wishes for.

To my editor, Laura Apperson—all I ever wanted was a voice in this country and you gave me my American dream.

To my author friends who have saved this book countless times: Sasha Vasilyuk—I would not have this book without you. I love you so much. Jacqueline Doyle, Rose Anderson, and Alia Volz, your edits helped me find my voice. I'm so honored to have learned from you. Thank you to Qian Julie Wang—without your book, I wouldn't have had the courage to write mine. And to Jill Damatac, who is an endless source of encouragement.

Thank you to the Looking Glass team for your unwavering support, energy, and brilliance in bringing this book to life. Thank you to the Future Of team, especially Amanda, Michelle, Saimah, Sara, Clara, Maurice, Kailey, and Andrea, you go above and beyond in ways I can't even describe. Thank you to Rebecca, Thai, Matt, Monica, Julia, and especially Katie of the Alcove team for your support, guidance, and kindness that I have so deeply appreciated. Thank you also to Emily Mahar, who designed such a poignant cover.

Terror, thank you for being my safe place all the way back to writing fanfics together after school. Taelor (@stylishsista), thank you for your unending cheerleading. Thank you for being an endless source of support and comfort. I love you so much and I'll be bothering you until my last breath. Jen, I am forever grateful for your insight, love, and patience, especially trudging through the earliest draft of this book. Lauren, you and Pixel gave me the hope I needed for this project and the housewives to save my sanity. Antonia (@blackgirlthatreads), your recommendations are flawless. I am so grateful UH brought us together. To Douglas, one of my oldest friends, our photoshoots are some of the fondest memories of my life. Thank you. To Phonc, BonBon, Tim, and Tina of Ivy's Nails: your friendship has meant the world to me. To Dan from Brick and Mortar books, thank you for creating such an incredible space for readers and authors alike. I am deeply grateful for my creative writing teachers at the University of Houston, especially Jameelah Lang and Aaron Reynolds. I truly would not have written this book if not for your wisdom. To my elementary school friends, T and J, thank you for being my friends when I needed it most. I think of you often. Also, "Lenora," you saved my family in a terrible time, and I'll never forget that. To Ms. Lynn, I wish you were still here. To Ms. P., thank you for not kicking me out of your room in the morning. I needed your kindness more than I ever let on. To Mimi, you inspire me, and I wrote this book thinking of you. Thank you to the friends and family who have helped more than they will ever know: Virgil, Sheri, Madeline, Payton, Brian, Inni, Eddie, Ginille, Mike, Barb, Dave, and Michelle. For pulling me out of a terrible place, Annie and Jennie, thank you for reminding me of my strength. Thank you to my fur babies, Babydog, Babycat, and Santa, for being more drawn to my keyboard than I am.

It was a long and winding path to rediscover my lost family, and I am deeply grateful to have never lost the support and love of my Papa, Stepmother, Dedushka, Uncle, Baba A, Aunt G, cousins A, D, and S, siblings big and little A, Babushka N, and my cousins V, D, and N. I love you guys immensely.

To everyone who has followed my story on social media, you are the reason I am able to tell this story. I am forever grateful for your support.

Finally, thank you, Mom, for bringing me to this country and sacrificing so much. I am eternally grateful.